DATE DUE

DEMCO 38-296

North Africa in Transition

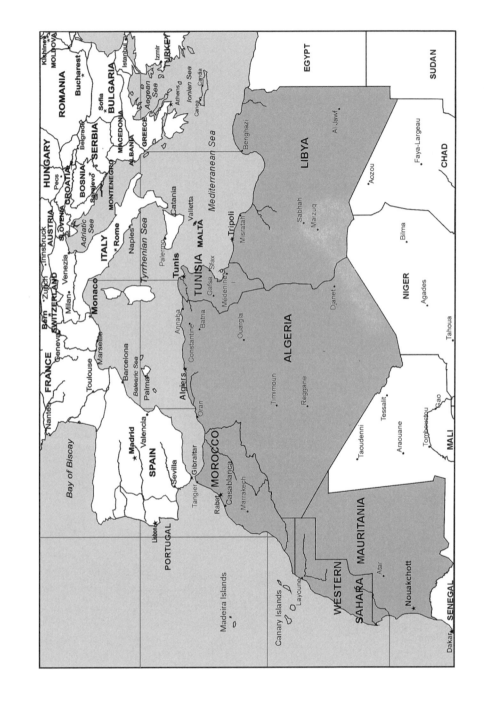

North Africa in Transition

State, Society, and Economic
Transfomation in the 1990s

Edited by Yahia H. Zoubir

Foreword by William B. Quandt

University Press of Florida
Gainesville/Tallahassee/Tampa/Boca Raton
Pensacola/Orlando/Miami/Jacksonville

North Africa in transition

Copyright 1999 by the Board of Regents of the State of Florida

Printed in the United States of America on acid-free paper

All rights reserved

04 03 02 01 00 99 6 5 4 3 2 1

Library of Congress Cataloging-in-Publication Data

North Africa in transition : state, society, and economic transformation in the 1990s / Yahia H. Zoubir, editor ; foreword by William B. Quandt.

p. cm.

Includes bibliographical references and index.

ISBN 0-8130-1655-X (alk. paper)

1. Africa, North—Social conditions. 2. Africa, North—Economic conditions. 3. Africa, North—Politics and government. 4. Islam—Africa, North. I. Zoubir, Yahia H.

HN781.A8N67 1998S

306'.0961—dc21   98-39084

The University Press of Florida is the scholarly publishing agency for the State University System of Florida, comprising Florida A & M University, Florida Atlantic University, Florida International University, Florida State University, University of Central Florida, University of Florida, University of North Florida, University of South Florida, and University of West Florida.

University Press of Florida

15 Northwest 15th Street

Gainesville, FL 32611–2079

http://www.upf.com

To my wife, Cynthia, and our children, Nadia, Jamel, and Malek

Contents

Figures and Tables

Foreword

North Africa often has been relegated to the margins of the primary concerns of scholars and policymakers alike. Those who focus on the Middle East and Africa tend to ignore developments in the Maghreb. Journalists flock to cover the most recent crisis in Israel/Palestine or the Persian Gulf, but serious reporting from North Africa is rare in the Western press. Few universities in America or Europe offer courses on the Maghreb.

Gradually, however, scholarship is catching up with the reality that North Africa is a region of some 75 million people, who are passing through a fascinating period of social, economic, and political change. The present volume, with its emphasis on developments in the 1990s, and with due attention to the socioeconomic transformations of the past generation, helps the reader see North Africa in all its complexity.

And the picture is worth studying. In Morocco, for example, the king, who has ruled for more than thirty years, is experimenting with a gradual opening of the political system. An opposition leader has assumed the post of prime minister, after winning the largest number of seats in parliament. Civil society is remarkably vibrant. Economic reform has generally gone well by regional standards. And thus far, Morocco has been spared the violence that has been so pervasive in its closest neighbor, Algeria.

Algeria's most recent decade has been dominated by political violence that has cost the country some seventy-five thousand lives. As the 1990s come to an end, there is some indication that the violence is ebbing. Large sections of the country are now calm, and the risk of full-scale civil war seems remote. Still, terrible damage has been done, and it will take years for the country to recover.

Algeria also presents a more complex picture than the horror stories that attract most journalistic attention. Of greater concern to many Algerians than the violence is the grim socioeconomic situation facing the country's youth. Unemployment is a perennial problem. Declining educational standards are also a source of concern, as is the abysmal housing situation. With all of these problems, Algeria nonetheless has been able to go further with a pluralistic political system and relatively free press than most countries in the vicinity. It is not so much a matter of a regime graciously bestowing a few benefits of liberalization, but rather a tough society clinging to the gains of hard-fought battles in the 1980s. It is not clear how Algeria's limited democratization will proceed, but there is more political vitality in the country than most outsiders would expect to find. Only a few years ago, some imagined that Algeria would become the next Iran, an Islamic republic hostile to the West. That seems unlikely today.

Tunisia is as much a surprise as Algeria, but in a different way. Tunisia's transition to independence seemed a model of national development: there was little violence; the leadership of Habib Bourguiba was reminiscent of Mustafa Kemal Ataturk's benevolent modernization/westernization/secularization of Turkey. Stability and progress seemed the order of the day. And, indeed, Tunisia has done quite well in terms of economic reform and social development. But the hoped-for democratization fell prey to the panic that seems to have struck the Tunisian elite as Algeria descended into violence. To prevent the same from happening in Tunisia, the regime cracked down on all opposition and has turned itself back into a harshly authoritarian state. Perhaps, with time and further economic diversification, pressures will mount for an opening of the political system, as occurred in South Korea and Taiwan. But for the moment, Tunisia allows far less pluralism of expression than either Morocco or Algeria.

This well-crafted volume of essays on North Africa shows that scholars appreciate what is happening in North Africa, but with several distinctive points of emphasis compared to typical area-studies approaches. First, all see North African states as grappling with issues that are familiar from other contexts. No longer is it odd to compare North Africa with Latin America or East Asia, as well as with the more familiar Middle Eastern cases. Each country, of course, has its own distinctive history and institutions, but that is not a reason to avoid comparisons. In the future, we can expect that North African studies will be part of the trend toward genuinely comparative political inquiry.

A second point about these essays is that they tend to privilege explanations rooted in social, economic, and political realities. This stands in contrast to a body of scholarship and journalism that has emphasized North Africa's dual cultural heritage, French and Arabo-Islamic. The specific cultural blends found in North Africa are not ignored here, but they are not seen as the key to understanding either the failures or the successes of these states. And that, it seems to me, is the right perspective to adopt: the Maghrebi crises are more political and socioeconomic than they are cultural.

A third point that stands out in this volume is the quality of writing and research now done by North Africans about their own societies. Look at the footnotes and bibliography in this book. Many, if not most, of the authors cited are from the region. The tension found in Middle East studies of highly politicized scholarship is less apparent here. Orientalism is less in evidence, and the interchange between Maghrebi scholars and their Western counterparts seems largely fruitful. True, authors differ on many topics, especially the place of Islamic movements. But the division runs within both subsets of authors—those from within the region and those without. It is not a dividing line between indigenous writers and outsiders.

The last two decades have been tough ones for North Africans. On the whole, the promises raised by independence in the 1950s and 1960s were dimmed in the 1980s. Hopes of economic betterment and democratization were raised, only to be dashed. But despite the obvious disappointments, the future is not so bleak for this region. Compared to others in the Middle East, Maghrebis do not have to see vast resources diverted to military expenditures. Nor will the demographic challenge of the future be as daunting as in the past. Sometime in the next twenty years, those leaving the job market will equal the numbers entering. That will change social dynamics considerably. In addition, North Africans seem to have had their fill of utopian projects, whether in the name of nationalism or Islam. The trend now toward more pluralism and pragmatism bodes well for the future.

The big challenges now in North Africa are to integrate the huge number of marginalized youth into the productive sectors of society, to improve the educational systems to prepare the next generation for the global economic challenges of the twenty-first century, and to open up political space for the increasingly complex social formations to express themselves through peaceful means. None of these problems will yield to immediate solutions. They are the work of a generation. But they are worthy challenges for people who deserve a better future and who seem determined to achieve it through their own efforts.

William B. Quandt
University of Virginia

Preface

The idea to compile the chapters in this book originated during a discussion that my friend Daniel Volman and I held while attending the International Studies Association annual meeting in San Diego, California, in April 1996. The intention was to bring together scholars from the Maghreb, the United States, and Europe. My experience in those three places was instrumental in helping me secure contributions from some of the leading scholars and some of the next generation of Maghrebi experts. I would like to express my sincere thanks to the contributors for believing in the project and for abiding by my rigorous deadlines for abstracts, submissions, and revisions. I would also like to thank Meredith Morris-Babb, editor in chief at the University Press of Florida, not only for giving serious consideration to the project but also for her continued support and encouragement throughout the process, and Jacqueline Kinghorn Brown, project editor at the University Press of Florida, for her collaboration and identifying areas where changes could be made to improve the quality of the manuscript.

Although authors traditionally acknowledge their families last, I would like to break that tradition by expressing now my heartfelt thanks to my wife, Cynthia, and my children, Nadia, Jamel, and Malek, for enduring my late hours, especially during the summer of 1997, when I worked ceaselessly on the chapters.

Had it not been for the diligence, dedication, and constant support of Georgia Lessard from Thunderbird's Center for Authoring Services, it is doubtful whether this book would have come to life. She did all the formatting, entered all the changes, and kept me going at every stage of the project. I can hardly express the full gratitude that I owe her. Professor Zeddic Lanham, from Thunderbird's Department of Modern Languages, helped with the editing of more than half the chapters. His contribution to the quality of this book is invaluable. I would like to express my gratitude to him for spending countless hours on the chapters.

I cannot thank enough Betsy Bryant and Diane O'Brien, administrative assistants in the Department of International Studies, for their support and encouragement. They have never failed to provide assistance whenever I needed it, especially during the toughest times in the summer of 1997. My gratitude to them is immeasurable.

I would also like to express my gratitude to Olufemi Babarinde, my colleague in the Department of International Studies, for his friendship and valued advice.

In my professional career, I have known individuals whose scholarly achievement, humility, and enduring friendship have been true inspirations in my academic endeavors. This acknowledgment is a modest tribute to them: Duncan L. Clarke and David C. Brown, both at the American University in Washington, D.C.; Steven I. Levine from Boulder Run Research in Hillsborough, North Carolina; Hugh Roberts at the London School of Economics; William B. Quandt of the University of Virginia; and Robert A. Mortimer, George Joffé, Clement Moore Henry, and Mary-Jane Deeb, contributors to this book.

Last but by no means least, I am deeply indebted to my father for assisting my research by regularly sending me various Algerian newspapers and any new publications from Algeria, and for sharing with me his penetrating knowledge of Algeria.

INTRODUCTION

Yahia H. Zoubir

In the late 1980s, world attention focused on the changes occurring in Eastern Europe and in the former Soviet Union. Few, however, seemed to notice that change had started even earlier in the Maghreb. Indeed, the "constitutional" coup d'état in Tunisia in November 1987 and the dramatic riots in Algeria in October 1988 marked the beginning of a new era in the region. New groups emerged to challenge the state and to question developments since independence. Emerging civil societies rejected authoritarian, "developmentalist" governments and called for governments that would institute more social justice. The governments established in Morocco and Tunisia in 1956, in Algeria in 1962, and in Libya in 1969 all failed to deliver the socioeconomic prosperity they had promised their citizens. Though somewhat successful in the first two decades, mostly because of workers' remittances and of hydrocarbon or other natural-resources revenues, the policies those governments adopted resulted in the impoverishment of the middle and lower classes. The absence of democratic freedoms, widespread corruption, the marginalization of large segments of society (especially young people), arbitrary rule, clientelism, nepotism, and human-rights violations caused the ruling elite in the Maghrebi countries to lose their legitimacy. The severe socioeconomic crises caused by inflation, soaring international debt, high unemployment, and mismanagement of resources, coupled with no means of redress through democratic institutions, led to a repudiation of the tacit social contract rulers had established with the ruled following independence from colonial domination. The new social groups challenged the authority and the legitimacy of the state with an intensity and on a scale never previously witnessed. Although radical Islamists were the leading force opposing the state, others including cultural groups, human-rights organizations, students' organizations, moderate Islamists, and women's associations became political forces. Pressures for change and reform arose from unprecedented social and economic crises, which often triggered violent upheavals. Failing economies induced the regimes to liberalize in order to bring about the necessary reforms and to implement the austere programs imposed by international financial institutions, such as the International Monetary Fund and the World Bank. To survive, the Maghrebi regimes allowed a degree of economic and political liberalization. They initiated liberalization in the hope that civil society would support them and would stop contesting their authority. The governments also hoped that such limited liberalization would curtail the potential for violence and destabilization.

Feeling threatened, Maghrebi regimes tried to confine or stifle their opponents. The inability of the regimes to respond to the increasing demands of their citizens, and of their previous social allies, forced them to disengage from sectors of which they had traditionally been in charge. The four governments concluded that they no longer could sponsor development and that they needed instead to promote at least a degree of domestic and international private investment for growth and prosperity. As the contributors to this volume demonstrate, however, these governments have not yet fully assessed all the implications of liberalization and privatization.

In the Maghreb, democratization has not developed along with economic liberalization and privatization. In Algeria, for instance, democratization resulted in the strengthening of radical Islamists who threatened the legitimacy and survival of the old rulers. The Islamists similarly threatened Tunisia. The unanticipated power of the emerging civil society has so grown, in fact, that the two regimes interrupted democratization. Morocco and Libya have also faced a much more potent opposition than they had ever before faced, and both countries may follow Algeria into violence and oppression.

This volume is divided into three parts. In the first part, the contributors have analyzed why development in the Maghrebi countries—Algeria, Libya, Morocco, and Tunisia—has failed. Mauritania, though part of the Arab Maghreb Union, is not included, because its development needs to be analyzed in a wider, African context. Although the central Maghreb consists of Algeria, Morocco, and Tunisia, Libya has been included because its foreign policy affects the Maghreb more than does that of Mauritania.

In spite of the different approaches and opinions of the contributors, readers may reach a number of conclusions from the first part. Civil societies have emerged in the Maghreb because the governments have failed in their development strategies while simultaneously disengaging from sectors of the economy that they long controlled; in other words, economic liberalization contributed to the advent of civil societies in the Maghreb.

Using a dialectical approach, Professor Clement M. Henry traces the development of civil societies in the Maghreb. He shows that as colonial rule produced a nationalist opposition, so nationalist governments have generated their own Islamist opposition. He believes that Islamists must be included in democratization; otherwise, they will appropriate civil society and the nationalist legacy.

Yahia H. Zoubir argues that economic liberalization in Algeria and the weakening of the state are the primary factors responsible for the emergence of a civil society. He believes, as does Henry, that moderate Islamists must be included; however, Zoubir believes that radical Islamists may destroy civil society.

Azzedine Layachi, too, agrees with Henry's assessment that the continued reluctance of the Moroccan monarchy to liberalize the political system will strengthen the Islamist movement, particularly its most radical factions. Layachi asserts that international pressure has helped in liberalizing the Moroccan political system but that the reforms are limited and will not prevent upheavals.

Robert King analyzes the tensions in Tunisia using the dialectic between international economics and domestic politics, on one hand, and between the demands for political development and the needs for economic development, on the other. He clearly shows that Tunisia's economic liberalization has not led to political liberalization. His analysis instead corroborates the view that repression has resulted from economic liberalization in Tunisia.

Mary-Jane Deeb provides an overview of the mounting opposition to Qadaffi's regime in Libya. The old social contract, which substantial oil revenues and a small population made possible, has eroded. The UN-imposed sanctions have widened the gap between the rulers and the population; a more forceful opposition, led mainly by Islamists, has threatened the stability of the regime.

The second part of the book deals with specific, salient issues pertaining to the Maghrebi countries. Claire Spencer's opening chapter provides an overview of the various approaches to change used in the study of the

Maghreb. Her investigation shows that most approaches reveal an obsession with the question of Islamism and its potential implications for the West. Indeed, many European studies, especially security studies, concerned themselves with the implications of the Islamist phenomenon for the continent. Those studies focus on migration from the southern shores of the Mediterranean to Europe. The rise of Islamism is perceived as a domestic threat, notably in France, Spain, Italy, and Belgium, where millions of North Africans reside. There is also concern that the instability in the Maghreb, mainly in Algeria, will spill over into Western Europe, resulting, for instance, in the export of terrorism. Unemployment in the Maghreb also encourages citizens of Algeria, Morocco, and Tunisia to emigrate to Europe, with all its economic and cultural ramifications.

The most striking aspect about the Maghreb is the youthfulness of its population. Mohamed F. Azzi examines the most important dimensions of the complex and multidimensional existence of Maghrebi youth and analyzes the socioeconomic conditions that constitute the primary ingredients of the turmoil in Maghrebi societies. The Maghrebi countries have experienced almost identical problems with their youth. Azzi's sociological-anthropological analysis, using empirical research, contributes to an understanding of the process of alienation of young people in the Maghreb. His study demonstrates unequivocally that unless their problems are addressed, the cycle of riots will continue and more youth will join the radical Islamists. In other words, governments' failure to meet the needs of their youth will invigorate the "movements of rage," which Zoubir highlights in the first part of the book.

Alienation and marginalization in North African societies are not unique to young people. Maghrebi intellectuals have also suffered from alienation in their own societies. Rarely do books on the Maghreb include chapters on the intellectuals. To fill the gap in the field of North African studies, Patricia Geesey has contributed a chapter dealing specifically with the role of francophone intellectuals, how they view their respective societies, and how they see their own roles in them. For obvious reasons, her chapter focuses primarily on Algeria, where intellectuals (both arabophone and francophone for that matter) have been targeted for assassination. Geesey investigates the reasons for the alienation of francophone intellectuals; she notes that socioeconomic conditions partially explain the indifference the populations show toward those intellectuals. Indeed, those populations often regard the intellectuals in their societies as privileged castes.

Despite its multifaceted problems, the Maghreb is a rich region and offers lucrative investments for foreign investors. The decision of Maghrebi regimes to liberalize their economies may transform the region into so-called emerging markets. Nora A. Colton examines the actions undertaken by the governments of Algeria, Morocco, and Tunisia to institute market economics, and although she sees those countries as emerging markets, Colton argues that the regimes have launched economic liberalization without being fully cognizant of its social and political implications. She also confirms the analyses of the contributors in the first part of the book that economic liberalization occurred in each of those states with no concomitant political liberalization.

The move toward political liberalization in the Maghreb has not alleviated the deplorable condition of human rights. In the mid-1980s, human-rights groups sprang up and began to challenge authoritarian political systems. Youcef Bouandel argues that the Maghrebi regimes have incorporated talk about human rights into their political discourse but only to legitimize their power. Foreign governments and donor institutions have, at least to a limited degree, succeeded in institutionalizing human rights. The three countries have even founded human-rights organizations. Human-rights conditions in Algeria have deteriorated, however, because of the fierce war between the security forces and Islamist extremists, on one hand, and the extremists' attacks against the civilian population, on the other. Morocco (where human rights were the most deplorable) made some progress, but the record still remains negative. Tunisia's case is the most dismaying. The Tunisian regime has used the crisis in neighboring Algeria and the threat of Islamist extremism to repress all opposition in the country, including democratic forces. All the contributors agree that Maghrebi regimes have resorted to repression and to human-rights violations to crush opposition to their rule.

The evolution of the Maghreb in the late 1980s promised to inaugurate a decade of peace and regional cooperation. However, as Robert A. Mortimer shows through his analysis of intra-Maghrebi relations, the Arab Maghreb Union (UMA), created in 1989, remains an illusion. Mortimer argues that the UMA is hibernating and that economic union failed mostly because of a lack of political consensus and political stability. The relationship between the two powerful regional states, Algeria and Morocco, has been at a low ebb because of a variety of factors, of which the twenty-three-year-old conflict in Western Sahara remains the most important.

Zoubir treats the importance of the Western Sahara conflict in the opening chapter of the third part of the book, which is devoted to the Maghreb in world affairs. In his examination of the geopolitics of the Western Sahara conflict, Zoubir concurs with Mortimer's observation that regional cooperation has been hampered by the poor relationship between Algeria and Morocco and by their failure to reach political consensus. In addition to dealing with the positions of Algeria and Morocco in the conflict, Zoubir analyzes the roles that France, Spain, and the United States have played in the regional conflict. The unstable situation in Algeria, which created fears of a spill-over into Morocco, and the existence of a UN-sponsored cease-fire between Moroccans and Sahrawis have strengthened Morocco's position. However, any resolution of the conflict will need to incorporate Algeria's interests if regional economic cooperation is to become a reality. Unless a definitive solution is reached in the conflict in Western Sahara, not only will Maghreb Union remain an illusion, but the threat of war will also persist in the region.

The conflict in Western Sahara has consumed substantial resources and has seriously impeded the economic growth of the two countries. Daniel Volman looks at the military balance in the Maghreb, primarily focusing on Algeria and Morocco. He notes that the conflict in Western Sahara led to substantial purchases of military equipment. He argues that Algeria, despite the Islamist insurgency it has faced since 1992, still holds a military advantage over Morocco, dissuading the latter from launching a war against Algeria, POLISARIO Front's main ally. In view of his analysis, one should add that Algeria's military superiority has also prevented Morocco from winning the conflict in Western Sahara.

Until recently, the United States did not regard the Maghreb as an entity. The post–Cold War era, however, has led to what may be a more regionally oriented U.S. policy. Stephen Zunes and Zoubir together analyze U.S. policy toward each Maghrebi state and examine how the United States defines its interests in the region. They believe that, although not yet congruous, a regional policy, the core of which is economic liberalization, may be emerging, denoting a shift away from the traditional U.S. position, which allowed the French to play the major role in the central Maghreb. Zoubir and Zunes also look at U.S. policy toward Libya (excluded from the emerging regional policy) within the context of the "rogue-states" doctrine that the National Security Council developed in the 1990s. In their opinion, that policy is counterproductive because it punishes the Libyan population and strengthens Qadaffi's dictatorial rule.

Although the United States has shown great interest in the Maghreb, the members of the European Union, especially those bordering the Mediterranean, have even greater interests. Therefore, the last part of the book concludes with a chapter by George Joffé, on the European Union's policy toward the Maghreb. Joffé examines the European Union's Association Agreements with the Maghreb in the wake of the Euro-Mediterranean Partnership arrangement that followed the Barcelona Conference in November 1995. Joffé analyzes how Europe has responded to the evolution of the Maghreb and assesses the effectiveness of the various measures adopted by the European Union, on one hand, and by individual European member states, on the other.

While the contributors to this book acknowledge the problems that the Maghreb has witnessed in recent years, they also recognize the potentialities of that region. The most hopeful sign is the rise of civil societies. The emergence of autonomous associations in the Maghreb demonstrates that democratic change, albeit slow, is achievable. A new social contract is inevitable. The Maghrebis are yearning for the exercise of freedom and for social justice. They have developed means of resistance that the regimes can ill afford to ignore. Both the state and civil society will have to redefine their relationship. The states in the Maghreb have no alternative to democratization and good governance. Authoritarianism, whatever its past merits in the area of development, is obsolete.

At the regional and international levels, there is no doubt that the Maghrebi states need to cooperate. Regional integration is a necessity if the regimes wish to overcome the problems that globalization and European integration have generated. The UMA offers a good framework for that to happen, assuming a genuine willingness on the part of the regional actors and the international community to resolve definitively this lingering conflict. Maghrebi states and societies enjoy a great deal of ingenuity; all they need is the determination to use it.

Part I

Polity, Society, and the Economy
in the Maghrebi Countries

1.

POST-COLONIAL DIALECTICS OF CIVIL SOCIETY

Clement Moore Henry

This chapter will discuss how the Maghrebi colonial experiences shaped Maghrebi civil societies and how these societies may overcome their respective colonial legacies. Civil society is understood by most writers, inside as well as outside the region, to offer the societal underpinnings for democratic forms of government. Paradoxically, it is a Western concept articulated in the eighteenth and nineteenth centuries by orientalist theorists such as Montesquieu, Hegel, Tocqueville, and Mill, who contrasted their dynamic civil societies with "static" oriental or Islamic ones. Yet much like English seventeenth-century Puritans and their American offspring, the contemporary Islamists committed to reconstructing Maghrebi society along Islamic lines are the principal stimulus to civil society in the region, as in other parts of the Middle East and North Africa.[1] The Maghreb is currently at a political crossroads: the future of civil society may well depend on the ability of the incumbent regimes to share power with some of the Islamist elements. Whether civil society actually reinforces democracy is a further question to be addressed in some concluding comments.

Civil society will be defined here, following Michael Walzer, as "the space of uncoerced human association and also the set of relational networks—formed for the sake of the family, faith, interest, and ideology—that fill this space."[2] This definition is deliberately broad. It has the virtue of including informal patterns of association as well as the formal associations, interest groups, and political parties that often are taken to constitute civil society. Authoritarian regimes, in the Maghreb as elsewhere, tend to constrain formal intermediaries in ways that make a mockery of narrower conceptions of civil society. Seeking positive international images, they claim to be promoting democracy by encouraging the development of an official "civil society," consisting of legally recognized political parties and unions, together with nongovernmental organizations (NGOs) under their control. Studies of formal intermediaries can reveal much about the nature and strategies of an incumbent authoritarian regime, but they reveal little about prospects for political transition, much less democratic consolidation. A broader conception also conforms more closely to North African understandings of civil society.

Earlier generations of Tunisian nationalists had sharply distinguished between the *pays légal* of the French Protectorate and the *pays réel* comprised of informal networks and formal associations that the authorities periodically suppressed. The idea of a *pays réel* conveys a broader understanding of civil society which may include illegal opposition parties and associations among its set of relational networks. During the colonial period, these networks struggled for official recognition and eventually replaced their oppressors. Today a similar process appears to be under way in the Maghreb, although the oppressor is no longer foreign. Each country, in its own way, appears to be replicating the struggle for national liberation against French colonialism. The Islamists now occupy some of the political ground that their nationalist forebears successfully contested, against states now dominated by indigenous rather than foreign elites. Just as Algeria's military republic recalls the military regime of French Algeria beefed up by the Mollet government in 1956, Zine El-Abidine Ben Ali's regime is reminiscent of the Corsican police state managed by hard-line French *Residents* such as Marcel Peyrouton in 1934 and Jean de Hautecloque in 1952. Political Islam appears weaker and less well organized in Morocco than in the other two countries. But perhaps Morocco, too, is running true to form, a generation "behind" the others, just as it was the last to have been colonized. Civil society is undergoing major transition in all three countries, and the contemporary struggles of their respective civil societies seem to reflect their respective patterns of anticolonial struggle.

Even when civil society is articulated in opposition to a given regime, however, it is not really separate and distinct from the state. Civil society may be conceived as a set of formal and informal intermediaries occupying a space "between" the individual and the state, but the spatial metaphor should not be taken literally. Informal as well as formal intermediaries are shaped by laws, regulations, and, this chapter will argue, by historical legacies of conflict and cooperation with authorities. It is the modern state, after all, that encourages or discourages intermediaries from becoming formal associations, makes them legal or illegal, and gives them public space or drives them underground. Legacies of state-building—and repression—crucially shape the structures and "civic culture" of civil society. The colonial experiences of North African civil societies therefore condition the contemporary struggles between incumbent regimes and Islamist oppositions in ways that deserve to be explored and clarified.

Colonial Dialectic

Inspired partly by Hegel's master-slave dialectic and Albert Memmi's intimate portraits of colonizer and colonized,[3] and partly by Bourguiba's own speeches describing the epic work of Tunisian nation-building, I originally viewed anticolonial struggle as a dialectical process progressing through three stages corresponding to three paradigmatic elite responses to the colonial situation.[4] The first response was to emulate the foreigner and assimilate Western values, including liberal constitutionalism and nationalism; the second was to reject them in the name of Islam and national authenticity; and the third, finally, was to appropriate them fully, in practice as well as in theory, for purposes of national emancipation. In the third moment of the colonial dialectic, the westernized elites prove themselves to be more capable defenders of Islam and national authenticity than their traditionalist predecessors. In a fully developed colonial dialectic, the American paradigm of modernization—vintage 1960—triumphs. Not that this schema was exclusively American: Abdallah Laroui, a Moroccan intellectual, developed an analogous schema inspired by a neo-Marxian dialectic in his *Idéologie arabe contemporaine.*[5]

In view of the Islamist resurgence since the 1970s, such a colonial dialectic may appear quaint and outdated, but I shall nonetheless defend my version of it. In the words of Ian Lustick, who recently criticized my work:

> The hegemonic status of his belief in nationalism as natural and inevitable, while giving his work clarity and elegance, also places a stringent limitation upon it. His model of the colonial dialectic and three moments of nationalist consciousness, presented as an explanation of the most likely path from European colony to national state, takes the national state form as the terminal condition of Middle Eastern political life. Such an approach rules out the possibility of a continuing dialectic involving Islamic or otherwise nonnationalist moments of political consciousness.[6]

We agree that the dialectic continued after independence, and, as Lustick observes, Islamism and comparable Jewish impulses arose in Turkey and Israel, respectively, as well as across the Arab countries of the Middle East and North Africa. At issue is how to interpret these new modes of political consciousness. Were the newly aspiring elites in these countries reverting from third- to second-moment orientations, upsetting traditional modernization theory?

With post-1967 Israel in mind, Lustick questions the hegemonic status of nationalism and draws a sharp distinction between nationalist and Islamic modes of consciousness. It can be argued, however, that the new elites have remained nationalist, much as Arab nationalists in the 1960s remained loyal to their respective countries (while occasionally invoking alliances with brother Arabs to overthrow incumbent regimes). By their respective political involvements, the new aspiring elites confirm the "hegemonic" status of the nation-state everywhere in the region except Israel, where borders and citizenship are contested but not (at least not yet) the parliamentary regime. While Islamism has indeed "opened 'wars of position' [in Antonio Gramsci's terminology] over the meaning of political identity in polities throughout the Middle East,"[7] it is the political regimes and their definitions or conceptual boundaries of citizenship, not the territorial political communities, which are at stake. Nationalism remains hegemonic, and indeed the political spaces of contestation have deepened in all Maghrebi countries since independence. Islamism in Tunisia or Algeria does not contest these countries' respective colonial boundaries, although it may offer new identities to Tunisian or Algerian citizens. The one outstanding issue of a national boundary, that of the Moroccan Sahara, unified rather than divided Moroccan elites in 1973 and compensated them for the "loss" of Mauritania in 1960. Regional and ethnic differences have also tended to reinforce rather than threaten Morocco's political regime by pointing to the necessity of a monarch-arbiter. And in Algeria, where ethnic and linguistic demands have challenged the regime, they did not contest the political community. Berberism, for instance, is about the distribution of power among national elites, not a call for a separate political community.

Postcolonial spaces have deepened, in the sense that more people in each state aspire to real citizenship, but the national boundaries of each political community remained more or less intact, accepted by regimes and oppositions alike. Incumbent regimes, however, steadily lost legitimacy after their independence honeymoons. Not only did they fail to deliver the promised goods, their actions encouraged the emergence of new counterelites, just as the preceding colonial regimes had given rise to nationalist elites. What is fascinating is how deeply the new responses were embedded in their respective colonial legacies. Were they backsliding, as their religious discourse might suggest, or deepening the dialectic?

The colonial dialectic had indeed assumed a progressive unfolding of elite interpretations of national identity: the third moment was presumed over time to supersede the religiously inspired appeals of the second moment. However, the triumph of the third moment was by no means inevitable during the colonial period. The full working out of a colonial dialectic required the "right" colonial situation, with a conflict sufficiently protracted to enable successive generations of nationalists to articulate the three stages.[8] In French North Africa, Tunisia was the only country that fully exemplified this dialectic before independence. The Young Tunisians prior to the First World War were superseded by the Destour in the 1920s and the Neo-Destour by the late 1930s. Tunisia was the only candidate in the region for a potential backsliding from third- to second-moment orientations. Moroccan nationalism lagged Tunisia's by a generation, yet independence came at the same time, empowering the second moment. In Algeria, the protracted conflict was too ruthless to permit the primacy of educated elites, whether of the first, second, or third moment.

Has there been backsliding, then, in Tunisia? It should be recalled that the third moment never excluded religion. While negating the elites of the second moment, it contained a broader mass movement of second-moment orientations articulated in the Maghreb by Koranic schools, village mosques, and other intermediaries attached to national elites through political parties. During the colonial period, Islamic reformism in fact had deeper roots in Tunisia, which had fallen under the domination of third-moment elites, than in the rest of the Maghreb. These roots eventually nurtured Islamist reactions to Bourguiba's brand of nationalism, but they were mediated by the third-moment elites, which had acquired legitimacy at the national level.

As Abdelkader Zghal has so astutely observed, Tunisia's leading Islamist, Rachid Ghannouchi, is very much the "illegitimate son" of Habib Bourguiba, and "both are above all the products of Tunisian civil society, well entrenched within the long tradition of exchange between the two shores of the Mediterranean."[9] Like Bourguiba, Ghannouchi came from a politically peripheral region and was socially and professionally marginalized in a political economy dominated by francophone elites.[10] Like Bourguiba, he appealed to the uprooted and the dispossessed and offered new understandings of collective identity based on fresh interpretations of Islam adapted to the contemporary world. Ghannouchi distanced himself from traditional Islamic reformism and came to accept Bourguiba's law banning polygamy, once Bourguiba himself was removed from power and the Islamist movement had the chance to become Tunisia's leading legal opposition party.

If Ghannouchi is an Islamist, attacking the westernized consumerism of Tunisia's upper strata, so also was Bourguiba, who had insisted in the early 1930s on Tunisian women wearing the veil to protect their Tunisian national identity against the ravages of colonialism. Each leader tried to extend the reach of Tunisian nationalism and citizenship by appealing to Tunisia's Islamic heritage. Each leader was also in principle a *destouri* (constitutionalist) committed to western constitutional norms. It is no accident that Rachid Ghannouchi, the indirect product of Tunisia's colonial dialectic, is the most progressive of contemporary Islamist thinkers. He is surely part of a deepened third moment of Tunisian nation-building, injecting Islamic civic conscience into Western constitutional norms which Bourguiba had betrayed.

Traditions of Conflict

The past never quite repeats itself, but history offers a useful perspective for understanding the current processes shaping civil society in the Maghreb. Earlier patterns of anticolonial struggle shed light on current struggles, and past outcomes may serve as warnings against similar futures. The colonial dialectic generated civil society in all three countries, but with important variations that illustrate relationships between types of struggle and outcomes.

In Algeria, a long and often brutal colonial occupation not only displaced and discredited the society's natural elites and intermediaries but prevented new elites from extending their associations and nationalist parties to broad segments of the population. Although the nationalist struggle involved virtually the entire society, the intense polarization of a protracted guerrilla struggle marginalized the educated elites along with the vast majority of people who just wanted to survive the ugly war. Civil society in the sense of relatively autonomous associations flourished only briefly after independence. Once Boumediene's Tlemcen group consolidated control over the colonial state apparatus, civil society escaped into informal networks of cousins and friends within the expanding administrations, including that of the ruling party. As Ali El-Kenz explains, "organic" intellectuals could not emerge during the Boumediene years.[11] They were either co-opted into the complex set of state bureaucracies or isolated in other ways from potential readerships or followings. Civility was driven underground into private family life.

One especially unfortunate victim of bureaucratic repression was El-Qiyam, an Islamist discussion group founded by the late Malek Bennabi. The association was disbanded in 1966 and formally dissolved in 1970. As Yahia Zoubir observes, the association accomplished "the important task of paving the way for future Islamist organizations in the country"; he also notes their intellectual poverty and the remarkable ignorance of their predecessor's teachings—despite the fact that "the only true democratic thought in post-independent Algeria came from the independent Islamic thinker Malek Bennabi."[12] Bennabi's pamphlet, *La démocratie en Islam*,[13] was being distributed in downtown Algiers in 1990 but had little impact upon events. Imitating their Front of National Liberation (FLN) forebears, Islamist activists resorted to guerrilla warfare in 1986 and again in 1992, provoked by a state apparatus that, like its colonial predecessor, discouraged other forms of political expression.

The colonial dialectic resulted in more open forms of civil society in Morocco and Tunisia. In the two protectorates, traditional elites survived the French conquest and assimilated French culture without losing their standing in the society. In Tunisia, a French educated elite was gradually broadened to include new families, notably from the Sahel. As early as 1940, Henri de Montety noted that the new elements were superseding the old families in an intergenerational struggle which was politically reflected in rivalries between the Destour and the Neo-Destour parties.[14] Despite periodic police repression, the Neo-Destour was able to deepen its appeal among broad strata of the society and, in alliance with the Union Générale Tunisienne de Travail (UGTT), encourage the formation of a wide array of associations. By independence, a vibrant civil society had come into being, but one-party government subsequently reshaped it into administrative hierarchies paralleling those of the government. Tunisified, the old colonial administration survived, to be challenged in the 1980s by dissident Destourians and a new generation of Islamists escaping the ruling party's embrace.

In Morocco, by contrast, the colonial struggle did not give rise to a hegemonic nationalist party. Just as the processes of colonization and the formation of new elites lagged a generation behind similar Tunisian developments, nationalist responses were similarly delayed. Within the nationalist movement, the old families still held their own as the dominant element within newly educated elites. The circumstances of independence favored the retention of the monarchy in 1956, just as they might have favored Moncef Bey in Tunisia if independence had been granted in 1942. At independence, Moroccan civil society remained a heterogeneous assortment of urban associations and rural notables representing the Protectorate's tribal constructs. It proved relatively easy for King Mohammed V to play upon divisions within the Istiqlal and to encourage other parties and associations in rural areas where the Istiqlal was weak. His successor selectively co-opted or eliminated the putative young Moroccan Bourguibas who aspired to hegemony. Consequently, independent Morocco preserved a richer and more active civil society of associations and political parties than Tunisia's—albeit at the cost of much more extensive violations of human rights. By the early 1970s, once King Hassan was obliged to face the consequences of having suspended the constitution and becoming dependent upon military support, there was precious little civil society in the sense of "uncoerced human association" left in any of the Maghrebi countries.

The differences between the Moroccan and Tunisian cases of nationalist struggle and civil society formation are instructive, however. Many observers, myself included, used to think that the Tunisians were fortunate to have been colonized longer because their protracted anticolonial struggle offered an exemplary incubation period for building up strong nationalist organization (and civil society).[15] In retrospect, however, the relatively high degree of consensus enjoyed by nationalist elites proved ephemeral and ultimately destructive because it facilitated a personality cult and a bureaucratization of civil society. The political polarization associated with the colonial dialectic, moreover, left an unhappy legacy. The Neo-Destour had tried to consolidate its hegemony in 1937 in bitter and occasionally violent confrontations with the Old Destour. Subsequently, the tragic Youssefist scission, repressed with the help of the French, was used to justify the official orchestration of consensus after independence. Today the same logic is used to justify repressing the Islamists.

Morocco was lucky to have escaped single-party rule. Civil society remained divided into distinctive political subcultures, talking past one another in ways that often lacked civility. The cacophony of discourses seemed as removed from political reality as the official *langue de bois* of neighboring Algeria. They could also be more easily manipulated than a hegemonic third-moment party. The better to divide and rule, the king encouraged the rebuilding of civil society in the 1970s and 1980s. Most of the parties were persuaded to play politics on the king's playing field, and many political prisoners were released and rehabilitated. The human-rights records of the three countries seem finally to have been reversed. Morocco's record, imperfect as it may be, seems to be less at issue today than those of Algeria and Tunisia.

This brief synopsis of patterns of nationalist struggle offers some insights into conditions for the development of civil society. Morocco and Tunisia highlight the critical roles of educated elites in the process. They were the intermediaries of the colonial dialectic, the carriers of new forms of association imported from Europe and from European settler communities and adapted to local conditions. In Algeria, where the intellectuals were marginalized, the new forms of association remained weak. Even at the regional and local levels, Morocco and Tunisia displayed richer associational life. In Algeria, Abdelhamid Ben Badis' movement of reformed *ulama* had greater political salience than comparable reformist movements elsewhere in the Maghreb, but its organizational base of modern Koranic schools was less extensive than those of Tunisia and Morocco. In Tunisia, for example, they reinforced the Neo-Destour's local base and provided key intermediaries between French-trained leaders and less educated populations.

Intellectuals were marginalized in Algeria for many reasons, but the underlying cause was that the colonial regime was too brutal, with so many major interests at stake, to tolerate a space for indigenous elites and their nationalist organizations. The more brutal and repressive the authoritarian regime, the less auspicious the environment will be for developing any civil society. The other important lesson offered by these brief histories is that even when a regime does tolerate some space (at least some of the time) in which nationalist movements are permitted to develop associations as well as informal networks, a protracted conflict may have destructive consequences that outweigh the "progress" associated with the third moment of the colonial dialectic. Too much apparent consensus in the face of a colonial or authoritarian adversary is likely to suffocate civil society. Moroccan society, reflected in the dissensus among its elites, remained buoyant and pluralistic. The colonial situation did not polarize elites into "forces of light" and "forces of darkness," as in Tunisia at the time of the Youssefist scission, because the conflict did not last as long.

Future Prospects

What can these lessons suggest concerning the future of civil society in the Maghreb? History does not repeat itself, and any resemblances be-

tween national liberation struggles and the contemporary struggles between Islamists and incumbent regimes must be qualified by the obvious
difference that the incumbent regimes, unlike French Algeria or the protectorates, are governed by their respective nationals. Each regime may
be at least as authoritarian as its colonial predecessor, and indeed each
has also inherited the disciplinary apparatus of the colonial police state.
But each regime now controls a sovereign state, and any change of regime—however desired and influenced by external pressures—must come
from within rather than be dictated from abroad. Unlike the anticolonial
consensus of the 1960s, there is no broad international consensus today
that states should Islamize, only—with many qualifications—that they
ought to democratize. Tunisia and Morocco more or less follow the fuzzy
international guidelines by running regular (if not quite "fair and free")
elections and by promoting official "civil society."

Another significant difference between the colonial and contemporary
periods is that the capitalist economies have been nationalized and in part
privatized, laying an indigenous groundwork for civil society, which in
the final analysis is a child of capitalism. Civil society also had economic
bases in the colonial period—such as Sahel peasant freeholders in Tunisia
and a Fassi bourgeoisie in Morocco—but they have grown dramatically
since independence with the takeover of colonial holdings, some
privatization of state assets, and modest amounts of private investment
in new assets. The private sector is strongest and most concentrated in
Morocco and weakest in Algeria, where, however, state housing was sold
off to their tenants in the mid-1980s and private lands were subsequently
restored to their owners. The occupational structures of these societies
have drastically changed since independence. In 1955, 78, 71, and 60
percent, respectively, of Algerian, Tunisian, and Moroccan Muslims were
employed in agriculture; in 1990, the percentages were down to 26, 28,
and 45, with Morocco changing the least, for the most part in the 1980s.
The labor forces employed in industry rose from 12.5 to 31 percent in
Algeria, and from 11 to 33 percent in Tunisia, but only from 23 to 25
percent in Morocco.[16]

Another major change, of course, concerns education and literacy. Even
in Morocco, where education, viewed as potentially destabilizing, was
least promoted, primary education soared from 17 to over 70 percent of
the population from 1955 to 1993; 29 percent of the eligible female population was enrolled in secondary school (compared to 55 and 49 for Algeria and Tunisia, respectively).[17] Far greater numbers of potential leaders, of sociologically competent people, are now available to participate

in associational life. In Algeria, the country historically most deprived of civil society, thousands of associations came to life in response to President Chadli Benjedid's political opening of 1988–91. Despite European fears of hordes of Algerian "boat people" invading their shores in the event of an Islamist takeover, it seems unlikely that any successor regime can again marginalize Algeria's educated middle and lower classes.

The lessons of the earlier efforts to build civil societies are still relevant, however. Protracted military conflict in Algeria may decimate civil society's natural leadership and delay its development. The war in Algeria meanwhile encourages repression in Tunisia by a regime that manipulates elite fears of Islamism to stay in power. Tunisia's prisons and camps were more populated in 1991–92 than during the bleakest periods of colonial repression, and apparently they remain so (see chapters 4 and 8). Protracted political conflict could result in the sort of polarization among elites that once had empowered Bourguiba and might eventually support a new authoritarian proselytizer. Whether the incumbent Algerian and Tunisian regimes retain the upper hand or lose out to the Islamists, civil society is at risk to new, better-organized, "bureaucratic" forms of authoritarianism in both countries as long as the conflicts endure. These regimes will require ever more repressive means to stay in power, as the pressures of the Islamists are compounded by the pains of economic adjustment. The counterelites, in turn will, develop more sophisticated "third-moment" cultures and techniques of survival. Guillermo O'Donnell's description of Latin America's ugly "bureaucratic-authoritarian" regimes of the 1960s may well apply to these North African regimes, premised as they are on the suppression on the Maghreb's equivalent of *lo popular.*[18]

Some scholars as well as supporters of the incumbent regimes may argue, against any quick resolutions of the respective conflicts, that the costs would be unacceptable and that civil society would be the victim rather than beneficiary of the probable settlement. Assuming that a settlement were possible in Algeria, the feared outcome would be an Islamist-dominated government and an Islamic republic of Algeria, with domino effects in Tunisia, Egypt, and Morocco. Islamic republics would proceed to destroy all non-Islamist forms of association.

In my opinion, this worst-case scenario represents too literal a rereading of colonial history; it underestimates the social and economic changes that have occurred since independence. Despite official Arabization of much of the educational system, French cultural influences have permeated broad segments of society, and Algeria's extensive middle strata of cadres and employees no longer can be managed by a narrow base of administrators, whether FLN or Islamist. The private sector, while weak, is growing and would probably be further encouraged by any Islamist regime. The worst-case scenario also misrepresents political Islam. Islamism is not a political doctrine comparable to Western ideologies. Although Islamists may agree in theory that "Islam is the solution" to all human problems, the consensus carries little practical socioeconomic content. Without a Khomeini or a doctrine of *velayat-e faqih* (rule of the jurisprudent), it is difficult to see how Algerian Islamists could govern without mechanisms for articulating differences of opinion. Islamism may or may not be compatible with parliamentary democracy, depending on how the Islamists come to power.

The worst-case scenario also fails for practical reasons to be convincing. To come to power, the Islamic Salvation Front (FIS) needs the support of the Algerian army. Guerrilla tactics might work if they sparked crippling dissension within the army, but the atrocities committed by the Armed Islamic Group (GIA) since 1993 have stiffened the army's resolve. The FIS today could hardly come to power with the help of the GIA because the guerrilla force is weak and disorganized. It is a poor replica of the FLN's internal guerrilla forces, deprived of support from any external army like Boumediene's National Liberation Army (ALN) in 1960–62. And it is worth remembering that in 1962 a much stronger FLN still needed a political peace with President Charles de Gaulle to achieve power, for its battered forces were no match for the French army.

Unfortunately, there are no signs that President Liamine Zeroual and the commanders of the Algerian army are preparing any political peace with the FIS. The hope in 1995 was that President Zeroual could discipline his hard-liners, successfully negotiate with the FIS leadership for new elections, and back FIS efforts to discipline their hard-liners and freelance Islamist desperadoes, with military support if necessary. The work of sharing power with the FIS then could have proceeded along the lines that were being negotiated by Chadli before he was dismissed. Were elections to be conducted freely, the non-Islamist parties gaining representation in parliament could encourage divisions within the FIS, which may have been better organized than other parties in the early 1990s but was hardly monolithic.

Perhaps pushed by hard-liners within the military establishment, President Zeroual instead rejected the "national contract" signed in Rome in January 1995 between Algeria's major political parties, including the FIS,[19] and took unilateral measures to create a semblance of constitutional legitimacy. His own election to the presidency was followed by a constitutional referendum leading to new legislative elections on June 5, 1997. Evidently, the regime was attempting to rebuild a facade of legitimacy as well as to eradicate the terrorists, and all of Algeria's principal parties participated, with the major exception of the FIS. The National Democratic Rally (RND), a government party newly created for the occasion, conveniently won 155 of the 380 seats in the new parliament, while two moderate Islamist parties gained 103. Voter turnout was officially proclaimed to be 65.5 percent nationwide, 43.3 percent in Algiers, and 33.3 percent among 663,251 registered Algerian voters living in France (see chapter 2). Caught between the military regime and Islamist guerrilla forces, however, civil society remained in limbo. Political space, suddenly opened up in 1989 and then closed down in 1992, was being slightly reopened, but it was far from certain that the official Islamist participants could relegitimate politics for the legions of Algerians who had voted for the FIS in 1991. The forces of civil society were still no match for the combined power of the military and its guerrilla opposition, which feed off each other,[20] and which have victimized a general population already suffering from Algeria's necessary but painful economic-adjustment policies. The faint hope was that President Zeroual might yet broker a peace after first convincing his military commanders of the legitimacy of Algeria's new constitutional facade.

A peaceful settlement in Algeria involving the FIS would clearly have positive effects elsewhere in the region. Even bringing leaders of the officially recognized Islamist parties into the government and strengthening their credibility might have salutary ripple effects. If the Algerian experience could somehow demystify the specter of Islamists sharing power, Ben Ali might have greater difficulty justifying his police regime as a bulwark against the Islamic movement Green Threat. The Nahda could be recognized as a legal opposition party, thereby enhancing the credibility of future Tunisian elections. Conversely, continuing bloodshed in Algeria reinforces Tunisian authoritarianism and deepens the historical parallel between the epic struggles of the Neo-Destour and the current tribulations of the Nahda. But just as Ben Ali's regime may be more intimidating than the French Protectorate, Rachid Ghannouchi lacks Bourguiba's stature. Still waiting in the wings, perhaps, is a Tunisian FIS, founded by Mohammed Ali el-Horani, which rejects Ghannouchi's policy of peaceful confrontation in favor of a more active, violent path.[21] Bourguiba might yet acquire another illegitimate offspring to displace Ghannouchi and emulate Bourguiba's dark side, betraying Tunisia's constitutionalist legacy. It seems premature to argue, as does Elbaki Hermassi, that Tunisia has already resolved the issue and that political Islam has faded away from the political scene, just because Ghannouchi has managed so far to parry calls for violent struggle.[22]

Tunisia's worst-case scenario would be a protracted struggle with the Nahda that undercut Islamist leadership committed to working peacefully for political and social change. Tunisian society, like Algeria's, has grown too complex to be ruled by administrators and the police. The apparent political stability that currently prevails has been bought at the price of massive violations of human rights, which have undercut the regime's legitimacy. Though Ben Ali is no Saddam Hussein, the title of a book about Iraq also applies to contemporary Tunisia, *The Republic of Fear*.[23] Many of the natural leaders of Tunisian civil society are afraid to speak out—whether or not they are in any sense Islamist—lest they and other family members suffer economic retribution or worse. Under these conditions, the presidential plebiscite and parliamentary elections of March 20, 1994, were "a mere formality."[24] Nineteen seats in parliament were reserved for token opposition parties, but two of their tame leaders were subsequently arrested and incarcerated for several months for doing their opposition duties.

Morocco seems better positioned to weather the Algerian storm. Its pluralistic facade of parties and elections enjoys greater credibility than Tunisia's, and the king's decision in March 1998 to appoint Abderrahmane El Youssoufi, leader of the opposition Socialist Union of Popular Forces (USFP), to form a new government gives the opposition greater credibility, at least for a time. By reserving key posts for his veteran administrators, however, the king makes it difficult for the opposition parties, confined to economic and technical ministries, to implement any major policies, despite mounting social hardship and unemployment.

The Commander of the Faithful's ability to co-opt and domesticate Islamist forces may be diminishing. Neither the USFP nor the other traditional opposition parties attract many university students. Like Ben Ali, the king has encouraged a wide variety of NGOs to represent a compliant "civil society" and thereby contribute to a "modernization of the clientelistic practices of the *makhzen*."[25] On the international stage, in fact, Morocco has jumped ahead of Tunisia. Although traditionally Tunisia has displayed a greater density of NGOs, the situation may be changing. Morocco sent twenty-seven NGOs to the International Conference on Women held in Beijing in September 1995—half again as many as Tunisia and twice as many as Algeria. That Morocco surpassed Tunisia in this area is quite surprising: since 1991 Ben Ali's regime has singled out women as "a possible rampart against 'fundamentalism,' and consequently they have been called upon to mobilize," especially through NGOs.[26] In Morocco, the power of the NGOs remains distinctly limited,[27] but they do contribute to a climate of greater political pluralism than in Tunisia and possibly offer more effective barriers or channels for rising tides of Islamists.

In addition to encouraging NGOs, another possible strategy, not yet attempted in Morocco, might be to foster Islamist business groups and invite them into the existing cartels controlled by the monarchy. So far, Morocco has resisted overtures to establish Islamic banks, whereas Algeria and Tunisia have accepted them. Moroccan reticence derives from the king's refusal as Commander of the Faithful to share his religious authority with any other potential power center. With a share in the country's finance capital, Islamic businesses could selectively sponsor Islamist associations much as other businesses support existing parties. The question is whether a moderate, pro-monarchical Islamist mainstream might encourage or discourage unconditional Islamist opposition. One lesson learned in the early 1970s was that suppressing unconditional non-Islamist oppositions without political cover made the monarchy vulnerable to military coups. Perhaps the political cover of moderate Islamists could prolong the monarchy and render it more constitutional. The Islamists would have to join and compete with other parties articulating constraints on the arbitrary exercise of power.

Conclusion

The longer the incumbent regimes resist political settlements with their Islamist oppositions, the bleaker the prospects for their respective civil societies. Delays will only reinforce the picture of history repeating itself, of Islamists acquiring the mantle of authentic nationalism pitted against alien regimes. Protracted colonial conflict was detrimental to civil society even when, as in Tunisia, the element of armed struggle remained peripheral and subordinate to the political leadership. The protracted conflict of the 1990s seems to be suffocating civil society in Tunisia as well as Algeria, and it shows few signs of abating, despite the legislative elections in Algeria, as these lines are being written (December 1997).

The lost opportunities seem especially tragic in Tunisia because its third-moment elite, including the Islamist opposition, could have retained a relatively high degree of national cohesion while practicing constitutional democracy. Civil society tended to integrate Tunisians into a functioning polity rather than dividing them into polarized camps. Rachid Ghannouchi had supported Ben Ali's "national pact" in 1988 and was ready to work within the system in 1990, when the regime refused to recognize his Nahda party and subsequently cracked down on the alleged terrorists and sympathizers alike.

Of the three countries under discussion, Morocco clearly offers the most fertile field for civil society. Predicated on a policy of divide and rule, the monarchy was adept at encouraging and manipulating civic NGOs as well as political parties. Indeed, just as privatization offered the *makhzen* new patronage resources,[28] NGOs were also contributing to the modernization of the king's patron-client networks. Would greater numbers of NGOs and volumes of NGO activity prepare the way for the more institutionalized restraints on political power required of a constitutional monarchy or other forms of constitutional democracy? This assumption underlying much of the civil-society literature deserves more critical attention. Sheri Berman reminds us that Weimar Germany was a nation of joiners and that associations disconnected people from mainstream political parties and trained many of them ultimately to serve the Nazis.[29] Could it be (repeating the experience of the Weimar Republic) that the NGOs encouraged by the Moroccan monarchy are simply weakening the political parties, further segmenting Moroccan society, and offering organizational skills to Islamists so that they eventually seize power?

Such a scenario, at least, points to differences between Morocco, where it has some plausibility, and Tunisia, where it does not. The colonial dialectic, which largely conditions the possibilities for civil society, already reached the third moment in Tunisia, whereas Morocco, still oscillating between the first and second moments (both of which are dominated by the king), might yet experience a revolutionary breakthrough to the third moment. In Tunisia, the third moment already domesticates the Islamists and renders them fit to coexist with other political forces deriving from Bourguibism, whereas Moroccan political culture offers no analogous anchor of elite consensus. Morocco also may be victim of the widest social inequalities in the region: as was shown earlier, it has made less progress than its neighbors in educating its citizens and creating jobs in industry, while its private sector, headed by industrial groups and agricultural enterprises owned by the king, is the largest and most concentrated in the region. By many accounts, its traditional parties are largely discredited; indeed some Moroccans say they are not even part of the civil society of more dynamic NGOs.[30] Islamists, of course, are not permitted to found political parties, but some Islamist politicians have obtained permission to form cultural associations after reaching the necessary informal understandings with the monarchy.[31] Economic policies designed to attract investment to Morocco and make its exports competitive may be increasing the social strains that feed Islamist tendencies. Morocco's pluralism, in short, does not insure a soft landing into constitutional democracy. Courageous leadership is needed—sooner rather than later, indeed, if Morocco's experienced political parties are to play a responsible role. Though Moroccan society is undergoing rapid change, its relatively large rural population can still cushion political change better than in neighboring Algeria.

Perhaps, as François Burgat has observed, regimes deserve their oppositions.[32] More open regimes, respectful of human rights, notably of the freedom to participate in associations of their choice, could strengthen the moderate mainstreams of the respective Islamist movements. The Maghreb's political regimes are the product of their respective colonial situations and traditions of nationalist struggle, but regimes are also people who can overcome structures. Alliances between the moderates and reformers within the respective regimes could hasten the progress officially advocated by their leaders toward greater democracy.

Notes

1. Goldberg, "Smashing Idols and the State," 3–35.

2. Walzer, "The Idea of Civil Society," 293.

3. Hegel, *The Phenomenology of Mind*; Memmi, *The Colonizer and the Colonized*.

4. Moore, *Tunisia since Independence*.

5. Laroui, *Idéologie arabe contemporaine*.

6. Lustick, "Hegemony and the Riddle of Nationalism," 27–28.

7. Ibid., 29.

8. Moore, *Politics in North Africa*, 36–38.

9. Abdelkader Zghal in Zartman, *Tunisia: The Political Economy of Reform*, 205.

10. Burgat, "Rachid Ghannuchi: Islam, nationalisme et islamisme," 109–22.

11. El-Kenz, *Algerian Reflections on Arab Crises*, 18–25.

12. Zoubir, "Algerian Islamists' Conception of Democracy," 68, 81.

13. Bennabi, *La démocratie en Islam*.

14. Montety, "Old Families and New Elite in Tunisia."

15. Moore, *Politics in North Africa*, 90.

16. Ibid., 54; World Bank, *World Development Report 1997*, 220–21.

17. World Bank, *World Development Report 1997*, 226–27.

18. O'Donnell, "Tensions in the Bureaucratic-Authoritarian State."

19. Mortimer, "Islamists, Soldiers, and Democrats," 35–38.

20. Addi, *L'Algérie et la démocratie,* 182–83. Also see interview with Roberts, "Under Western Eyes," 39–42.

21. *Middle East Economic Digest,* August 19, 1994, 24.

22. Hermassi, "The Rise and Fall of the Islamist Movement in Tunisia," 105–28.

23. Al-Khalil, *The Republic of Fear.*

24. Denoeux, "Tunisie: Les élections présidentielles et législatives," 49.

25. Denoeux and Gateau, "L'essor des associations au Maroc," 23.

26. Daoud, "Les femmes tunisiennes," 33. For the United Nations Development Program's on-line list of NGOs attending the United Nations Fourth World Conference on Women held in Beijing, September 1995, see gopher:// gopher.undp.org:70/11/unconfs/women/ngo.

27. Laurent and Denoeux, "Campagne d'assainissement au Maroc," 133.

28. Henry, *The Mediterranean Debt Crescent,* 82–87.

29. Berman, "Civil Society and the Collapse of the Weimar Republic," 401–29.

30. Laurent and Denoeux, "Campagne d'assainissement au Maroc," 133.

31. Burgat, *L'Islamisme en face,* 120; *The Islamic Movement in North Africa,* 170–73.

32. Burgat, *The Islamic Movement in North Africa,* 306.

2.

STATE AND CIVIL SOCIETY IN ALGERIA

Yahia H. Zoubir

A crisis cannot give the attacking forces the ability to organize with
lightning speed in time and in space; still less can it endow them with
fighting spirit. Similarly, the defenders are not demoralized, nor do they
abandon their positions, even among the ruins, nor do they lose faith in
their own strength or their own future.

Antonio Gramsci

The Concept of Civil Society

This chapter reviews the relationship between the state and civil society
in Algeria. The emergence of civil society in Algeria may be linked to a
dual process: economic liberalization and the weakening of the state due
to the failure of its authoritarian developmentalist policy. Furthermore,
the indisputable existence of an increasingly resolute civil society provides the potential for genuine democratization.

"Civil society" embraces many "private," yet potentially autonomous,
public sectors distinct from the state. Such sectors are regulated by various associations existing within them, preventing society from degenerat-
ing into a shapeless mass. At least two ingredients characterize civil society: distinction and autonomy from the state. Civil society consists of a
network of economic, intellectual, political, and religious associations.
Those associations are independent of the state and of the family but not
totally separate from them.[1] In other words, as Larry Diamond explains,
"civil society is the realm of organized social life that is voluntary, self-
generating, (largely) self-supporting, autonomous from the state, and
bound by a legal order or set of shared rules. . . . It involves citizens

acting collectively in a public sphere to express their interests, passions, and ideas, exchange information, achieve mutual goals, make demands on the state, and hold state officials accountable."[2]

Civil society is also what Antonio Gramsci described as the space for the ideological struggle and for ideological hegemony,[3] an aspect of civil society often overlooked in the contemporary literature.

The concept of civil society, as opposed to the more general concept of society, helps analysts to distance themselves from the statist approaches, which dominated the analysis of Middle Eastern and African polities until the late 1980s. Indeed, Arab and Maghrebi intellectuals in general were state-centered and criticized the state only to demand a more important and more efficacious intervention of that very same state, but they totally ignored the concept of civil society.[4]

Civil society figures even more importantly in the theories on the transition from authoritarian to democratic regimes because it plays a crucial role once the liberalization of the authoritarian regime has begun. One of the consequences of authoritarian regimes is, of course, the depoliticizing and atomizing of society through repressive measures, ideological domination, and the restriction of the space of political action to the mere pursuit of private goals. In other words, the state totally controls the public sphere and prevents organizational or group autonomy where political identities could be expressed.[5]

As has been the case in most Middle Eastern countries, civil society has been the victim of authoritarian rulers who have succeeded in controlling it to a degree. The rentier states, in particular, succeeded in eliciting and maintaining a considerable level of consensus from both the masses and the elite. The intellectuals provided a justification for a strong state and overlooked its repressive measures in the name of modernization and nation building. The intelligentsia in the Middle East, in fact, never became the catalyst of new critical associations within civil society; if anything, it considered the nascent pluralism to be a factor of disunity, or *fitna*, for the revolution.[6] Central power gained almost total control over society. The "opposition"—muted, as it were—consisted only of supporting the power in place so as not to create divisions within the nation. It was forbidden from seeking power or from attempting to weaken the established regimes, let alone presenting itself as a different or autonomous component,[7] and those regimes, supported by the so-called progressive Left, proved that they could mobilize quickly against any true opposition.

Although frequently the target of revolutionary rhetoric, the "business class" (bourgeoisie) agreed to a tacit pact with the regime. They gave up any conspicuous political role and followed the state's main economic guidelines in exchange for the state's acquiescence in allowing them to make substantial profits. The state therefore controlled the working masses through a combination of social benefits and repression.[8] The intellectuals, the new capitalist class (concentrated in the public sector), and the trade unions (controlled by the state through the single party) formed a common front favoring authoritarian control instead of forming the basis for a new civil society.

Such fundamental concepts as tolerance, dedication to democracy, and civility are known to be among the most vital factors in the transition to a democratic order. Yet one of the most neglected aspects of democracy is the idea of "civility," which one may define as "an attitude and pattern of conduct."[9] Civility is a recognition of and devotion not only to the organizations that make up civil society but also to all its layers and categories. An even more important defining characteristic of civility is that "as a feature of civil society [civility] considers others as fellow-citizens of equal dignity in their rights and obligations as members of civil society; it means regarding other persons, including one's adversaries as members of the same inclusive collectivity, i.e., as members of the same society, even though they belong to different parties or to different religious communities or to different ethnic groups."[10]

The significance of civility stems from its capacity to attenuate the degree of conflict in society. But how are civility and tolerance—two necessary ingredients of democracy—developed? They are developed in civil society. In a civil society, the stakes are lower and force is used solely to maintain the peace. In a civil society, "all the associations are equal under the law."[11] In other words, civil society is the realm where the evolution of various democratic virtues—including moderation, inclination toward compromise, and deference for diametrically opposed beliefs—takes place.[12]

In Algeria, democratic virtues are critical in order to prevent the breakup of national identity. The severity of the crisis since 1988 and the armed conflict among various forces in the 1990s have exacerbated all the socioeconomic contradictions, which the authoritarian regime had succeeded in concealing for almost three decades. Even at the peak of liberalization (1989–91), opposition groups showed little civility toward one another— the radical Islamists and the secularists sought to negate the existence of the other. A fact often overlooked in studies on Algeria is that a segment of civil society encouraged the military to annul the second round of the legislative elections in January 1992 because of the fears the radical Islamists provoked among many Algerians.

State and Society in Algeria

Until the October 1988 riots, which shook the stability of the state, the Algerian political system fell under the control of a variety of military and civilian actors organized around a clan. The leader, surrounded by a clique of associates and a disparate clientele, unified the group. The unity of the group in power was neither ideological nor necessarily regionalist, but primarily clannish. The single party, officially charged with the task of ruling over society, was in fact only the conduit between society and the bloc in power.

Despite the authoritarian regime's attempts to impose total control over society, parallel forces (such as the underground economy and dissident groups) challenged the policies the regime had instituted. A divorce between state and civil society resulted from the policies that successive regimes pursued without regard for society's wishes. Regardless of its instinctive defense against the state, civil society was still not conscious of its potential power and organizational capabilities. The weakening of the state shortly before and after the October riots and the emergence of radical Islamism created the awareness about the potentiality.

Although limited, an Algerian civil society existed under French colonial rule. Innumerable civic, religious, athletic, and even political associations were active throughout the country. But the regimes that have ruled Algeria since its independence in 1962 have always distrusted all types of autonomous associations, whatever their nature; even the Boy Scouts fell under the control of the state.[13] The FLN party or the concurrent bureaucracy absorbed autonomous organizations. The majority of "autonomous" associations were limited to athletic, parenting, or religious activities. In 1966, for instance, the leaders of the Union Nationale des Etudiants Algériens (UNEA) were imprisoned, and the union fell under the authority of the party. The UNEA was banned for demanding the right to organize independently of the state. The Union Nationale de la Jeunesse Algérienne (UNJA) continued for a while the autonomous activities of the UNEA. Eventually, however, it colluded with the regime of Houari Boumediene, especially after he launched the agrarian revolution in 1971. The UNJA obtained a noteworthy degree of support for the organization of summer volunteer work in the countryside for students. The Union Générale des Travailleurs Algériens (UGTA) was forced into submission to the party in

1969, though it offered strong resistance to the single party on many occasions. The authorities created their own associations, such as the FLN Youth (JFLN) to support the regime's development policies, and the Woman's organization (UNFA). After independence, schools and students began to increase rapidly. Universities could not accommodate the increase, so they, too, became merely an extension of the state. The universities fulfilled only an economic and social function; they did not provide a base from which an Algerian intelligentsia could challenge the state. Thus, "by becoming more socialized and more democratized, the university in Algeria seems paradoxically to have lost the intellectual hegemony it might have exercised in society's cultural realm."[14]

Although far from being monolithic, the regime nonetheless felt apprehensive about the possibility of dissension. Decree 63–297 of August 14, 1963, prohibited any political association other than the single party. The Communist party was the first to be banned in November 1962, but other parties suffered the same fate following the promulgation of the 1963 decree. The Parti de la Révolution Socialiste (PRS) and the Front des Forces Socialistes (FFS) were therefore banned in August and September, respectively. Algeria's rulers argued that their opposition to a multiparty system stemmed from the experience of the period preceding the war of national liberation, in which the quarrels among the various parties and within the main party (MTLD) slowed nationalist advance. The argument prevailed under the rule of President Houari Boumediene (1965–1978). President Boumediene once declared that "the plurality of parties under disguised forms, within the single party, should be fought and destroyed because it represents a danger which threatens to decimate the party and will transform it into a dead body without a soul."[15] His attitude persisted until the political liberalization which the successor regime initiated in early 1989. The regimes overlooked the fact that under French colonial rule, Algerians managed to participate in associative activities. In fact, those activities made up the nuclei of the nationalist movement which eventually defeated French colonial rule.

Although created by the regime, a semblance of "civil society" did in fact exist in postcolonial Algeria. The FLN party's mass organizations were active, even though their role was more that of a conduit than a mediator between society and the state. Moreover, those organizations were close to the masses, so they served as quasi "interest groups" which the regime could not ignore. In the euphoria of development and the "anti-imperialist struggle," most intellectuals endorsed, albeit critically, Boumediene's regime. Under Boumediene's rule, Algerian society underwent profound socioeconomic, cultural, and psychological changes. In order to succeed in his policies, Boumediene used his political strength to control a relatively solid bloc in spite of the deep, often irreconcilable, ideological and political differences permeating it. Clearly, despite the rhetoric, the leadership was not unanimous in its support for the socialist ideology.[16]

The media, an important element of civil society, were, like the other elements, subordinated to the state and the party. They served to mobilize and to communicate state policies. Although the various constitutions guaranteed freedom of the press, the regime's monolithic conception of society resulted in an interpretation of that freedom different from that prevailing in liberal democracies. As in the other Maghrebi countries (and in the rest of the Arab world), the Algerian press was conceived as an "instrument of dialogue between the authorities and the masses within the framework of the options defined in a definitive and unanimous manner by the social body. It must favor the participation of the citizens to the realization of national goals."[17] The authorities thus expected the press to perform a civic task of educating and enriching the masses, to help in their mobilization and organization, and to explain to them the objectives of development. The goal was not to have a neutral press but to have one that was committed to a holistic, unified vision of society, as the FLN state conceived it. The press was, however, one of the main spaces for confrontation among the various dissenters within the single party.[18]

The cataclysmic events of October 1988, triggered by society's accumulated grievances against corruption, marginalization, arbitrary rule, and injustice, revealed that the ruling bloc, which had begun to disintegrate in the mid-1980s, had reached a point of no return. The disintegration of the bloc resulted from the general crisis of the rentier state because of prolonged socioeconomic difficulties. The ruling bloc had grown too complacent and failed to perceive its diminishing capacity as a "welfare state" or its diminishing legitimacy inherited from the prestigious war of independence. Postindependence youth, who make up more than 70 percent of the population, did not, and do even less so today, share any of the values of the wartime FLN and its army of liberation. Most Algerians have lost all faith in the state's elites, accused of corruption and incompetence, and have rejected the overused nationalist ideology that the system propagated for three decades. Algerians, young people in particular, have become disenchanted because of the rise of a new, unproductive caste of nouveaux riches, who have conspicuously displayed, against ethics and traditional teachings, their often unlawfully accumulated wealth. In the meantime, the youth were denied much of what they expected: opportunities for good education, housing, travel, and marriage. The contradictions between the official, socialist discourse and the everyday reality have caused young people to lose faith in patriotic and national values, the values that helped the country make important strides in the first two decades of its independence.

The Democratic Opening and the Process of Democratization

In the 1980s, even before the tragic events of October 1988, autonomous cultural (Amazigh/Berber), feminist, human-rights, syndicalist, trade, and Islamist associations had begun to blossom throughout the country. A cyclical pattern of riots—on a small scale but affecting most of the country—induced the regime to introduce some timid reforms, favoring the recognition of a limited range of cultural and community associations. The regime even went as far as recognizing the Algerian Human Rights League, albeit in the hope of countering two otherwise independent human-rights organizations. In fact, in 1987, the government acknowledged the right of citizens to create nonpolitical associations around issues, such as consumer defense and cultural activities.

The mounting debt-service payments, the increasing power of the new bourgeoisie, and the drop in oil prices prompted President Chadli Bendjedid to initiate economic reforms and economic liberalization. The reforms and economic liberalization also served as a stratagem for eliminating rivals in the regime and served to advance the interests of a particular faction entrenched in the private sector. That faction had support in the military, the administration, and the regions and consisted mostly of those who had not found favor and promotion under Boumediene. Following the riots of October, however, the regime had no option but to initiate political reforms, then fearing for its survival. The reforms soon generated their own dynamic, beginning a process with many ramifications, in many ways irreversible.

On February 23, 1989, Algerians approved a new constitution.[19] Its adoption amounted to a revolution because the new constitution rejected the FLN as an organization charged with a political function. The FLN was no longer mentioned as playing the supreme role and as having supremacy over political life.[20]

More important, freedom of expression, association, and assembly were guaranteed under the 1989 constitution. The most meaningful amendment was the recognition of the right of the citizens "to create political associations" (Art. 40). That amendment permitted the subsequent establishment of a multiparty system, thus terminating the hegemony of the FLN and making the latter a *parti comme les autres* (a party like any other). Law No. 89–11, which established the rules for the existence of political associations,[21] (read political parties) complemented the constitution. The liberalization process underlined the deep contradictions which have pervaded the Algerian state and society. Clearly, one of the results of liberalization was to allow the new caste to propagate openly its ideology; thus, the socioeconomic contradictions were now reflected, albeit in vague terms, in politics.

After the introduction of the new Law on Political Associations, numerous parties (such as PAGS, PST, FFS, MDA, MDRA) formed or emerged from clandestine life or were proclaimed (such as RCD, FIS) after long years of struggle against succeeding FLN regimes. Thus by 1992, the authorities had approved more than sixty parties. The proliferation of parties reflected genuine ideological orientations in a few cases; but the regime in place and the FLN encouraged such a proliferation of parties in order to obstruct strongly organized alternative political forces. The state had encouraged the emergence of civil society because it could no longer play its traditional role of provider.

A civil society, therefore, revealed its existence following the October events. In addition to human-rights leagues, literally thousands of associations were created. They publicly expressed their opposition to such practices as torture and imprisonment of individuals without due process of law. Other associations, whose members focused on such concerns as ecology, religion, and consumer protection, sprung up everywhere. Women all over Algeria created associations to proclaim their right to full citizenship and to demand the abolition of laws that they felt were discriminatory, such as the 1984 Family Code. Trade associations, such as the Association of Chief Executive Officers, the General Confederation of the Algerian Economic Operators, and the Algerian Confederation of Businessmen, also made their appearance in civil society. Even retired military personnel created their own association, AR-ANP. Artists, writers, and peasants forged their own associations. Such associations do not necessarily have a political nature: they often react to the various societal problems that the country has faced (unemployment, the promotion of market economics, and the advancement of the Arabic language, for instance). It is worth noting that even organizations such as the UGTA and the UNJA, historically linked to the ruling party, developed an autonomous existence.

The main and most popular and appealing party to have emerged and to have benefited from the liberalization of the political system in 1989–91 was the now-banned Islamic Salvation Front (FIS). A populist party and the most radical Islamist organization in the country, its leaders contended that they expressed the general will of the Algerian people and promised to implement the *Shari'a al Islamiya* (religious law), once in power.[22] Such a promise, of course, implied disregard for any republican constitution[23] and inaugurated the "divinization" of politics, hence implicitly precluding the expression of temporal views and the existence of a genuine civil society. Whatever the intentions of the FIS, the claims of its leadership to represent the only legitimate path contradicted "the pluralistic and market-oriented nature of civil society."[24] In other words, the party, at least in rhetoric, sought to establish its hegemony over the public. But, the FIS and the more moderate Islamist associations, such as the Movement for Islamic Society (HAMAS), formed their own syndicalist and women's organizations, which played an active role in society, especially in providing help and moral support to the needy. The emergence of such groups confirmed the disengagement of the state and its perceptible weakening.

Islamism and Civil Society

Whatever their authoritarianism, successive Algerian regimes never succeeded in totally muting opposition to their rule. Groups from within and without always had challenged, with different degrees of effectiveness, their absolute authority. Opposition to the regime came from all social categories. However, opposition to the regimes in Algeria traditionally has come from either Marxist-Leninist or Trotskyite groups or from Islamist organizations. The two groups, of course, were incompatible with each other but managed to enter periodic alliances.[25] The struggle between the two ideological groups and the violent clashes between them were much stronger than their common fight against the regimes in power. In fact, the Marxist groups, for instance, extended critical support to Boumediene's regime for many years and exercised considerable influence inside the mass organizations. The regime of Chadli Bendjedid exploited the antagonism between the two groups; it succeeded in playing the Islamist groups against the Marxists. The Marxists had withdrawn their support from the socioeconomic policies once Bendjedid's "liberal-reformist" orientations became obvious. But that withdrawal did not prevent the regime from repressing the Islamists when they abused their prerogatives by attempting to establish a moral order through violence, such as attacks on bars and aggression against women dressed in Western clothing.

Even though one can speak of a quasi-war of attrition, in the Gramscian sense—in that the Islamist movement was well anchored in the political system, in the FLN party, and in the mass organizations in order to propagate its own ideology—it failed to establish its cultural hegemony over the entire civil society. Yet it compelled the regime to make concessions, notably in the educational and justice systems.

In dealing with civil society, it is somewhat problematic to consider the FIS as a movement favoring the blossoming of civil society. Its totalitarian tendencies presumably would have repeated the experience of Algerians under the FLN's single-party rule. Clearly, unlike the moderate Harakat mujtama al silm (Movement for a Peaceful Society [MSP], formerly known as Harakat al-Mujtama al Islamiy [HAMAS]), for instance, the FIS, from its inception and despite its popular appeal, had alienated large segments of civil society. Not only did the FIS target the regime, but it also attacked the so-called democratic parties, the moderate Islamists, and women who did not share the party's ideological outlook. This is not to say, however, that Islamists are not part of a positive development of civil society. Indeed, contrary to the FIS, which refused to form alliances with secular or other Islamist organizations, the MSP has sought unambiguously to work within the system in place and adopted a less threatening attitude toward the incumbent rulers. In an interview that Mahfoud Nahnah, the party's president, granted me in Algiers in June 1997, he declared unequivocally that "I am not like those [FIS leaders] who say '*la mithak, la destur*' [no charter, no constitution—one of the FIS slogans]; I say: 'I operate within the legal framework of the state and am willing to work with any Algerian party, whatever its ideological inclination, as long as its members seek the best interests of society and the country'." Whatever one's reservations about the genuine design of the Islamists in Algeria, the Islamists have undoubtedly participated in the resurrection of civil society and have compelled the regime to liberalize. The FIS, HAMAS/MSP, and the smaller Nahda party created their own associations, at various societal levels: women, unions, youth, children, and students. They also founded their own newspapers. These activities largely explain, for instance, why the FIS succeeded, in 1989–91, in mobilizing important segments of the population against the discredited regime. They also account for the continued popularity of Islamism (at least its moderate variant) despite the atrocities that extremist Islamist groups have committed in the country, especially in the 1992–93 and 1996–98 periods.

Undoubtedly, civil society played a role in the shaking of the Algerian state. Civil society grew and gained visibility because of the October events, but it has yet to provide a strong democratic alternative. At the same time, though, in face of the violence-repression cycle since 1992, civil society has resisted either being reabsorbed by an ascending powerful, authoritarian state or being swept away by yet another populist, totalitarian movement.

The tragedy in Algeria is that parallel to the emergence of civil society and a vibrant political life, especially in the period from 1989 until May 1991, the manifold crisis has also bolstered "movements of rage," or "violent nativist responses to failure, frustration, and perplexity."[26] Frustration, rage, and violence have somewhat overshadowed the advent of civil society, but never before has such opposition from civil society confronted the Algerian state. Despite the high degree of violence, a consensus on norms defining a "civil sphere" is in the making in Algeria. "Civil society would then not be a set of *groups* but a *space* or *realm* defined by newly constituted norms about what the state should and should not do and by the rules of politics in that space, *including* politics by non state actors."[27]

The transition in Algeria is similar to the transitions from above which have characterized democratic openings in many Latin American countries. In the Algerian case, the various associations might exploit the openings that the old authoritarian rulers offered (under pressure from civil society to be sure), assuming, of course, that the norms of civility discussed earlier are learned. The strategy the Algerian regime has pursued since 1995 could therefore create conditions conducive to a democratic evolution. Those conditions, of course, suppose that opposition parties will seize each opportunity and use it to push for greater democratization.

The June 1997 Elections: The Way out of the Crisis?

Following the cancellation of the elections in January 1992, the Algerian regime lacked any strategy to overcome the ensuing political crisis. The weakness of the regime led to an intensification of violence that almost destroyed the state in 1993–95. By late 1994, a new approach seemed to be forming, which included an attempt to create legitimate institutions and to allow the opposition to participate, albeit to a limited degree. The first step was the presidential election, which took place on November 16, 1995. It was the first pluralist presidential election since the country's independence. Liamine Zeroual won the election against three other contenders, of whom the most challenging was the moderate Islamist Mahfoud Nahnah. The regime continued its strategy and rejected an alternative offered by other opposition parties, including the FLN and the FIS. The propositions contained in the San't Edigio [Rome] Platform were aimed at rehabilitating the FIS and at resuming the political process where it had stopped in early 1992. In November 1996, the regime held a referendum on a new constitution, which banned the use of regionalism, of Islam, and of certain national values for political purposes. Later, the regime compelled parties whose names or platforms contained any of the banned elements to change their appellations and tenets to conform to the new legislation. In order to avoid a repetition of the December 1991 elections—in which the Islamists won the majority, resulting in yet another cancellation of the elections by the military—the authorities founded in March 1997 a presidential party, the National Democratic Rally (RND). The new party was reminiscent of the short-lived National Patriotic Rally (RPN), created by President Mohammed Boudiaf (January–June 1992) to mobilize Algerians and revive nationalist sentiment in the country. However, unlike the RPN, which died shortly after the assassination of its founder, the RND benefited from overwhelming administrative support. Few therefore doubted that, in spite of its recent creation, the party would garner a major share of the June votes.

As expected, the RND gained 156 seats in the 380-seat legislature, followed by the Movement for Society and Peace, with 69 seats. The FLN won 63 seats while the second Islamist party, Nahda (formerly Islamic Nahda), obtained 34 seats. From that event, many analysts have drawn the conclusion, regardless of the irregularities in creating a (sociological and political) balance in the National Popular Assembly (APN), that the institutionalization process represents a step in the right direction: a weakening of the authoritarian system and a concomitant strengthening of civil society. Moderate Islamists (MSP and Nahda) occupy 103 out of 380 seats in the assembly. Unlike their counterparts in Tunisia or Egypt, Islamists in Algeria are allowed to function and to represent constituents under their designation, one of the most positive aspects of this change. In fact, the new assembly, where ten political parties and independents are represented, is pluralistic. Close to eight thousand candidates, representing no fewer than forty-one political parties, competed for seats during the June 5 elections. The APN now constitutes the forum where ideas clash and where the elected deputies are learning to form coalitions, to work together in committees, and to debate government policies. Already, a grand coalition, composed of the RND, the MSP, and the FLN, has produced a government in which the MSP and the FLN each hold seven ministries and state secretariats. If one adds to the pluralistic legislature an independent critical press, one of the most vibrant in the Arab world, then one may discern a genuine civil society. The independent press in Algeria, despite its shortcomings, is an important actor in civil society. In its edition of December 15, 1997, *El Watan* reported that more than two hundred publications are available in the country. Neither state repression nor Islamist extremists have succeeded in stopping the ascension of an increasingly freer, more critical, and more professional press.

As civil society grows, the military, wearied of direct involvement in political life during the years of crisis, may choose to concern itself less with politics and more with its professional functions. In other words, civil peace, the absence of a threat from radical Islamists, the preservation of the military's corporate interests, and a government of national unity will result in stability and national reconciliation, which, in turn, will stimulate economic growth and initiative.

The expectations associated with the nascent civil society may seem too optimistic, but skeptics should remember that Algeria is a new nation-state, so it should not be analyzed as though it were an accomplished democracy. Students of democratization know all too well that transitions to democracy are complicated, take time, and make advances and retreats. What is certain today is that the political situation in Algeria is changing, and even though patterns of authoritarianism still persist and conservative forces dominate the legislature, the slow march toward democracy may have begun. The proof that civil society is strengthening could be seen in October 1997, following the municipal and departmental elections. Clearly, the regime rigged those elections to favor the presidential party, the RND. But the vehement way in which that vote was denounced proved that six years of violence had done little to stifle civil society. That secular and religious parties demonstrated side by side against the administration's abuses of power proves that civil society has indeed become the space in which political rules are contested and where the rules of the political game, including civility, are learned. The deputies in the national assembly continue to denounce the government for its failure to contain violence and to protect citizens. There are clear signs that the deputies may bring down the government and force the appointment of a new prime minister. Furthermore, in late January 1998, the Algerian press denounced the president for not addressing the nation during the religious holiday (*Eid al Fitr*), following a bloody month of Ramadan, during which thousands of innocent civilians were massacred. In no other country of the Middle East can the press be so critical of a head of state.

All these events constitute clear evidence that civil society in Algeria has succeeded in gradually eroding the old political system and is forcing the rulers to be more accountable to their people. The end of violence in Algeria will undoubtedly allow the new societal forces to advance further demands on the state for democracy and full citizenship.

Notes

1. Shils, "The Virtue of Civil Society," 4.

2. Diamond, "Toward Democratic Consolidation," 5–6

3. Bobbio, "Gramsci and the Conception of Civil Society," 30. For a different view, cf. Buci-Glucksmann, *Gramsci and the State*, 70 ff. and n. 5, 412–13.

4. Zghal, "Le concept de société civile et la transition vers le multipartisme," 225–26.

5. O'Donnell and Schmitter, *Transitions from Authoritarian Rule*, 48 ff.

6. Waterbury, "Une démocratie sans démocrates," 101.

7. Ghalioun, *Le malaise arabe—État contre nation*, 104.

8. Waterbury, "Une démocratie sans démocrates," 101.

9. Shils, "The Virtue of Civil Society," 11.

10. Ibid., 13.

11. Walzer, "The Civil Society Argument," 101.

12. Diamond, "Toward Democratic Consolidation," 8.

13. For a similar point, see Farès, *Algérie—Le bonheur et son contraire*, 86.

14. El-Kenz, *Au fil de la crise—5 études sur l'Algérie et le monde arabe*, 23.

15. Boumediene speech given in Oran on March 21, 1966, cited in Camau, *La notion de démocratie dans la pensée des dirigeants maghrébins*, 205.

16. Bennoune and El-Kenz, *Le hasard et l'histoire—Entretiens avec Belaïd Abdessalem*, 244 ff.

17. Camau, *La notion de démocratie*, 390.

18. Brahimi, *Le pouvoir, la presse et les intellectuels en Algérie*, 154. See also Garon, *L'obsession unitaire et la nation trompée—La fin de l'Algérie socialiste*.

19. "Constitution de la république algérienne démocratique et populaire," 188–210.

20. For a critical analysis of the 1989 constitution, see Cubertafond, "La constitution algérienne du 28 Février 1989," 3959.

21. "Loi no. 89–11 du 5 Juillet 1989," 604–7.

22. *Projet de programme du front islamique du salut* (Algiers: March 7, 1989).

23. For a full treatment of the FIS's attitude toward the 1989 constitution, one should refer to Lavenue, "Le FIS et la constitution algérienne," 127–43.

24. Diamond, "Toward Democratic Consolidation," 67.

25. A good discussion on these two groups can be found in Bernard Cubertafond, "Algérie," in *Contestations en pays islamiques*, Badie, Coulon, Cubertafond, et al., 31–62.

26. Jowitt, *New World Disorder*, 275–77.

27. Callaghy, "Civil Society, Democracy, and Economic Change in Africa," 235.

3.

ECONOMIC REFORM AND ELUSIVE POLITICAL CHANGE IN MOROCCO

Azzedine Layachi

Like many other countries in the Middle East and Africa, Morocco has faced in the last two decades important challenges at the domestic, international, and regional levels. At the domestic level, these difficulties have resulted from major social changes: a high urbanization rate, a high ratio of youth to total population, and increasing impoverishment. Moreover, this country also has been facing a prolonged economic crisis, a political malaise (especially after the controversial 1993 parliamentary elections), and a rising Islamist tide. At the international level, changes in the global economy, especially in Europe, have pushed Morocco to seek a special association with the European Union (EU); economic negotiations with the EU were, in turn, often accompanied by pressures for democratization and for the respect of human rights. At the regional level, the bloody confrontation in Algeria between armed Islamists and the state has caused fears of a possible spillover into the kingdom, and the continuing dispute over Western Sahara still causes concern.

This chapter examines the nature of Morocco's efforts at dealing with these domestic, international, and regional challenges. It focuses on issues raised by economic and political liberalization and tackles the following two questions: What relationship exists between economic and political liberalization in general and in Morocco in particular? And have Morocco's economic liberalization and structural adjustment been accompanied by political liberalization, especially in the area of state-society relations?

The combined effects of a deep political malaise, a lasting economic crisis, and international pressures made the ruler of Morocco, King Hassan II, decide in 1996 to reform parliament and its mode of election. Most political players accepted the reform in a referendum on September 13. This constitutional reform took place in the context of a deep crisis prompted by the 1993 parliamentary elections. In these two-round elections, the opposition parties, which had obtained very good results in the first round of June 1993, received a disproportionate and insignificant number of seats in the second round. The Koutla opposition coalition (left) of the USFP, PI, PPS, and OADP obtained 99 out of 222 seats on the first ballot and only 15 seats out of 111 on the second ballot; the previous progovernment majority (MP, UC, RNI, MNP, PND) received 116 seats in the first round and 79 in the second. The opposition parties felt that this disproportion resulted from direct manipulation of the vote by the state bureaucracy and the monarchy in order to prevent the opposition bloc from gaining control of both parliament and government.

The outcome of the 1993 elections led to a deep political crisis; the parties of the Koutla refused to participate, as junior partners, in a government formed and controlled by the king. A serious political malaise set in also among the opposition parties themselves, as their leaders disagreed on a common response.

To avoid a repetition of the setback experienced in the 1993 parliamentary elections, the opposition parties sought a firm commitment from the king that future elections would not be manipulated and that their results would be respected. For his part, the king wanted the reintegration of the opposition into the political process, regardless of the outcome. To this end, the king and the opposition parties reached a formal agreement prior to the 1997 elections. On the basis of this agreement and the revised constitution, new municipal elections took place on June 13, 1997. Despite having doubled the number of municipalities it controlled (from 219 in 1992 to 405 in 1997, out of a total of 1,517), the Koutla gained, in fact, very little in these elections. The progovernment and center blocs today control most local offices.

The parliamentary elections that followed on November 14 brought no substantial change to the existing political map of Morocco. Three major party blocs, the Koutla, the Wifaq (progovernment right), and the center received an almost equal number of seats (102, 100, and 97, respectively). The USFP won the largest number of seats (57) in the lower house but not the majority. However, as expected and as many observers had wished, the king appointed this party's leader, Abderrahmane Youssoufi, as prime minister and asked him to form a coalition government.

This event constituted a major departure from past practices, but does it alter the political map and political process in Morocco? To what extent do recent institutional reforms and the opposition's access to government constitute the start of a genuine political pluralism and democracy in Morocco? Finally, what role did economic change play in the political crisis and the political "adjustment" that the king has made?

There is no agreement among existing theories and empirical findings on the relationship between economic crisis and political instability, on one hand, and economic development and political liberalization, on the other. Some early works on this issue stated that economic development can stimulate political liberalization as an incipient middle class seeks to influence public policy and succeeds in doing so by providing those in power with an essential coalition of supporters.[1] Modernization theory suggested that praetorian political regimes are more likely to result from social mobilization at a time of economic crisis.[2] However, in the case of Morocco, the lasting economic crisis aroused popular discontent and even violent clashes, but the political regime was not fundamentally shaken or altered. Further, when the Moroccan state radically reformed the economy through an IMF-sponsored structural-adjustment program, systematic and sustained political liberalization did not follow. Therefore, neither economic crisis nor economic liberalization has caused any substantial political change. Only recently have there been some institutional changes, and their long-term impact is difficult to predict. These changes, which resulted mostly from strong domestic and international pressures, included the release of political prisoners in 1994, a constitutional reform in 1996, new municipal and parliamentary elections in 1997, and the nomination of an opposition leader as prime minister.

To fully understand the particular relationship that has existed in Morocco between economic reform and political change, one needs to begin with an overview of Morocco's social, economic, and political evolution in the last two decades.

The Economy: Crisis and Reform

With an area of 172,419 square miles, Morocco has a population of 28.6 million, which grows at 2.3 percent per year.[3] Its per capita GNP of $1,110 in 1995 makes it a lower middle-income country.[4] Morocco's economy is based on the free market, but the public sector has always played a major role in it. Since the beginning of structural adjustment in 1983, the state slowly diminished its participation and engaged in a privatization program whose main beneficiaries have been powerful business conglomerates such as the Omnium Nord-Africain (ONA) and some foreign investors.

Morocco's main export commodity is phosphate. The kingdom is the largest phosphate exporter in the world and holds 75 percent of the world reserves. It also controls rich fishing waters and has developed a sophisticated tourist industry, which, along with other exports, brings in much-needed hard currency. Moroccan migrant workers send home approximately $2.5 billion a year.

The country has a small manufacturing industry and a mostly traditional agricultural sector, which provides significant quantities of food for export. Agriculture remains a major source of wealth for the Moroccan bourgeoisie, while millions of peasants on their small parcels eke out an income well below the poverty line. Three-fourths of rural households own less than two hectares each and account for only 16 percent of all arable land; about one-third of rural households have no land at all or extremely small parcels.[5] Agriculture contributes 20 percent of Morocco's GDP and employs 50 percent of the total labor force (10 million workers).[6] However, agricultural land has been controlled by fewer and fewer landowners, who are linked either to industrial conglomerates, to the royal family, or to both. This skewed land distribution resulted from many factors, including rural migration, urbanization, and government policies that benefit modern, export-oriented businesses controlled by a handful of landowners and agricultural businesses.

Morocco has been particularly vulnerable to external shocks and to shifts in the policies of its main trading partners, the Europeans. In recent years, the country's economic performance has been severely affected by Europe's recessions and increased integration. Its tourist industry was adversely affected by the 1991 Persian Gulf war (which resulted in a decline of tourism in all Arab countries) and by the rise of militant Islam in North Africa. The war in Western Sahara and the annexation campaign that followed it affected Morocco's economy more than any other factor.[7] The annexation efforts cost Morocco close to $1 billion a year in the 1970s and 1980s.[8] Even though Saudi Arabia provided many of the funds, 45 percent of Morocco's budget went into these efforts.[9]

The economic crisis of the early 1980s (the heavy burden of the Western Sahara war; major external economic shocks, including a drop in the price of phosphates; an unbearable balance of trade deficit; and a rising foreign debt, $8,475 billion in 1980),[10] prompted the adoption, in 1983, of an IMF-sponsored structural-adjustment program.

Orthodox austerity measures were taken to restructure the economy and to stimulate growth. These included the elimination of food subsidies; the freezing of government wages, of public hiring, and of investment; the devaluation of the dirham; the deregulation of interest rates; the withdrawal of support for agriculture through the deregulating of most prices; the liberalization of imports; the promotion of exports and investments; and the liberalization of foreign trade. All export duties and licenses were abolished, and a series of fiscal and financial incentives encouraged export. Privatization was started with the creation of a Ministry of Privatization and the adoption of Law 39–89, which allowed the sale of 112 enterprises in a variety of sectors—even those considered "strategic," such as oil, petrochemicals, transportation, and communications. Privatization was also extended to industrial production, banking, agriculture, food processing, textiles, leather, tourism, and various services.

After more than ten years of intense restructuring, the economy was stabilized and its structures overhauled, notably through the privatization program and the gradual retreat of the state. By the early 1990s, the state's budget deficit had declined from 12 to 3 percent of the GDP, exports increased by 9.7 percent, the debt to GDP ratio fell from 123 to 81 percent, and the debt-servicing ratio fell from a high 70 percent to 33 percent.[11] (Foreign debt had reached more than $20 billion in 1993.)[12]

In spite of the selling off of some major public interests, privatization has fallen short of its objectives: only twenty-five corporations were sold by 1997. Morocco's exports still lag far behind its imports in dollar value. In the 1990s, export earnings did not cover more than 59 to 68 percent of imports.[13] The export sector is insufficiently diversified and is dominated by a few products and services which are directly affected by international prices and demand fluctuations.

Except for a major gas pipeline linking Algeria with Europe through its territory since the end of 1996, Morocco's economic exchanges with its Maghrebi partners constitute less than 10 percent of the country's total international commerce. King Hassan believes that Morocco's prosperity will be better guaranteed through a close association with Europe. He has little faith in the Arab Maghreb Union (UMA) (see chapter 11).

The failure of integration in North Africa, coupled with such changes as the Maastricht Treaty in Western Europe and the fall of socialist regimes in Eastern Europe, has compelled Morocco to seek some special economic relationship with the European Union. Its ten-year-old application for full membership in the EU was rejected many times but, in 1995, the European Union agreed to establish a special relationship with the kingdom. This new relationship entailed membership in a free-trade zone, fishing agreements, and financial aid—all contingent upon Morocco's economic liberalization.

In spite of the implementation of aggressive economic reforms, Morocco remains a poor developing country. The bourgeoisie has become wealthier in recent decades while the urban poor have become poorer because of dwindling opportunities for employment at home and abroad and fewer available social services. In the end, structural adjustment carried a heavy social cost: a decline in real wages; a rise in unemployment; inflation; and increased urban migration which, in turn, feeds a dangerous concentration of poor in the overgrown cities of Casablanca, Fez, Tangier, Marrakech, and Rabat-Salé.[14] Some of those cities were shaken by riots in 1981, 1984, 1990, and 1996 in protest against worsening living conditions. All of these riots resulted in heavy casualties and imprisonments. By the mid-1990s, recurring droughts aggravated the economic conditions and led to an increase in the food-import bill. Between 1995 and 1998, strikes and street protests by workers and demonstrations by unemployed graduates affected such sectors as transportation, banking, health, and education. At universities, Islamist militants often organized student walkouts.

The Political System

As a result of Morocco's profound economic overhaul, people's perception of the state's economic role has undergone a major change. The state is providing much fewer services than it used to, especially as the public sector keeps shrinking because public institutions are abandoning what they no longer wish to or are able to engage in or support.

In contrast to these rapid economic changes, political reforms have come at a much slower pace and have yet to stimulate change in the political regime or the structures that sustain it. Since independence in 1956, a formal political pluralism and a regime that fluctuates between an absolute monarchy and a flexible authoritarianism have characterized Morocco's political system. One thing, however, has always been constant: the king is the most important and most powerful institution.

After assuming power in 1961, King Hassan II, who claims kinship with the prophet Mohammed, strengthened his power at the expense of the parties, which, because of their nationalist endeavors against French colonialism, had asked for a share of power. The king put the security forces under his direct control and neutralized the opposition by repression, imprisonment, and even assassinations. His legitimacy derives from tradition and religion. He is considered *amir al-mu'minnin* (the Commander of the Faithful); as such, he commands high respect among the masses. However, he was challenged twice in the 1970s by the army, which tried to overthrow him.

After an early period of political uncertainty and crisis, King Hassan silenced the opposition and even succeeded in rallying some of the parties to his side when he engaged Morocco in the annexation of Western Sahara. Opposition to the monarchy was equivalent then to opposition to the territorial claims over Western Sahara, which had become a popular cause. The second half of the 1970s witnessed a temporary political respite as the opposition was kept tightly in line during the popular irredentist campaign for Western Sahara.

However, as the conflict over Western Sahara lingered and its cost rose, the Moroccan economy suffered, as did most Moroccans' standard of living. The wave of popular discontent and unrest that ensued in the early 1980s was followed by yet another period of repression. After King Hassan reasserted his control over the situation, another period of political truce set it. Moderate opposition was allowed to function, while radical challengers were eliminated.

In sum, King Hassan's governing style keeps shifting from a concentration of powers, repression, and intimidation to relative parliamentary politics. The monarchy also resorts to patronage, clientelism, and a selective distribution of privileges.

As a condition for continued economic cooperation, Morocco's international partners demanded economic reform, a minimum of political change, and respect for human rights. At home, the negative consequences of economic reform on the poor and on unemployed youth generated additional pressures for change. In response to these pressures, the king released political prisoners in July 1994 and 1998; parliament repealed an unpopular 1935 law on detention; a 1996 constitutional reform created an upper house in parliament and altered the electoral mechanism; new municipal and parliamentary elections were held in 1997; and, for the first time, the king allowed the opposition to form a government and allowed nine members of the Islamist tendency to sit in the legislative body.

The main purpose of the political reforms was to calm the rising tide of popular discontent, of social tensions, and of international criticism. Far from affecting the nature of the political system, those reforms had all the marks of a "regime survival strategy" beyond the reign of King Hassan himself.[15]

Limits of Economic Reform and the Elusive Political Change

Morocco's economic liberalization program was vigorously sustained through the 1990s, mostly because it was required by a severe economic crisis and also because of strong societal calls for better living and working conditions. Except for a relatively slow privatization, Morocco's economic reforms were praised by international institutions and European partners; however, the vast majority of Moroccans have yet to benefit from these reforms.

In contrast to some of the most daring economic changes, political reform has been markedly slow and even stagnant at times. Though relatively important, the measures the government took in the 1990s have yet to translate into actual and effective change in the power structure and in the political practice in Morocco.

While economic reforms have been important in reducing the overwhelming weight of the state and the monarch on the economy, they do not necessarily indicate, however, that King Hassan and the powerful state apparatus (especially the mighty Ministry of Interior) are willing to share power with an increasingly independent-minded parliament or ready to hand over important ministries to the new government of the leftist leader, Youssoufi. In fact, the powerful Interior Minister Driss Basri was one of a few ministers who remained in their function after the opposition took control of the government.

For the great majority of Moroccans, political change appears more elusive than real, and the benefits of economic reform have not been felt yet. Unemployment has steadily risen, reaching 20 to 30 percent in the urban centers in 1997, and public expenditures on social services continue to be reduced. The number of new job-seekers continues to increase faster than job creation, especially for the youth (60 percent of the population is below age twenty-five), and the gap between rich and poor has widened even further in recent years.

The business and government elites have been the primary beneficiaries of economic reforms. The reforms have not produced jobs as anticipated or increased foreign-exchange earnings. Several obstacles and weaknesses in the Moroccan economy and bureaucracy caused the reforms to fall short of their expectations.

Unless they are addressed soon, these problems not only may hinder economic progress, but also could threaten the overall stability of the kingdom. A combination of negative consequences of economic reform may cause a powerful social explosion, such as the one that rocked Algeria in 1988 and throughout the 1990s, especially when the channels for peaceful expression are limited.

Morocco has been marred since 1995 by a series of strikes in a variety of sectors and a rising mobilization of many segments of society. That mobilization recently has been set in motion not by traditional unions and political parties but by new formal and informal movements, including independent unions and Islamist associations.

A lasting crisis has the potential of invigorating a radical challenge to the system. "Unorganized labor, the urban unemployed, those in the informal sector, shanty-town dwellers, students, and rural agricultural workers and peasants . . . will lose most from austerity and structural adjustment, will oppose the regime, and are the most violence-prone sectors of the population."[16]

Because of the relative failure of the traditional political parties and their labor unions to channel and control protest, independent forces may come to play a leading role as guardians of societal interests and could challenge the authority of the state, the monarchy, and the power elite. This may then usher in either a genuinely democratic experience—where absolute power will be replaced by a constitutional regime—or a violent clash between revolutionary forces and a conservative system, with unpredictable results.

Because it can be difficult to reconcile economic liberalism with a highly centralized political system, economic liberalization must necessarily be complemented with a relative political opening, which includes some representation of most strata of the social and economic orders. Even though a policy of inclusion may not automatically bring about rapid and tangible improvement in the living and working conditions of most people, it would at least help to channel and control the rebellious opposition.

Economic reforms can be more effective if they are accompanied by political reforms that open the door to popular participation through the development of a civil society. A civil society may bring in the missing voices, but is it possible in the current economic and political reality of Morocco?

Civil Society: Shortcomings and Potential

Civil society refers to the independent association of groups and individuals for protecting their particular interests and for influencing public policy. It "checks state arbitrariness while serving as a buffer between state power and private spheres."[17] It includes associations, political parties, unions, various informal groupings, an independent press, and individuals such as intellectuals and opinion leaders.

Associative life in Morocco is old and was consecrated by the royal charter and the Dahir of November 1958. Many of the traditional associations, which focused mainly on communal works, ritual gatherings, and utilitarian purposes, have been replaced in the last twenty years by modern groupings. Many associations were born in urban centers and led popular action after parties and unions lost some of their power. However, their role and actions are severely limited by the nature of the regime and an omnipotent state.

The new urban groupings provoke the suspicion of those in power but are, at the same time, courted by political parties and urban notables for electoral purposes. The ambiguity with which the new urban groupings are viewed substantially limits their independence, and some of them are even used by the state for ideological integration.

The activities of these urban associations cover a wide spectrum of areas: sports, arts, religion, professional interests, humanitarian aid, human rights, and the environment. Associations representing liberal professions (lawyers, doctors, architects, and pharmacists) are among the most important, along with those representing the managers and owners of private enterprises, which are very influential in the area of economic policy. Associations of human rights, consumers' rights, and environmental protection are relatively young.

Associative life is mostly concentrated in large cities, such Casablanca, Fez, Rabat, and Marrakech, and attracts mainly young and educated people. Some associations (such as those of writers and of economists) are partly or totally controlled by political parties, some (such as regional cultural associations) by the state. Others maintain a relative independence.

Secular Associations

Among the most effective associations are those of business. They affect labor policies, pricing, production, and trade. Their leaders are often businessmen as well as government officials or high-level bureaucrats. The most important business associations are those representing large corporations, such as the Confédération Générale Economique du Maroc, the Union Marocaine Agricole, the Comité Professionnel de la Minoterie Marocaine, the Fédération des Industries de Conserve du Maroc, the Fédération Marocaine des Sociétés d'Assurance, the Fédération des Industries des Corps Gras, the Association Professionnelle des Industries de Tannerie, the Association Marocaine de l'Industrie Textile, the Association des Industries Minières, the Association Professionnelle des Importateurs de Matériel, and the Association Marocaine des Producteurs d'Agrumes.

Associations for human rights have also been active and relatively effective in spite of constant harassment by the state. Their efforts, along with international pressure, paid off when hundreds of political prisoners were released in 1994 (see chapter 8). They include the Ligue Marocaine des Droits de l'Homme (LMDH), the Organisation Marocaine des Droits de l'Homme (OMDH), and the Association Marocaine des Droits de l'Homme.

Women's associations are also relatively active; their action developed mostly in the 1980s and focused on the promotion and protection of women in rapidly changing societal and economic environments; however, their work is limited by divisions among the leadership. Some women leaders favor a focus on the defense of women's rights, while others prefer humanitarian and cultural actions. Strong state control through financial incentives or administrative limitations and also strong control by political parties have contributed to the overall weakness of women's associations.

There are many types of women's associations. Strictly humanitarian associations include the Croissant Rouge and the Association de Soutien à l'UNICEF. Family protection associations include the Association Marocaine de Planning Familial, the Association pour la Sauvegarde de la Famille, and the Association pour le Conseil des Familles. Feminist organizations comprise the Union Nationale des Femmes Marocaines. Professional associations are composed of the Fédération des Femmes de Carrières Libérales et Commerciales, the Ligue Nationale des Femmes Fonctionnaires dans le Secteur Public et le Secteur Privé, the Association des Femmes de Carrière Juridique, and the Amicale Nationale des Cadres Féminins des Administrations Publiques et Semi-Publiques. Finally, the Association Démocratique des Femmes Marocaines, the Union de l'Action Féminine, and the Organisation de la Femme Istiqlalienne constitute the main political associations.

Several youth and student associations cover a wide range of areas. However, they are generally weak, and many of them are affiliated with political parties. The most noteworthy are the Jeunesse du PPS, the Fédération Marocaine des Associations de Chantiers, the Association des Chomeurs Diplomés, the Union Nationale des Etudiants Marocains (UNEM), and the Union Générale des Etudiants Marocains (UGEM).

Several Amazigh-based (Berber) organizations promote the Tamazight language and the Amazigh culture in Morocco. These include the Association Tellili (freedom), the Association Marocaine de la Recherche et d'Echange Culturel (AMREC), the Association Assala du Bassin Méditerranéen, the Association Bine al Ouidane, and the Association Culturelle de Soussa.

There are many other types of relatively independent associations whose success and activism vary. There are several environmental associations, such as the Association Marocaine pour la Protection de l'Environnement (ASMAPE) and the Mouvement National des Ecologistes Marocains and Société Marocaine pour le Droit de l'Environnement (SOMADE). In the health sector, several associations offer support and counsel to people afflicted with certain disorders or diseases and to their families, including the Association Marocaine pour la Lutte contre le SIDA (ALCS).

The state has also encouraged the development of regional cultural associations. These are used for ideological integration and for the recruitment of local notables and loyal civil servants. This category includes the Association Angad el Maghreb Acharqui, the Association Hawd-Assafi, the Association Doukkala, the Association Ahmed Al-Hansali, the Association Illigh, the Association Annahda-Association Nador, and the Association Al-Mouhit.

Most of the organizations mentioned above constitute elements of a potential civil society, but their mere existence does not necessarily translate into a civil society. They are not fully independent, and their impact on public policy is very limited. Under adequate conditions and a strong political momentum, this rich associative map can become the backbone of a genuine civil society.

Islamist Associations

Religious associations have also been fairly active in Morocco. They are of two main types: traditional associations of preaching and teaching and modern associations seeking a radical change. Associations of the first type are mostly active in rural areas (traditional pillars of support for the monarchy), and those of the second type are found in urban centers.

Created in 1965, al-Tabligh wal-Da'wa Lillah (Preaching) is a promonarchy association that wants to revive the Islamic Umma (Muslim community) and the implementation of the *Shari'a* (Islamic law). It calls for peaceful change and has thousands of urban members. Jam'iyat al-Shabiba al Islamyyia (Association of Islamic Youth) is a radical group created by Abdelkrim Moutii in 1970. It seeks rapid change by any means; however, factionalism and divergent viewpoints on action have weakened its structure and appeal. Al-Rabita (the League), a benevolent religious association, focuses mainly on social and humanitarian issues, while working to protect the Shurafa (nobles) and their descendants. Al-Adl wal Ihsan (Justice and Benevolence), the movement of Abdesslam Yacine, currently under house arrest, claims moderation and legalism and enjoys a wide support among the disaffected urban youth. It denounces social injustice and ethical degradation in Morocco and calls for the peaceful return to the "rule of God." Recently, the government rejected its request to form a political party that abides by the constitution.

Except for Jam'iyat al-Shabiba al-Islamiyya, which is almost nonexistent today, most Islamist associations born in the 1970s "have evolved toward an 'Islamism of compromise' with the regime. Most known leaders have chosen the strategy of 'pressure' for the moralization of the political and socio-cultural life."[18] Radical organizations were subdued by repression and weakened by their internal division and inability to stage a popular upheaval. There exist, however, a few underground ultra-radical Islamist groups, some of which are suspected of alliance with the Algerian al-Jama'at al-Islamiyya al-Mussalaha (Armed Islamic Groups, GIA).

In recent years, the Islamists have infiltrated various parts of society, especially the poor neighborhoods and the schools and universities of major cities, and have even recruited many urban professionals. Their infiltration was facilitated by their social and charitable services in poor neighborhoods, by their championing of the demands and grievances of students, and by their denunciation of corrupt political leaders. They also have infiltrated political parties, labor unions, and civic associations and have used them as legal outlets for criticism and demands. In the last parliamentary elections, members of the al-Tawhid wal Islah movement (Unity and Reform of Abdelilah Benkirane, now led by Ahmed Rissouni) ran as candidates of the Popular Democratic and Constitutional Movement (MPDC), a party of Islamist leaning. Both movements hold nine seats.

Radical Islamists do not yet constitute a real threat to the regime, but they may effectively challenge it if a crisis arises over the transition of power (when Hassan II vacates power), or if they manage to move from the margins to the center of the political process through organized political action.[19] Although the king has co-opted, coerced, and contained the visible manifestation of Islamism, the Islamist challenge remains a threat. Up to now, the Islamists have not succeeded, for three main reasons: (1) the king's own claim to ultimate religious leadership, (2) the relative control (albeit weak) of social and economic contestation by the traditional unions and parties of the left, and (3) a fierce state repression (seven hundred Islamists were arrested in 1982 alone and many others in subsequent years). Furthermore, to weaken their appeal, the king established a whole system of expression of "official Islam" and promoted the creation of several apolitical and promonarchy religious organizations. In recent years, however, and in the context of an invigorated religious life (albeit under the stimulation and control of the "official Islam") independent Islamist groups grew and developed as a moral force among the urban youth and disaffected segments of society,[20] which tend to respond to calls for the resurgence of religion, egalitarianism, and social solidarity. These groups may become an uncontrolled opposition that can mobilize the masses for a radical change under the banner of Islam. They may succeed if the economic crisis lasts, if the gap between rich and poor widens, and if the traditional opposition continues to be effectiveness

Political Parties

Political parties appear conservative in the face of a society which calls for change. Multipartyism has existed in Morocco since the colonial era and has not clashed with the monarchy; in fact, it reinforced it. The king encourages division among the opposition and presents himself as a unifying figure above conflicting party politics. Most parties support the monarchy and oppose it very little. "It is very difficult in this context to link the proliferation of political parties to democracy or to equate multipartyism with political pluralism."[21]

The monarchy has always manipulated the parties by including and excluding parties from government or by repressing some of them and promoting promonarchy blocs in parliament. The "Moroccan system of client-patron relationships reproduces itself in the political parties, which are more or less clienteles."[22] Opposition parties often clash with one another over policy and tactics; only on a few occasions did the major parties unite as an electoral bloc, such as the Koutla in 1993 and 1997. After a deception in the 1993 parliamentary elections, the opposition felt that the system had failed to deliver on its promise of a democratic opening and became torn by a sharp internal division, which diminished even further the parties' ability to affect public policy.

There are many parties in Morocco, but only a few are constantly active and visible. The Istiqlal Party (PI), which was founded in 1943 as a nationalist movement for independence, is committed to a tolerant Islam and "represents a traditional, defensive, and status-quo oriented segment of a small urban and rural population, with traditional strongholds in Fès and Meknès."[23] It is highly supportive of the monarchy. The Socialist Union of Popular Forces (USFP) was created in 1972; it is committed to establishing a socialist democracy after capturing power by way of elections. This promise will soon be put to the test now that the USFP is in charge of the government. The Party of Progress and Socialism (PPS), formed in 1968 by members of the banned Moroccan Communist Party, compromised its revolutionary line when it moved from the far left to the center in order to remain legal. The Organization of Democratic and Popular Action (OADP) was at first driven by a revolutionary zeal, but after suffering repression, it opted for a democratic path to socialism. In 1996, when it opposed the constitutional reform and called for a "no" vote, the state excluded it from all official activities (even elections) and suspended its newspaper. The National Assembly of Independents (RNI) is known as "a party of the monarchy" because of its close link to the throne and its appeal to the high bureaucratic elite and high bourgeoisie. The National Democratic Party (PND) is another promonarchy formation. The Constitutional Union (UC) is a moderate party which enjoys the king's support and promotes national unity behind the monarchy. The Popular Movement (MP) is an Amazigh-based promonarchist party, which promotes an Islamic socialism and the recognition of the Amazigh character of Morocco.

What was said above about civic associations applies also to political parties. They are relatively active but within the confines of what the state and the monarchy find acceptable. The rules of the game are known by all, and any party that violates them is harshly punished. Also, "the representation of political currents has a meaning only in so far as it primarily helps in the control of these currents by those in power; the expression of political parties, which goes as far as a recognition of the opposition, is always carefully conditioned by the acceptance of a political pact which could neither question the essential principles of the regime, nor influence its fundamental equilibria."[24]

Conclusion: Prospects of Comprehensive Change

Up to the nomination of an opposition leader as head of government, all recent political reforms seemed to constitute merely a cosmetic response to domestic and international pressures rather than meaningful change.

The opposition's relative control of government does not mean that it exercises real power. The same forces that wielded power in the past still dominate.

The stringent economic reforms, which have been undertaken, necessitated a compliant society and an acquiescent political elite as well as cooperative international institutions and foreign governments. To secure such compliance, acquiescence, and cooperation, a minimum of political reforms had to be undertaken.

In the second half of the 1990s, Morocco's economy performed well below expectations as a result of a series of severe droughts and the negative consequences of economic reforms themselves. Workers in a variety of sectors (railroads, banks, health, and education) organized strikes and demanded better working conditions and higher wages. In late 1996 and early 1997, students joined the movement by calling for better study conditions and employment prospects. It is important to note that Islamist militants mostly led their movement.

As the state curtailed its roles in the economy, in welfare, and in social integration, discontent grew among the many sectors of society which suffered from the fallout of structural adjustment. The suffering prompted occasional rebellions against public policies or their absence. The nonexistence of institutionalized and genuinely free channels for expression of grievances and demands contributed to aggravating an already explosive situation in several large cities in Morocco.

In the intermediate term, if economic liberalization stimulates a serious political challenge to the regime, the latter may respond either with a meaningful democratic opening, where an absolute monarch and a hegemonic state are replaced by a constitutional monarchy and responsive government, or with repression of the forces calling for a real change. In order to avert repressions (similar to those imposed in Tunisia and in Algeria, where they caused death and destruction), economic liberalization needs to address the difficulties of the lower social strata and be complemented with a political opening that allows the expression and representation of most societal interests. Maybe then economic restructuring will become more effective and a societal uprising will be prevented.

No meaningful initiatives should be expected from the established opposition groups and leaders, because many of them have vested interests in the existing order. Only a wise and creative initiative from the king can prevent a deterioration of the economic and political conditions. Revolutionary fervor otherwise may spring up from a new and young vanguard, Islamist or leftist, with no stakes in the current system, or from the military once the Western Sahara question is resolved. In the latter case, the demobilization of the military could be worrisome for the monarchy. "No matter what the outcome of the Western Sahara conflict will be, the problem of reintegrating the army into society will affect the equilibrium of the system. The government will need to mobilize new resources in order to continue satisfying the demands of the army, unless, after the Sahara, the army becomes engaged in reconquest of the Presides,"[25] or the Algerian and Mauritanian territories still claimed by Morocco.

The best alternative for King Hassan, then, may be to share power with a "tolerated" traditional opposition, rather than for him or his successor to have to contend with a radical opposition. It would also be to the king's advantage not only to respond forthwith to the most urgent economic needs of the masses, but also to allow an independent associative life—not to say civil society—to thrive and to form a counterweight to a potentially hostile partisan opposition in parliament and in government.

Morocco can evolve peacefully and incrementally toward democracy because of some favorable conditions such as an established (albeit controlled) associative life and multipartyism, a growing urban middle class, and international incentives for economic and political liberalization. The constitutional reform of 1996 can help bring about such evolution if it leads to effective electoral processes, a decentralization of state power, a real empowerment of the new government, and a substantial freedom of expression and association. Moroccans need to be enabled and empowered to look after their own interests under a state that respects human dignity and promotes social and economic justice.

Notes

1. Deutsch, "Social Mobilization and Political Development," 493–514; Lerner, *The Passing of Traditional Societies;* Binder, *Crises and Sequences in Political Development.*

2. Huntington, *Political Order in Changing Societies.*

3. "World Population Data Sheet."

4. World Bank, *World Development Report 1995.*

5. Sabagh, "The Challenge of Population Growth in Morocco," 32.

6. Report by the *Centre Marocain de Conjoncture* (CMC), relayed by Reuter dispatch on April 10, 1997.

7. Zoubir, "Political Economy of the Western Sahara Conflict."

8. Damis, "Morocco and the Western Sahara," 166.

9. Tessler, Entelis, and White, "Kingdom of Morocco," 376.

10. World Bank, *World Development Report 1995.*

11. Reuter news dispatch, "Morocco's 1994 Budget," November 29, 1995. One dollar equals approximately nine dirhams.

12. World Bank, *World Development Report 1995.*

13. For a comparative analysis of Morocco's structural-adjustment policies, see Pfeifer, "Between Rocks and Hard Choices," 25–63.

14. Ibid., 39.

15. On regime survival strategies, see Brumberg, "Authoritarian Legacies and Reform Strategies," 229–59.

16. Farsoun and Zacharia, "Class, Economic Change and Political Liberalization," 276.

17. Layachi, *State, Society and Democracy in Morocco,* 10.

18. Lamchichi, "Les incertitudes politiques et sociales," 10–11.

19. Shahin, "Secularism and Nationalism," 184.

20. Benani, *L'islamisme et les droits de l'homme.*

21. El-Benna, "Les partis politiques au Maroc," 130 (translation mine).

22. Waterbury, *The Commander of the Faithful,* 169 ff., cited in Tibi, *Islam and the Cultural Accommodation of Social Change,* 170.

23. Entelis, *Comparative Politics of North Africa,* 70.

24. Santucci, "État et société au Maroc," 428 (translation mine).

25. Ibid., 431 (translation mine).

4.

REGIME TYPE, ECONOMIC REFORM, AND POLITICAL CHANGE IN TUNISIA

Robert J. King

For many, the Middle East is the Bermuda Triangle of area studies. Observations are distrusted, explanations are challenged, and generalizations are dismissed.[1] Analysts expect—and exhort—states and societies in North Africa and the Middle East (MENA) and less developed countries (LDC) to transform themselves dramatically in response to a rapidly changing international environment. "Traditional" political forms are considered mostly undesirable and probably futile. Apparent successes are dismissed as transitory because they are based on disintegrating social pacts which must be "completely abandoned."[2] For those who agree, change—especially political change—is expected; the failure to change needs to be analyzed, and the analysts assume that the favored teleology (usually democracy) determines the degree to which MENA and other LDC nations resist.[3] The logic assumes the need to explain why LDC political systems have *not* moved in the "required" direction.

Empirical analysis suggests a different view. Despite the keen anticipation of imminent political liberalization found in many MENA analyses, change in MENA and other developing countries tends to be slow and incremental. As often as not, domestic political requirements win out over international economic and political pressure. One observes a dialectical rather than any uniform movement toward imagined goals. This chapter will attempt to explain why Tunisian realities have not fulfilled Western expectations by using a broader comparison, based on East Asian cases, by which to understand the Tunisian political and economic system.

State-Society Relations, Regime Type, and Economic Adjustment

When analyzing a process such as economic adjustment that has been important for over four decades, it is useful to review the fundamental logic of the process. The international economic system, the dictates of which are set by Western industrial nations, requires a state's commitment to a market-driven, decentralized economy. This competes squarely with the desire of LDC governments and rulers to stay in power, usually by arrogating all the consequential levers of power to the central government. In this way, the preference for political centralism clashes with the necessity of economic decentralization. The developmentalist policies of the 1960s and 1970s, and the neo-classical policies that followed, failed because they emphasized only one side of the equation.[4] A third wave of analysts looked at both sides, suggesting that too much centralization could be as undesirable as too little; in addition, the governments of South Korea and Taiwan, the showcases for neo-classical liberalism, did not significantly reduce their intervention in the domestic economy but rather changed how they managed the economy. Instead of disengaging from the economy, the LDC state was required to engage an unwilling, and sometimes inept, private sector in its development program.[5] For these analysts, the state's authority was embedded in a broader set of relations with society in a dynamic relationship labeled "embedded autonomy."[6]

The framework for the present chapter, "structured engagement," also examines both sets of preferences, analyzing in particular the role of regime type in the attempts of centralized authoritarian states to reconcile international economic requirements with national political needs. The claim here is that regime type will influence how the state-private sector relationship interacts with the phase of economic adjustment to affect the outcomes of economic adjustment programs (EAPs).[7] Specifically, it is expected that stabilization measures will thrive in more-centralized regimes, while restructuring measures will require the closer understanding of market preferences that a more decentralized regime, with an autonomous private sector, can provide.[8]

The regime types considered in the present chapter are, like most LDC regimes, centralized and either hegemonic or exclusionary. Hegemonic regimes brook no significant dissent, requiring universal acceptance of the national political and economic agendas. Exclusionary regimes do not allow significant political power centers other than the central government, but they do permit limited autonomy (*because of* the exclusion) for functional tasks (for example, economic adjustment). The characterizations are based on two of the most successful East Asian cases, Taiwan and South Korea. There is evidence that although both have experienced considerable adjustment success, the success is in different phases, reflecting very different regime types.[9] The most recent troubles in Asia also provide evidence: the difficulties South Korea (an exclusionary regime) has experienced are at the macroeconomic level. The "Asian flu," as of this writing, has not afflicted Taiwan (a hegemonic regime).

Tunisia: Hegemonic Centralism and Economic Adjustment

As Haggard reminds us, "External pressures, even the most powerfully constraining ones, are filtered through the prism of domestic political life,"[10] in this case, through regime type. It is necessary, then, to determine the regime type and then to analyze adjustment success. The evidence for Tunisia's regime tends to point to a hegemonic regime. The state bureaucracy, since independence, has excluded any claim for autonomous interest groups,[11] reserving for itself an ideological universality. We will see that this arrangement has resulted in good stabilization results but much weaker restructuring. This is to be expected, because the informational and implementational requirements of restructuring suffer from the functional uniformity that hegemonic regimes demand.[12] A review of Tunisia's state-building and economic reconstruction will show that Tunisia has developed a hegemonic regime which has enjoyed some macroeconomic success but less microeconomic success.

Development of the Tunisian State

The current regime in Tunisia dates from soon after independence in 1956, but it is firmly rooted in the country's colonial and precolonial past. Today's centralized control in Tunisia first developed in the mid-1800s, primarily through Ahmad Bey's reform of the military and the repression of a countryside rebellion, leaving the state, *faute de mieux*, as the principal force in the rural areas. That repression both strengthened the central administration and weakened traditional kinship and tribal ties which dominated rural Tunisia. The development of the French Protectorate "insured the continuity of the bureaucracy established earlier and of the clientelist political structures it had spawned."[13] The growth of government resulted in a continuing penetration of the bureaucracy into the hinterlands, further weakening tribal authority and strengthening that of the central government. In short, Tunisia at independence was "an established bureaucratic state."[14]

Independence "changed the resources available to the players but not the rules of the game."[15] Bourguiba, despite pluralistic tendencies at the beginning, moved forcefully to create a system that revolved around him and his party. (He once commented that *he* was the system). Even the "national associations," ostensible intermediaries between state and society which had served Bourguiba faithfully under colonialism, saw their limited autonomy even more circumscribed after independence.[16] Most of the major economic associations (UTICA, UNAT) were *political* creations of the Neo-Destour party.[17] Only UGTT could claim any independence, but it, too, was ultimately harnessed for Bourguiba's political ends. Facing the monolithic state was a decentralized, family-oriented, private sector, not yet ready, according to one observer, "to stand on its feet."[18] Its main representative, UTICA (Union Tunisienne de l'Industrie, du Commerce, et de l'Artisanat), the principal producer organization in Tunisia, began as a political, not an economic, counterweight to the colonial-French producer union. The political conditions and the resulting economic conditions created a weak, unwilling private sector which was also risk averse[19] and family oriented, preferring to concentrate ownership and capital among family members and close associates.[20] Even the secretary general of UTICA describes the organization's role as seeking "to rectify rather than propose" economic policies.[21] In general, UTICA and UGTT have been "fragile and weak social partners."[22] Given such a strong state and weak private sector, Tunisia's success at economic reform was not assured, at least according to neo-classical expectations.[23] As we shall see, the economic history of Tunisia from independence to 1986 also offered little hope that the Tunisian government would accomplish anything other than failure.

The Statist Path to Failure

After a decade of socialist-style collectivization in the 1960s, Tunisia had created a bloated public-enterprise (PE) sector; it had become *le tout état,* the all-pervasive state. A new strategy, designed in the 1970s and led by the new prime minister, Hedi Nouira, was to make private-sector entrepreneurs the "masters of the country."[24] Instead, they became the state's servants, dominated by regulations as before.[25] The substantial increase in oil and phosphate revenues caused the state to become not an engine of development but a center of employment. Far from becoming a liberal state, Tunisia became *l'état-providence,* the provider state:[26] state participation in economic activities actually increased during the period (see Table

4.1). The precipitous decline of world oil prices in 1982 forced Tunisia to face the consequences of its statist policies. In 1986, with another fall in world oil prices, Tunisia experienced its first year of economic loss since independence.[27] Faced with internal imbalances and mounting external debt, Tunisia negotiated its first EAP, an IMF standby, in 1986.

Economic Adjustment

Since then, Tunisia has succeeded in steadily instituting reforms. Analysts in international financial institutions (IFIs) have praised Tunisia's progress as "one of the best examples of how a developing country can overcome apparently intractable difficulties."[28] The confidence of IFIs in Tunisia was exemplified in the 1988 Extended Fund Facility (EFF) loan (a long-term loan that is more difficult to obtain but imposes more lenient conditions), which was extended a year after its initial due date, an almost unheard-of vote of confidence in an LDC's economy.[29] International creditors have also recognized Tunisia's efforts: throughout the 1990s, Tunisia's country credit rating has been near the top of all countries in Africa (including South Africa) and was the top-rated country for two of those years.[30]

Tunisia's reform success has been mainly at the macroeconomic level, especially in controlling state expenditures. When we compare 1981–85 (the beginning of Tunisia's crisis) with 1986–90 (see Table 4.2), Tunisia's *real GDP growth* fell slightly, from 3.8 to 3.4 percent, before rising in the post–Gulf War period to 4.2 percent. *Current account deficits* were reduced from an average of 8.5 percent of GDP (1981–85) to 3.3 percent.

Table 4.1. Relative importance of the state sector in Tunisia, 1970–80

Relationship	1970	1980
Share in gross domestic product	26.0	25.0
Share in gross domestic investment	31.0	34.0
Share in nonagricultural employment	21.0	22.5
Share in total nonagricultural salary payments	20.0	30.0
Ratio of salary payments to value added	39.0	47.5
Share in country's merchandise exports	80.0	75.0
Ratio of government capital transfers and subsidies to sector's gross investment	10.0	52.4

Source: Grissa, "Tunisian State Enterprises," p. 112.

The ranges during this period are striking. In 1984, the current account deficit was 10.9 percent. Just four years later, there was a precedent-setting 1 percent *surplus*. The post–Gulf War period saw a return to higher deficits but to lower levels than those of the prewar period. The *budget deficit* declined marginally between 1981–85 and 1986–90, from 5.0 to 4.3 percent, but saw a significant reduction to 3.5 percent in the period 1991–95. *Inflation* also declined from 9.6 percent (1981–85) to 5.8 percent (1991–95). The *debt-service ratio* averaged 17.2 percent in the 1981–86 period, climbed to 24.9 percent in 1986–90, and then decreased to 20.4 percent in 1991–95.[31] *Total debt as a percentage of GDP* was reduced, from 58.9 percent in 1986–90 to 53.5 percent in 1991–95. In trade, Tunisia has eliminated quantitative restrictions on most items and has liberalized price controls. Reforms, especially macroeconomic reforms, can be expected to continue for the foreseeable future, given Tunisia's accession to GATT/WTO and its recent accord with the European Union (EU), which has "locked" the country into continued stabilization efforts and further price liberalization.[32]

SOEs and Privatization

In contrast to its success at stabilization (for example, controlling spending), Tunisia's restructuring reforms, especially privatization, have been weak. The public-enterprise (PE) sector, which had accounted for 55–60 percent of all investment in Tunisia by the end of the 1960s,[33] grew even larger in the 1970s, despite the encouragement of the private sector by the state.[34] On the eve of the 1986 EAP, the PE sector still claimed 40 percent of all investment in Tunisia and 30 percent of all formal-sector employment. Even now, government estimates put PE investment at 25 percent of total investment.[35] Privatization laws have continued the trend by centralizing privatization in the prime minister's office, with the help of a commission dominated by bureaucrats.[36] As a result, Tunisia's biggest "success" at reducing the PE sector was in redefining what a PE was.[37] Other attempts, through 1991, resulted in fifty-one totally or partially privatized firms out of the nearly two hundred identified under the 1989 law, representing a mere 1 percent of the book value of the two hundred PEs.[38] More recently, between 1992 and 1993, Tunisia completed seven privatizations, almost all of which were hotels, totaling about $60 million and bringing in some $19 million in foreign exchange.[39] Despite Tunisia's stated intentions, privatization, according to one neutral observer, "has so far been a marginal phenomenon that in no significant way has

Table 4.2. The Tunisian economy: key indicators, 1981–95

Indicator	1981–85*	1986–90*	1991–95**
Real GDP growth	3.8%	3.4%	4.2%
Current account deficit	-8.5	-3.3	-5.3
Budget deficit	-5.0	-4.3	-3.5
Inflation	9.6	7.2	5.8
Debt-service/exports	17.2	24.9	20.4
Total debt/GDP	46.3	58.9	53.5

*Nsouli et al. (1993).
**IMF staff, *Tunisia: Recent Economic Developments*.

reduced the extensive role of the state in the production of goods and services.[40]

The structured-engagement argument would claim just such limited success in privatization. Because hegemonic regimes claim ideological universality, they allow very little autonomy, which is just what entrepreneurs and firms need in order to respond to market preferences. In consequence, tension results between the goal of privatization (decentralized decision making) and the goal of a hegemonic regime (centralized control).[41]

Regime Type and Political Change

Regime type and economic change having been reviewed, it is important now to explore the relevance of the framework for political change in Tunisia—and the outlook, at first, does not seem good. Like many single-party regimes, the Tunisian government has controlled politics by repeatedly creating sharp dichotomies between "acceptable" opposition and "unacceptable" opposition.[42] In the 1950s, Bourguiba's new government was challenged by Salah Ben Youssef. When opposition to the government turned violent, Ben Youssef was driven from the country with the help of French forces. In the 1970s, it was Bourguiba and the ruling party, the PSD (RCD), pitted against the principal labor union (UGTT), and its leader and political rival of Bourguiba, Habib Achour.[43] When a general strike in January of 1978 resulted in a riot and severe police repression,[44] Achour, head of the UGTT and former Politburo member, was jailed, leaving no serious opposition in the country. In the 1980s and 1990s, the secular Tunisian state has fought against the threat of Islamism.[45] The

Islamist party became increasingly important in the 1970s as a protest of the economically disenfranchised. Bourguiba banned the Islamist party (MTI) just before the 1981 elections.[46] The ban continued under Ben Ali, though warmer relations between the state and the Islamists developed in the early days of the new government.[47] The culmination came in the early 1990s, when an attack on a RCD party office resulted in the death of a night watchman. Horrified Tunisians silently consented to a severe (and continuing) crackdown on the Islamists and their renamed party, En-Nahda (Renaissance).[48] The crackdown explains, in part, the absence of a significant "threat" from the Islamic opposition.

Because of this lack of attention to human rights and Western norms of political democracy, Tunisia's political practices have figured prominently in the analysis of politics in the Middle East. Indeed, much of Western political analysis of the Middle East has been suffused with the "desire to combat despotism";[49] for the MENA region, the desire is not misplaced. In Tunisia, despite periodic pluralistic noises, the government has persisted in its authoritarian control of Tunisian society. Critics of the regime are not lacking, and examples abound. Especially noticeable is the contraction of space allowed for dissent. As noted above, despite the heady first days of the post-Bourguibist "New Era," which included the previously outlawed MTI, parties based on religion have since been banned. Even "legal" opposition parties have narrow limits for voicing dissent. When Mohammed Moada, head of the leading acceptable opposition party in Tunisia (MDS), printed an open letter criticizing "the return to single-party hegemony" and calling for a "gradual" move to a "pluralist culture and democratic choice," he was arrested, tried, and sentenced to eleven years in prison. His lawyer was also arrested and imprisoned.[50] (They have since been released, though some have labeled this "cosmetic.")[51] In a similar vein, during the 1994 elections, despite the promotion of opposition parties through a set-aside of seats specifically reserved for them, the openness did not extend to the presidential race. The Tunisian government arrested Moncef Marzouki, former head of the Tunisian Human Rights League, for declaring his candidacy for president. Space for dissent in other forums is equally narrow: the press is described as "suffocated" and journalists as "harassed."[52]

What, then, are the prospects for political reform in Tunisia? Based on the structured-engagement framework, political change will come about only insofar as the hegemonic hold of the RCD on Tunisian politics loosens. Some small signs may suggest that the Tunisian government is trying to increase political decentralization. Opposition parties "won" nineteen seats in the legislature in the 1994 elections—the first time they have done so since independence. Ben Ali has promised to subsidize "legal" opposition parties and to allow their representation in the parliament to as much as 20 percent of all seats.[53] The promises constitute only pro forma reform, but for the government, pro forma reform is better than formless (and potentially violent) opposition. And as a keen observer of North Africa noted, "controlled" liberalization, even when limited to the economy, may not always be controllable;[54] nevertheless, serious doubts about liberalization efforts remain, and significant political change may have to wait. In the 1994 elections, the RCD seemed to have rid itself of the demoralization it had been experiencing. The elections seemed to have rejuvenated the party's mobilizing mission through "a renewal of the party leaders, a balancing of the regions, a neutralization of certain 'barons,' and the promotion of the 'president's men,' [who are] younger, more technocratic, and less political."[55]

For those hoping for "real" political reform, they may need to look for a "Trojan horse" to bring about change from within.[56] If one looks eastward, Taiwan, and especially South Korea, show that sustained economic success can lead to political liberalization.[57] The principal element of liberalization seems to have been the decentralization that took place in economic restructuring policies and in the consolidation of interest groups which developed some degree of autonomy from the state.[58] In other words, the decentralization required for restructuring the economy may also lead to the opening up of the political system; that is, the dynamics of political liberalization resemble those of economic liberalization. In sum, *economic reform can be a type of (or at least a precursor to) political reform;* moreover, the present framework suggests that political change, like economic reform, will reflect and be constrained by the regime type of the country. The "universalism" expected in hegemonic regimes greatly differs from what one expects to prevail in other, exclusionary states that allow some degree of economic decentralization. A nearby neighbor (Morocco), for example, employs a divide-and-conquer strategy by adding, not eliminating, adversaries to compete with existing opposition.[59] When disagreements between the new and old groups become destabilizing, the king enters the fray as a *rex ex machina,* easing tensions and rallying groups around a national agenda. Such a strategy has the double advantage of allowing the king to remain above partisan politics, while at the same time providing him with information about the principal elements of political debate in the country.

As we have seen, and in contrast to Morocco, Tunisia has employed a divide-and-eliminate strategy with its most significant opposition. Given the continuing campaign against Tunisian Islamism, it will be instructive to examine in detail how this developed with the Tunisian government's most significant opposition in the present political context.

The Islamist movement first became important when, according to some, the government encouraged it in the 1970s as a counterweight to the radical left.[60] The relationship between the ruling party (the RCD) and the Islamist movement in Tunisia could be described as two sides of the same nationalist coin. For Bourguiba, Islam was an impediment to national development, both political and economic. It had to be made to serve the national good. This resonated with another famous, though much older, reformer, Mohammed Kheireddine, who argued for the integration of Western technology with the ideals of Islamic principles.[61] Bourguiba, however, went beyond this conception of reform: rather than integrating Western norms with Islamic practices, he sought to alter, and even eradicate, some Islamic practices as part of a larger campaign to "desacralize" Islam in Tunisian society.[62] One high-profile example was the Ramadan fast, which he attacked as "an abusive interpretation of the religion"[63] and which he tried to transform into a matter of personal conscience rather than religious requirement.[64] Riots at Kairouan, the holy city of Tunisia, ensued. Other, less salient changes included the outlawing of polygamy (which is specifically allowed in the Koran), as well as banning the veil for women and the *chechia* (a traditional religious hat) for men.

From the Islamist side, the development (and perceived anti-Islamic) models that Bourguiba was advocating were Westernization attempts at levels "not even achieved during colonial times."[65] Given Bourguiba's actions, one could see Islamism as a response to a native political system that has repressed the country's cultural symbols more systematically than the former colonizing power had ever done. In this context, the Islamists believed that their nationalism was purer, and more indigenous, than Bourguiba's. Furthermore, the precursors of MTI believed that Islamism required national social action rather than personal Muslim piety.[66]

Bourguiba rightly believed that the Islamist conception of nationalism provided a clear alternative to his own. In a hegemonic regime, one interpretation had to go. The government-Islamist clash of ideas came to head in 1981, when, in order to burnish the international profile of his political liberalization efforts, Bourguiba allowed "openly contested" elections.[67] The Islamists established the MTI at this time in order to contest the elections. However, after antigovernment speeches were delivered in some mosques, MTI was banned from the elections, and many of its leaders were arrested, tried, convicted, and sent to jail.[68]

Since then, MTI experienced two critical events. The first was in 1987, when political tensions were quite high under an enfeebled Bourguiba administration. The accession of Prime Minister Zine El-Abidine Ben Ali to power in a "medical" coup that ousted Bourguiba considerably lessened the tension. The main consequence was a government-MTI détente, which resulted in the short-term defanging of the Islamist threat. MTI joined the government and other opposition groups in the National Pact of 1988.[69] MTI renamed itself Hizb En-Nahda (or simply Nahda—Renaissance, or Renewal) in order to circumvent the law banning all parties that referred to religion (among other things) in its name. Rachid Ghannouchi, the head of the outlawed MTI, agreed to work within Tunisia's political framework, calling the Personal Status Code "liveable."[70] He even suggested that the law forbidding polygamy was the expression of an *ijtihad*—that is, a legitimate interpretation of holy texts.[71] In essence, he accepted the rules of republican politics, including the renunciation of violence.[72]

These measures were not enough for Ben Ali, who issued a presidential decree outlawing all parties that had anything to do with religion.[73] The pressure to rid Tunisian political life of all traces of Islamist influence led to the second critical event, in 1991. The mysterious fire in a local RCD party office that killed a night watchman on duty was blamed on Nahda, resulting in a frontal attack on Islamism. Reaction to the violence by shocked Tunisians resulted in the Islamist movement being "delegitimized."[74] Even more, they silently consented to a severe (and ongoing) crackdown on the Islamists and Nahda. This widespread sentiment explains, in part, the current absence of a significant "threat" from the Islamic opposition.

This is, in microcosm, the political tendency of the regime: demand ideological conformity but nurture pliant opposition; stamp out all nonconforming, and therefore threatening, opposition. The lesson seems to be that Islam as religion is not a threat. Islamism, as an alternative vision of Tunisian nationalism, *was* a threat and hence had to be removed.

Conclusion

Throughout the chapter, there has been an effort to connect the economic logic of adjustment to the political logic of regime type; however, if one is looking for definitive causal links, this chapter does not provide them. There is no getting around the "small *n*" problem and hence the preliminary nature of the findings, but if one values the heuristic character of research, then perhaps this chapter will contribute to the understanding of economic adjustment in Tunisia, and LDCs generally. It is also hoped that the framework has something to offer to analysis of political change. It is possible that economic liberalization may be the most auspicious way to political liberalization. For instance, South Korea, an exclusionary regime, provides the example of the two most recently elected presidents, both of whom had been major opposition figures, as well as the example of ex-presidents being sentenced for committing crimes during their tenure. Holding leaders responsible through the rule of law may have taken decades to develop, but those analysts who demand immediate political change—with or without economic reform—need only look to Algeria and Russia (among other countries) for counterexamples of an all-or-nothing approach. Rather than looking for signs of developing "civil society" or searching cynically for evidence that Islamists will take over, observers of Tunisia should analyze the *structures* of Tunisian politics for possible political developments. Analysts who criticize Western prescriptions for economic adjustment[75] have in the same breath praised Western visions of democracy as the only viable political "trajectory."[76]

This chapter suggests that neither view is correct. Both economic *and* political liberalization, though borrowed from Western models, are implemented in regional and domestic ways. This chapter has maintained that regime type will play a key role in determining outcomes of EAPs in Tunisia and other LDCs. The hegemonic system in Tunisia will result more in stabilization than in economic restructuring or in political liberalization. Regime type does matter, but not always in the way many analysts think.

Thus, although chronicling abuses is an important task (because doing so has brought about some changes in Tunisian political practices), political narratives—no matter how powerful—do not explain outcomes, and so their analytical use is limited. Citing democratic shortcomings is a meaningful enterprise, but lasting reform comes only through adjustment of basic political and economic structures, a process that demands more than a narrative account of reform failures. Certainly, ignoring Western political models would deprive LDCs of democratizing aspirations, but dismissing domestic constraints will create unrealistic expectations.

Much of Middle East political analysis, then, "reveals more about the preoccupation of Western scholars" than about the nature of Middle East politics.[77] What is needed is a shift to analyses that "combat the tendency toward Middle East exceptionalism and invite comparative, cross-regional analysis"[78] and that move away from the study of the Middle East as a sui generis form of research to a broader, more comparative approach. To escape the Bermuda Triangle of Tunisian, and MENA, studies, it will be necessary to employ a more comparative understanding of the region. Though perhaps overly facile, the aim should be for students of the region to refocus on "*politics* in the Middle East" and away from "*Middle East* politics."[79] That aim is a tall order, and the present chapter claims only to offer one attempt at a broader understanding of how Tunisia has managed economic adjustment and political change.

Notes

The author wishes to thank Thomas Lancaster and especially Richard Doner for their penetrating readings of early drafts of this paper, Christopher Alexander and Jeffrey Coupe for their engaging discussions, the Emory Political Science Department and especially AIMS for their support of my research in Tunisia, Jeanne Mrad of CEMAT for her constant competence and endless patience, Yahia Zoubir for his editorial deftness, and finally one anonymous reviewer and Debra Denzer for their contributions to the final draft.

1. Bill, "The Study of Middle East Politics," 503.

2. Hermassi and Vandewalle, "The Second Stage of State Building," 39.

3. For the Tunisian government's role as an "impediment to the advance of civil society," see Bellin, "Tunisian Industrialists and the State," 510.

4. Gerschenkron, *Economic Backwardness*; Hirschman, *The Strategy of Economic Development*. See Killick, *A Reaction Too Far,* chap. 2, for an excellent overview of the theoretical reasons for the failure of state intervention in the economy. For an empirical study of the failure of state interventionist policies in Tunisia, see Grissa, "Tunisian State Enterprises."

5. See Bellin, "Civil Society," 428, for examples of such "engagement" policies in Tunisia.

6. The term and the concept of "embedded autonomy" is from Evans, "The State as Problem and Solution."

7. In the stabilization phase, relatively more emphasis is placed on reducing demand (e.g., for domestic credit and in particular for state borrowing). The restructuring phase aims at reducing distortions (e.g., price controls) and increasing output capacity (e.g., through privatization).

8. Rueschemeyer and Evans suggest a similar linkage ("The State and Economic Transformation," 52).

9. Space does not allow for detailed evidence of the East Asian cases. Good accounts of Taiwan as a hegemonic regime that is more successful at stabilization

(i.e., highly centralized) include Gereffi, "Paths of Industrialization" and "Big Business and the State"; Wade, *Governing the Market;* and Cheng "Political Regimes and Development Strategies." For South Korea as an exclusionary regime (limited decentralization) with relatively good restructuring success, see Amsden, *Asia's Next Giant;* and Wade, *Governing the Market.*

10. Haggard, *Pathways to the Periphery,* 270.

11. Bellin, "Tunisian Industrialists and the State," 59; Schmitter, "Still the Century of Corporatism? 108.

12. Rueschemeyer and Evans, "The State and Economic Transformation," 55.

13. Anderson, "The Traditions of Imperialism," 7.

14. Anderson, *The State and Social Transformation in Tunisia and Libya,* 231.

15. Anderson, "The Traditions of Imperialism," 18.

16. Moore, *Tunisia since Independence.* The national associations were the UGTT, UTAC (later UTICA), UNAT, UNET, UNFT (respectively, the workers' union, the producers' union, the agricultural union, the student organization, and the women's organization).

17. Moore, *Tunisia Since Independence;* Salah Brik Hannachi, interviewed by the author, Tunis, May 17, 1993.

18. Richard Rousseau, interviewed by the author, Tunis, May 19, 1993.

19. Ezzedine Larbi, interviewed by the author, Tunis, May 18, 1993.

20. Eveleth, *The Private Sector Strategy,* 4.

21. However, given that some of the biggest private conglomerates in Tunisia are run by men who are not part of the inner circle of Ben Ali (nor of Bourguiba before him) and who have not been party stalwarts, the role of the private sector may change (Moncef El-Aoud, interviewed by the author, Tunis, May 20, 1993).

22. Abdeljalil Bedoui, interviewed by the author, Tunis, May 25, 1992.

23. Geddes, "The Effect of Political Institutions," 14.

24. Bellin, "Tunisian Industrialists and the State," 50.

25. Eveleth, *The Private Sector Strategy,* 1.

26. Delmasure, *L'économie tunisienne.* Tunisia could also have been described as a "rentier state," one that provided much and asked little of its citizens, all for a general acquiescence to the prevailing political system. See Chaudhry, "The Price of Wealth," for a discussion of this concept.

27. Eveleth, *The Private Sector Strategy,* 8.

28. O'Sullivan, "Grappling with the Legacy of the Past," 5. See also Chauffour, "Growth and Financial Stability," and Nsouli, "The European Union's New Mediterranean Strategy," for more recent reports on Tunisia's progress in economic adjustment.

29. Both Morocco and Algeria were denied EFFs at about the same time.

30. Ratings appeared in the May and September issues, 1990–94, of *Institutional Investor.*

31. Debt-service ratio is the cost of servicing external debt as a percentage of exports.

32. Nsouli, "The European Union's New Mediterranean Strategy," 15. See also Rodrik, "Credibility of Trade Reform," 14, who has called this governmental

"tying of its hands" a hedge against later governmental second thoughts.

33. Bouaouaja, "Privatization in Tunisia," 235.

34. Grissa, "Tunisian State Enterprises," 112.

35. *Le VIIIème plan en bref,* 17.

36. CAREPP, Commission d'Assainissement et de Restructuration des Entreprises à Participations Publiques (Commission for the Restructuring of Public Enterprises), established that members included the ministers of National Economy and Finance, Plan and Regional Development, Interior, and Social Affairs; the governor of the Central Bank; designated high-level bureaucrats; and the secretary-general of the government (Saghir, *Privatization in Tunisia,* 12).

37. Saghir, *Privatization in Tunisia,* 16.

38. Of course, the figure for PEs would have been much higher, and the revenue percentage much lower, if the pre-1989 definition for PEs had been used.

39. World Bank, *World Debt Tables,* 1:142, 155.

40. Saghir, *Privatization in Tunisia,* 17.

41. See Geddes, "The Effect of Political Institutions," for a rational-choice approach to the political difficulties of privatization. This is not in conflict with the present framework. While Geddes details the conditions under which privatization would go slowly, structured engagement suggests when, and why, such conditions would likely obtain.

42. Huntington has called these dichotomies "bifurcations" ("Social and Institutional Dynamics," 15).

43. The ruling party's name has gone through a number of changes, reflecting its choice of ideology. At independence, it was called Parti Néo-Destour, *destour* referring to the Arabic term for *constitution.* In the early 1960s, when the collectivist program was under way, the name was changed to Parti Socialiste Destourien to reflect its economic and social activism. After Ben Ali took power, he changed the name again, both to create distance between his predecessor and himself and to offer a new ideological vision for the 1980s and 1990s: Rassemblement Constitutionnel Démocratique (Democratic Constitutional Rally). As for the UGTT, it is the principal workers' union (Union Générale des Travailleurs Tunisiens).

44. The government numbered the dead at forty-seven; other estimates ranged as high as two hundred.

45. *Islamism* here refers to the practice of creating political forces, often in the form of political parties, to enhance the role of Islam in the political and social life of a country's citizens.

46. Anderson, *The State and Social Transformation in Tunisia and Libya,* 245.

47. This was short lived. Ben Ali soon insisted that there would be no religious party as long as he was in power (Limam, "Focus: Interview with Ben Ali").

48. Reaction to the violence by most Tunisians resulted in the Islamist movement being "delegitimized" (Ahmad and Zartman, "Political Islam: Can It Become a Loyal Opposition?" The quote comes from Zartman). Others have called the movement "moderate" (Ramonet, "Main de fer en Tunisie"; "Cosmetic Changes").

49. Bellin, "Civil Society," 509.

50. Boucher, "La société tunisienne privée de parole," 2.

51. "Cosmetic Changes."

52. Boucher, "La société tunisienne privée de parole."

53. "Cosmetic Changes."

54. Michel Camau, interviewed by the author, Tunis, May 19, 1993.

55. Denoeux, "Tunisie: Les élections présidentielles et législatives," 65.

56. I owe this image to Vandewalle, "Ben Ali's New Era."

57. Many would dispute the logic for Tunisia. One long-time observer of North African politics once commented to me that he did not want to hear of economic adjustment, let alone adjustment success, until there was significant improvement in Tunisian democratization.

58. This is much less true for Taiwan than it is for South Korea.

59. His "encouragement" of new political parties is one example of this (Zartman, "King Hassan's New Morocco," 19–22).

60. Anderson, *The State and Social Transformation in Tunisia and Libya,* 245.

61. Micaud, *Tunisia: The Politics of Modernization,* 9–10.

62. Ibid., 60–62.

63. Ibid., 143.

64. Moore, *Tunisia since Independence,* 58.

65. Rachid Ghannouchi, cited in Zghal, "The New Strategy of the Movement of the Islamic Way," 207.

66. Magnuson, "Islamic Reform in Contemporary Tunisia," 176.

67. Anderson, *The State and Social Transformation in Tunisia and Libya,* 246.

68. Ibid., 247.

69. Hermassi, "The Islamicist Movement and November 7," 197.

70. Hermassi and Vandewalle, "The Second Stage of State Building."

71. Zghal, "The New Strategy of the Movement of the Islamic Way," 208.

72. Hermassi, "The Islamicist Movement and November 7," 194, 197.

73. Limam, "Focus: Interview with Ben Ali."

74. Ahmad and Zartman, "Political Islam: Can It Become a Loyal Opposition?" The quote comes from Zartman.

75. See, for example, Mahjoub, "État, secteur public et privatisation en Tunisie," who calls EAPs a type of neocolonialism.

76. Boucher, "La société tunisienne privée de parole," 4; Rossevsky-Wickham, "Beyond Democratization."

77. Rossevsky-Wickham, "Beyond Democratization," 509.

78. Bellin, "Civil Society," 510.

79. There are exceptions to this general trend, including Alexander, "State, Labor, and the New Global Economy in Tunisia"; Anderson, *The State and Social Transformation in Tunisia and Libya;* and Vandewalle, *North Africa: Development and Reform,* to name only a few. See also Bill, "The Study of Middle East Politics," for an emphatic demand for comparison.

5.

POLITICAL AND ECONOMIC DEVELOPMENTS IN LIBYA IN THE 1990S

Mary-Jane Deeb

This chapter will look at some of the major problems Libya has faced since 1992, when the United Nations imposed economic sanctions on that country for its alleged involvement in the blowing up of Pan Am Flight 103 in December 1988 and French UTA Flight 77 in September 1989. It will discuss the political and economic impact of those sanctions and the attempts of the Libyan state to have them lifted. This chapter will also analyze some of the internal developments in the country, especially with regard to the rise of Islamist opposition groups and the more tribally based protest movements that have created major problems for the government. The analysis will conclude with an assessment of the future of the regime, taking into account the problems it faces and the resources it has at its disposal.

The Islamist Opposition

Although the 1992 UN sanctions appear to have isolated Libya internationally, regionally Libya has become, in the 1990s, more mainstream and has gravitated slowly but surely toward the political center of Arab politics. One of the main reasons is that the Libyan regime has come up against a powerful Islamist opposition that is perceived as a threat by all the regimes in power in the Maghreb and elsewhere in the region.

Libya is physically and politically in the very midst of that crisis. The Qadaffi regime, like those of presidents Hosni Mubarak of Egypt, Zine al-Abidine Ben Ali of Tunisia, or Liamine Zeroual of Algeria, is perceived by militant Islamists as a regime that is secular and anti-Islamic. As in other countries of North Africa, the Islamist opposition has called for the overthrow of the regime and its replacement by an Islamist government. In order to deal with this situation, the countries of North Africa (including Egypt) have been sharing intelligence on the activities of those movements through their interior ministries and their security services. Muammar Qadaffi has been included as an equal partner with the other regional leaders and has cooperated in sharing intelligence and in arresting Islamists fleeing from neighboring countries to Libya.[1]

The present Islamist opposition in Libya is made up of a large number of groups with somewhat different agendas. The more established ones are rooted in the al-Ikhwan al-Muslimin (the Muslim Brothers) movement, which was founded in the 1950s as the result of the impact of the Muslim Brothers of Egypt on Libya. Their ideas were spread through the schools and universities in the first decade of independence, when many Egyptians came to Libya as teachers and university professors.[2]

The Hizb al-Tahrir al-Islami (the Islamic Liberation Party) is an offshoot of the Muslim Brothers and appears to be linked to other similar organizations in North Africa and in Jordan, where the party was originally founded in the 1950s. It is popular with students and has made deep inroads in the military. It believes in the restoration of Islamic values and approves of the use of violent means to achieve its objectives.[3]

The Islamist wing of the National Front for the Salvation of Libya (the major Libyan opposition group), which was formed in 1981 in Khartoum by Muhammad Yusuf al-Maqarif, has been one of the most vociferous and best organized of all the Libyan opposition groups. Some of its members are high-level government officials who defected and sought safe haven abroad in Egypt, the United Kingdom, and the United States. It has members both inside and outside of Libya, and in 1984 it carried out a major attack on the Bab al-Aziziya military barracks in an attempt to overthrow the regime. The attack failed, and the movement was battered in Libya but survived abroad.[4]

The Jihad al-Islami (the Islamic Struggle) was formed in the early 1970s, again modeled after its Egyptian counterpart. It became very active in the mid-1980s, when twenty-six of its members were arrested in September 1986 and accused of two assassinations and various acts of sabotage.[5]

Another well-established Islamist group is al-Jama'a al-Islamiyya Libya (the Islamic Group—Libya), founded in 1979. It has added "Libya" to its name to differentiate itself from al-Jama'a in Egypt, although the addition could also mean that it is the same organization but simply the Libyan branch of that movement.[6] Like a number of its counterparts, it publishes a magazine, *al-Muslim,* and a newspaper, *al-Ra-id.*

Finally, al-Haraka al-Islamiyya Libya (the Islamic Movement—Libya), which was founded in 1980 and publishes *al-Shuruq,* is an opposition movement with links to other Islamist groups outside Libya, as indicated by the addition of "Libya" to its name.

There are also other more shadowy groups that appeared in the late 1980s and early 1990s, about which little is known. Those include al-Takfir wal-Hijra (Apostasy and Migration), which seems to be a counterpart to the Egyptian organization of the same name; al-Tabligh (the Warning);[7] Harakat al-Shuhada al-Islamiyya (the Martyrs' Islamic Movement); and al-Jama'a al-Islamiyya al-Muqatila (the Fighting Islamic Group), which was founded in 1991 and publishes a magazine called *al-Fajr* (The Dawn).[8]

In the past decade, these groups have been active, in Libya and abroad, in publishing materials discrediting the Libyan government as well as attempting to destabilize the Libyan regime. There have been numerous reported incidents of assassinations, attacks on military posts, and ambushes of government dignitaries attributed to or claimed by Islamist organizations. The Fighting Islamic Group, for instance, has claimed a number of operations inside Libya since 1995, the most recent being in May 1997 when the group attacked a military post and reportedly seized one hundred machine guns.[9] The Martyrs' Islamic Movement has also claimed that its members attacked some security posts in Benghazi in February 1997, killing a number of security officers and losing eight of their own when they were apprehended by the Libyan authorities.[10] There is, however, no accurate record of the activities of Islamist groups in Libya. The government blames all disturbances on these groups, and the Islamist opposition may in turn exaggerate its role in order to enhance its credibility.

The Military Opposition

What is clear, however, is that there has been a significant amount of unrest in Libya in the 1990s. The Libyan military has been behind a number of reported coup attempts aimed at overthrowing the regime. One of the most recent confirmed attempts took place in October 1993, when a military plot was hatched to ambush Qadaffi in Bani Walid, a town one hundred miles southeast of Tripoli. The plot was headed by a colonel in the army. The plot failed, and fifteen hundred people were arrested and hundreds killed.[11]

The reasons are many, not the least of which is the perennial question of unpaid salaries. Since the mid-1980s and perhaps even earlier, soldiers and officers have gone unpaid for months due to economic-reform measures aimed at restructuring the economy and cutting the budget. Officers' perks, including overseas training, were also radically curtailed if not cut altogether.[12]

Another major reason for the military unrest in Libya has been the defeat of the army by the French-backed Chadian forces in 1987.[13] This was followed by a complete forced withdrawal from the Aouzou Strip in 1994, when the International Court of Justice in The Hague ruled in favor of Chad on the issue of the appurtenance of that region.[14]

A third source of military dissatisfaction has been cuts in weaponry purchases and the consequent loss in the operational capability of the Libyan military. The decline in oil earnings in the mid-1980s was the principal reason for this reduction in arms purchases. More than half of Libya's estimated 2,210 battle tanks are out of commission, and over 50 percent of its 417 aircraft are in storage.[15] The sanctions have prevented Libya from purchasing spare parts for its aging weapons system, thus endangering the whole military infrastructure. It was reported that as recently as November 1995, ten tons of spare parts for Libya's combat aircraft, including its MiG fighters, were seized by the Italian police.[16]

Tribal Opposition

There also has been discontent among the tribes, especially those of Cyrenaica. That is nothing new, as that region has always been loyal to the Sanusiyya movement, which was headquartered in Bayda in prerevolutionary Libya. The overthrow of King Muhammad Idris I in 1969 was never fully accepted by his followers and fellow Sanusiyya members. From the first year Qadaffi assumed power in Libya, he had to contend with tribal unrest in Cyrenaica. In the early years, he tried to co-opt some tribes by spending lavishly in their region while undermining the power of others by imprisoning their leaders and redrawing administrative boundaries that had coincided with tribal lines to splinter the tribes.[17] In 1984, to ensure that there would be no resurgence of the Sanusiyya movement, Qadaffi had the remains of the founder of the Sanusiyya and his family disinterred from their tomb in the Jaghbub oasis and sent to

Algeria. The remains of the female members were placed in tombs throughout Libya.[18]

Throughout the 1990s, there have been reports of tribal uprisings and their quellings by the government's security forces. Most of the unrest has occurred in Cyrenaica, although there have been reports about attacks on security posts in Fezzan and Tripolitania as well. In some cases, there is an overlap between tribal and Islamist opposition to the regime; for instance, in October 1995, forty Ubaydat tribal leaders protested that the former minister of justice, Ibrahim al-Baqar, had been assassinated by government forces when he was killed in a car accident. He apparently had refused to condemn Islamists to death.[19]

The Secular Opposition

The other opposition organizations were formed outside of Libya by prominent dissidents and appear to be divided among themselves. They have ideological differences but also, and perhaps more important, personality differences that make a united democratic opposition unlikely.

A number of traditional organizations support the monarchy such as al-Ittihad al-Dusturi al-Libi (the Libyan Constitutional Union), which was formed in Manchester, England, in 1981. Others are ideological, like the pro-Iraqi al-Haraka al-Wataniya al-Libiya (Libyan National Movement), formed in 1980 by Umran Burways, which operates primarily in Europe.[20] And some, such as Munadhamat al-Tahrir al-Libiya (the Libyan Liberation Organization), appear to have been formed around prominent individuals; the latter organization was formed in Cairo in 1982 by Abd al-Hamid Bakkush, a former prime minister under the king.

Then there are groups that are offshoots of a major organization. For example, al-Tajamu' al-Watani al-Libi (the Libyan National Rally) was formed in 1976 by Umar al-Muhayshi and Abd al-Mun'im al-Huni, who were members of Qadaffi's Revolutionary Command Council and who defected to Egypt in 1975 after an abortive coup. They were joined by Mahmud Sulayman al-Maghribi, a former prime minister, and Fadil al-Mas'udi, a prominent journalist. In 1978 the group split, and al-Muhayshi and al-Mas'udi formed their own organization, al-Haraka al-Wataniya al-Dimuqratiya al-Libiya (The Libyan National Democratic Movement). Al-Huni, with a former Libyan diplomat, Muhammad Yusuf al-Maqarif, became founding members in 1981 of al-Jabha al-Wataniya li-Inqadh Libya (the National Front for the Salvation of Libya). In 1982, al-Maghribi and al-Mas'udi reconciled and formed a new organization, al-Tajamu' al-

Watani al-Dimuqrati al-Libi (the Libyan National Democratic Rally), which represented the coalescence of their two organizations, the Libyan National Democratic Movement and the Libyan National Rally.[21]

But it would be Al-Huni's organization, the National Front for the Salvation of Libya (NFSL), which he cofounded with a number of people including Muhammad Yusuf Maqarif, that would become the major opposition front against Qadaffi's regime. In 1988, it established a military wing, the Libya National Army, which immediately attracted over twelve hundred volunteers. The NFSL has published a magazine, *al-Inqadh* (Salvation), since 1982 and a monthly newsletter entitled *Akhbar Libya* (News of Libya) that covers Libyan politics. As its name denotes, it is a front that has brought together under one umbrella Islamists, leftists, monarchists, prodemocracy people, and others. It supports a pluralist alternative to the present regime in Libya.[22] This organization was responsible for a number of attempts at overthrowing the regime, the most important being the attack on the Bab al-Aziziya barracks mentioned earlier. The NFSL, however, is very divided along ideological and personality lines and has not posed a real challenge to the Qadaffi regime over the years.

The Changing Economic Environment

The UN Security Council unanimously adopted Resolution 731 on January 21, 1992, implicating Libyan government officials in the blowing up of Pan Am Flight 103 in December 1988 and the French UTA Flight 77 in September 1989. The UN resolution asked that the Libyan government "respond effectively" to requests by the United States, Great Britain, and France "to cooperate fully in establishing responsibility for the terrorist acts." Three months later, in April 1992, when the Security Council determined that Libya had *not* responded effectively to those requests, it passed Resolution 748, which banned flights to and from Libya and prohibited the sale of aircraft, aircraft parts, or craft maintenance equipment, as well as the sale or transfer of military equipment of any kind, to Libya. The resolution also encouraged all states to reduce their diplomatic personnel and staff in Libya and ask Libyans to do the same around the globe.[23] The sanctions have been renewed several times since then.

The sanctions have certainly had a negative impact on the Libyan economy, although less than had been anticipated. An excellent article appeared in August 1995 in the French *Marchés Tropicaux et Méditerranéens* which discussed some aspects of the Libyan economy. It argued that Libya's economy was in relatively good shape, since the country's economic and financial activities were based on petroleum revenues and those were not significantly affected by the UN sanctions. It cited a number of indicators to bolster its argument. First, Libya was investing heavily in Europe through its holding company, Oilinvest, and doing well. It owned 2,730 service stations and gasoline distribution centers in Europe, as well as a number of refinery plants in Italy and Switzerland. It was also expanding its economic activities in Germany, France, and Spain.[24] Second, Libya's adjusted real GDP per capita, despite a significant decline, was somewhat higher than those of Algeria, Morocco, or Tunisia, at about $5,869 in the mid-1990s.[25] Third, Libya's total debt (a significant portion of which was owed to Turkey, India, South Korea, and Russia) fell from $5 billion in 1990 to $3 billion at the end of 1994. Repayment of short-term debts to Middle-Eastern and European commercial banks accounted for a significant portion of this reduction.[26]

However, there were also signs that the economy was faltering, although that was not necessarily due directly to the UN sanctions. Until 1986, for instance, Libya's balance-of-trade sheet always showed a surplus, often exceeding $3 billion. However, with the fall of oil prices at that time, it began showing a small deficit, which rose to $1.7 billion in 1996.

The expulsions of Palestinians from Libya, which began in September 1996, were heralded by the Libyan authorities as a protest against peace with Israel. Those expulsions were meant to demonstrate that, despite Oslo II, Palestinians living abroad could not return to their "homeland" and that, consequently, those agreements had failed to meet the demands of the Palestinian people.

On closer examination, this explanation does not hold. Palestinians were not the only ones being expelled from Libya that year. Tens of thousands of Sudanese and Egyptian workers had also been expelled without fanfare or publicity. The reason for those expulsions is primarily economic. All the theatrics about the Palestinians were just a smoke screen to hide the fact that Libya's foreign labor force had become too large and that they lacked jobs and housing. In fact, the Libyan press published articles on the "foreign work force." The Tripoli news agency JANA, in one such article, reported that "the main reason for dispensing with foreign workers is care for [the] public interest . . . with regard to . . . food, health and environment security . . . the humanitarian condition of those workers attracted . . . attention as well. While we considered them our guests, we were ashamed when they slept in the streets or when they worked at menial tasks."[27]

A third indicator that all is not well with Libya's economy is that there has been a decline in demand for Libyan oil, due to a decrease in petroleum consumption in Europe. Libya had to reduce its production from 1.3 million to 1.2 million barrels per day in 1993; then the price of oil fell in 1994.[28] The government decided to cut imports to save, which resulted in shortages in almost all sectors of the economy.

But the decline in production is not only due to a decline in demand. Libya's oil industry, which was built in large part with U.S. technology, is unable to purchase U.S. equipment because of the UN sanctions. This, in turn, is having a negative impact on that critical sector of the economy. In 1993, for instance, the Waha fields had to cut production from 500,000 to 350,000 barrels per day when spare parts could not be found to replace damaged equipment. Cuts in production from 40,000 to 2,300 barrels per day also took place in the Bu Attifel field when water injection equipment could not be imported.[29]

Decline in Libyan oil production is also due to a natural decline in oil reserves. Libya's oil fields have been producing oil for an average of twenty-seven years and are showing signs of aging. For instance, production at one of the largest Mediterranean offshore oil fields, the Bouri field, dropped from 85,000 to 65,000 barrels per day in 1995 because of natural decline.[30]

A boom period in the 1990s, however, began when Iraq invaded Kuwait in August 1990. Between May 1990 and August of the same year, the price of a barrel of oil jumped from fifteen to thirty-seven dollars, and total exports increased by 58 percent over the preceding year. The trade balance registered a surplus, as did the current transactions balance. In March 1991, the oil market regained its stability, and oil prices fell to their pre–Gulf War levels.

The sector most significantly affected by the UN sanctions was the transport sector. Tens of thousands of Libyans used to travel abroad every year on vacation, for business, or on pilgrimage. The sanctions have made travel more difficult and more expensive. In 1991 Libyan travelers transferred $784 million in hard currency abroad. That figure declined to $452 million in 1992 and $166 million in 1993 as fewer Libyans traveled abroad.[31] The cost of transport, on the other hand, soared as people and merchandise had to move by land to the borders of Egypt or Tunisia before they could fly on aircraft from those countries.

There is also another, lesser known aspect to the UN sanctions that involves petroleum receipts. While revenues from oil are not frozen, they are deposited directly in a bank in Europe. Each firm doing business with Libya must have proof of this deposit, and Libya can open letters of credits in order to purchase items that are not on the list of embargoed goods.[32]

All these factors have affected the value of the Libyan dinar and, consequently, the cost of living. Officially, the dollar is worth 0.363 dinars, while on the black market it is worth at least 3 dinars.[33] More and more transactions take place in hard currencies, especially when those have to do with purchases of goods from abroad, or with major products domestically. It has become very difficult for people to buy cars, for instance, or such major household goods as refrigerators if they do not have hard currency. There is also a thriving black market in almost everything to meet the real and artificial shortages (due in part to hoarding and in part to illegal sales to neighboring states).[34]

According to French reports, the cost of living doubled in 1995 and tripled since 1992 when the sanctions were first imposed.[35] The Agence France Presse also reported that the Libyan Union of Workers denounced the loss of 20 to 30 percent of the purchasing power of agricultural workers because of the increase in the cost of living.

The State's Response to the Political and Economic Challenges

Qadaffi has tried every means to have the embargo lifted, short of turning two suspects over to the United States or the United Kingdom. He has attempted to have the sanctions lifted by addressing the issue of terrorism: in response to UN Resolution 731, Qadaffi reportedly ordered the closing down of Abu Nidal's offices in Tripoli in April 1992; a month later the People's Committee for External Liaison and International Cooperation issued a statement formally renouncing terrorism.[36]

Since that time, no major terrorist incident has been linked directly to the Libyan government. There have been accusations, however, of actions taken against Libyan opponents of the regime. For instance, Mansur Kikhia, a prominent dissident, disappeared in Cairo in December 1993 after attending a conference of Libyan opposition leaders in Washington, D.C., a few weeks earlier; Libya was accused of having kidnapped him. Ali Muhammad Abu Zayd, a founding member of the National Front for the Salvation of Libya, was assassinated in London in November 1995, and the NFSL maintained that the Libyan authorities were behind the murder.[37] The house of another important opponent of the regime, Abd al-Mun'im al-Huni, was bombed in Cairo in May 1997. Libyan agents were accused of having planted the bomb.

The United States also alleged in 1990 that the Libyan government was building a chemical-weapons factory in Rabta. International observers visited the facility and found it empty, after which Germany made accusations that another chemical weapons factory was being built in Tarhuna.[38] Neither accusation has been substantiated, although that certainly does not mean that Libya is innocent of those charges.

Qadaffi also has enlisted the support of his neighbors—primarily Egypt, Tunisia and Morocco—as well as the assistance of the League of Arab States. In the past five years, President Mubarak of Egypt, King Hassan of Morocco, and President Ben Ali of Tunisia have made numerous personal appeals to U.S. president Bill Clinton and to the United Nations to have those sanctions lifted. As recently as May 1997, Ben Ali called for an end to the embargoes on Libya and Iraq at a state dinner at Italy's Quirinale Palace in Rome, and Mubarak made a clear statement in a televised speech, saying, "The embargo has gone on for too long. When an embargo is prolonged, it loses meaning."[39]

Some Arab countries as well as a number of non-Arab Muslim countries have interceded on behalf of Libya at the United Nations. The Secretary-General of the Islamic Conference Organization (ICO) in 1993 was quoted as saying that the ICO reaffirmed its solidarity with Libya and that it would "continue . . . contacts with the United Nations and the Security Council so as to lift these measures."[40]

On May 31, 1993, a group of about two hundred Libyans crossed from the Rafah area into Israel to visit Muslim holy places on the occasion of Id al-Adha. Egyptian authorities and the Israeli tourism ministry helped coordinate the visit. Concomitantly, Qadaffi invited Libyan Jews who live in Europe, Israel, and the United States to come and visit Libya. Rafael Felah, head of the World Association of Jews from Libya, claimed that the visit was planned in mid-February 1992, when he visited Qadaffi. An Israeli businessman, Yaaqov Nimrod, cooperating with Saudi businessman Adnan Khashoggi, apparently was also involved in the planning of this episode and made statements to the effect that Qadaffi would visit Israel within the year.[41]

This visit was most probably a ploy to use Israeli goodwill to help lift the UN sanctions imposed on Libya and improve Libya's image in the West. This would not be the first time that Qadaffi had attempted to manipulate Jewish public opinion to his own ends. The French press reported that the first contacts between Qadaffi and Jews of Libyan descent took place in 1986 after the U.S. raids on Libya.[42] This incident, however, demonstrates to what lengths Qadaffi is willing to go to have the sanctions lifted.

In reaction to the Islamist opposition, Qadaffi has taken the same stand as other North African leaders: namely, denouncing the movements in no uncertain terms and cracking down on the various Islamist groups while simultaneously trying to appeal to his people by playing the Muslim leader. For instance, in April 1993, Qadaffi appeared on national television and called for a stricter implementation of *shari'a*, stating that thieves ought to have their hands amputated and that adulterers should be flogged publicly.[43]

The expulsion of foreign workers in 1995 was not only motivated by economic reasons, as mentioned above; it was also due to the links that some of them (especially the Sudanese, the Egyptians, and the Palestinians) had with Islamic groups in their home countries and the support they were providing for the internal Islamic opposition groups in Libya.

To deal with the country's economic difficulties, the Libyan leader has continued his liberalization program started in 1987 after the fall of oil prices on the world market.[44] A law was passed in March 1993 allowing for the establishment of private commercial banks;[45] and in July of that year, a decree permitted private-sector companies to engage in wholesale trade. Local private companies were also given the opportunity to compete for construction projects. The aim was to save foreign-currency earnings and create jobs for Libyans that were not subsidized by the state.[46]

Conclusion

As one assesses the situation in Libya in the 1990s, certain trends emerge. First, Libya's economy is not doing very well despite the optimistic evaluation of some. This situation is due in part to the UN sanctions but also to two other factors, namely, the falling price of oil on the world market and years of mismanagement of the economy under a socialist system. The half-hearted economic-liberalization measures have certainly not been very successful and have permitted the emergence of a thriving black market in foreign goods. Libyan-subsidized foodstuffs are also being sold in neighboring countries, causing severe shortages domestically.

What are the prospects for an economic recovery? They appear rather dim at the moment. But any crisis in the oil market (caused by war, civil strife, terrorism, or the like) could send the price of oil shooting up and help, temporarily, the Libyan economy to recover. There is no doubt, however, that it needs a major overhaul and significant investment in the infrastructure. The government also needs to allow the market to operate without trying to control or manipulate it.

Politically, the domestic situation has deteriorated gradually in the past decade. The regime does not have a solid base of power, and the major political forces in the country (namely, the military and the tribes) have turned against the government. Furthermore, both secular and Islamist opposition groups have become better organized (although as yet very divided) and more sophisticated and brazen in their attacks against the regime.

After more than a quarter-century in power, Qadaffi has become one of the longest-ruling leaders in the Arab world. As such, he no longer can claim convincingly to be a young revolutionary. For high-school and university students in their teens and early twenties, Qadaffi is an "elderly" politician in his mid-fifties. Thereby, he has lost his popular base—the Libyan youth, who identified with him and with what he had to say. Today his rhetoric is passé and out of touch with the changes taking place in the world around him.

It may be too soon to speculate about succession. What is clear, however, is that when the time comes, the transfer of power will not be smooth or easy. Not only is conflict to be expected, but there is no clear indication that a secular, democratic alternative has positioned itself to take over power. The military and the Islamists appear to have, at least at the time of this writing, a more forceful presence on the Libyan political scene.

Notes

1. Reuters reported in May 1997 that the Algerian Brotherhood in France, an offshoot of the Islamic Salvation Front (FIS), had complained officially that five hundred FIS members had been arrested nine months earlier and were still in jail in Libya.

2. See Marius K. Deeb, "Libya," 376.

3. Mary-Jane Deeb, "Militant Islam and the Politics of Redemption," 60.

4. Joffé, "Islamic Opposition in Libya," 628.

5. Report in *Foreign Bulletin Information Service—Near East and South Asia* [hereafter *FBIS-NES*], February 18, 1987, Q1.

6. Many Islamist groups do this; for instance, Hizballah exists in various regions of the Muslim world and puts a regional addendum to its name, like Hizballah-Gulf.

7. *FBIS*, May 5, 1993, 16.

8. Information on this latter group appeared on the internet—it may very well have been posted by the group itself.

9. "Libyan Chronology" for May 1997, on the internet.

10. *Al-Hayat* (London) report that appeared on the internet chronology "Libya: News and Views," March 9, 1997.

11. *Washington Post*, October 28, 1993, A32.

12. Ibid.

13. Economist Intelligence Unit, *Libya: Country Profile 1992–1993*, 7.

14. Mary-Jane Deeb, "Libya," 272.

15. Petroleum Finance Company, *Country Report: Libya*, 13.

16. Ibid.

17. El-Fathally and Palmer, *Political Development and Social Change in Libya*, 58.

18. Petroleum Finance Company, *Country Report: Libya*, 11.

19. Ibid., 13–14.

20. For a discussion of all these organizations, see Mary-Jane Deeb, "Libya," 367–79.

21. Ibid.

22. Marius K. Deeb, "Militant Islam and Its Critics," 192–96.

23. *New York Times*, April 1, 1992, 12.

24. Article in *Marchés tropicaux et méditerranéens*, quoted in *FBIS-NES*, September 15, 1995, 25.

25. United Nations Development Program, *Human Development Report 1997*.

26. Petroleum Finance Company, *Country Report: Libya*, 5.

27. JANA news agency, *FBIS-NES*, October 4, 1995, 31.

28. *Marchés tropicaux et méditerranéens*, 27.

29. Petroleum Finance Company, *Country Report: Libya*, 16.

30. Ibid., 17.

31. Ibid., 25.

32. Ibid.

33. Reuters reported that the dollar was worth three Libyan dinars ("Libya News and Views," on the internet, March 18, 1997).

34. Khalid Mizran, interviewed by the author, April 1997, Washington, D.C.

35. According to Agence France Presse in "Chronology," *Monde Arabe Maghreb-Machrek*, no. 152, 94.

36. *FBIS-NES*, May 14, 1992, 12.

37. "Chronology," *Monde Arabe Maghreb-Machrek*, no. 151, 85.

38. *Middle East Economic Digest*, March 5, 1993, 27.

39. Extract from Mubarak's speech, reported by Reuters, that appeared on internet.

40. *FBIS-NES*, April 12, 1993, 1–2.

41. Yared, "Kaddafi-Israel: Qui a piégé qui?"; *New York Times*, June 3, 1993, 10; also, *Washington Post*, June 1, 1993, A13.

42. Soudan, "Quand le Maghreb retrouve ses juifs . . . La loi du retour?" 14.

43. *Middle East Economic Digest*, April 16, 1993, 15.

44. For a discussion of the attempts at economic liberalization in Libya, see Vandewalle, *Qadaffi's Libya 1969–1994*, 203–22.

45. *Middle East Economic Digest*, April 2, 1993, 31.

46. *Middle East Economic Digest*, February 26, 1993, 27.

Part II

Dynamics of Change in the Contemporary Maghreb

6.

THE MAGHREB IN THE 1990S: APPROACHES TO AN UNDERSTANDING OF CHANGE

Claire Spencer

The 1980s and 1990s have been decades of rapid change in the key Maghrebi states of Morocco, Algeria, and Tunisia. The same may be said of a number of regions adjusting, first, to the global, economic changes of the 1980s and, second, throughout the 1990s, to the political as well as economic aftermath of the end of the Cold War. In the first period, when international preoccupations were still with the gradual thawing of the Cold War, the outside world—namely, North America and Europe beyond France—was only marginally interested in developments in the Maghreb. In the second period, the proximity of the region to Europe and the increase in the populations of Morocco and Algeria in particular have combined to focus more external attention on sociopolitical developments in the region. The perceived links between Islamism, demographic strains, and economic insufficiencies and their potential spillover effects have stimulated most new interest. These same developments have also posed tough questions within Maghreb societies themselves about the kinds of identities they seek to espouse for the new century. The key to resolving these issues lies not just in a classical struggle among competing domestic interests—economic, social, and political—but also in how the parameters are set for the expression of nationhood and national identity, on one hand, and political legitimacy, on the other.

The struggle has forged new landscapes in North Africa, the consequences of which have still to unravel. "Revolution" may be too strong a word to describe the changes in governance in the Maghreb, except in the cataclysmic case of Algeria, torn apart by a violence approaching civil war from the onset of the 1990s. Well before the fall of the Berlin wall, however, developments in the Maghreb had already triggered processes through which the Maghrebi states, both individually and collectively, had to face new international alignments, priorities, and realities, particularly of an economic kind.

This chapter will examine the background to the more detailed analyses of change, adaptation, and challenges to the stability of the Maghreb earlier in this volume. The purpose is to look at some of the ways in which outside observers have chosen to approach the question of change in the Maghreb, particularly where their primary focus has been on Maghrebi security and the stable transformation of the region. The rationale for this overview is to argue in favor of greater cross-fertilization between the studies undertaken by regional and disciplinary specialists and the policy-oriented literature on the Maghreb written by security analysts. The contention in this chapter is that the greater interest shown by the security-studies community in only some aspects of change in the Maghreb (above all the growth of Islamism) runs the danger of limiting the kind of explanations sought for the differing degrees of change and adaptation witnessed in the Maghreb. In an era of globalization, it would appear that more-diversified and encompassing explanations may be needed in order for external policymakers to assist in the gradual transformation of the region rather than to react—perhaps belatedly—to its alternative: namely, the spillover effects of abrupt, unforeseen, and potentially more-damaging change.

Background to Change

In each of the Maghrebi states, economic, then political, restructuring plans undertaken from the early to mid-1980s had differing short-term goals, as well as differing results and impacts. A standard explanation for the differences held that the catalysts for change, however, were broadly similar throughout the region and came as much from within as from without. Most reform plans arose from strains on internal distribution systems, built up since the early days of independence in the mid-1950s and early 1960s from inefficiencies of scale and financial management and from political systems that were becoming dysfunctional through their lack of response to the social and political demands of the peoples of each state. The stimulus for these strains arose, for the most part, from the consequences of a rapidly growing population. Even where demographic growth rates had slowed from over 3 percent to less than 2 percent per annum, governments still faced a younger, more volatile, and increasingly unemployed population. Statistical evidence identifying the age of half the Maghrebi population as fifteen years or less is not unusual and lends weight to the difficulties of transferring the collective memory from one generation to another.

From outside, the traditional motors for growth, such as the migration of workers to Europe and the expanding markets for Maghrebi exports, were dwindling under the pressures of the global debt crisis and world recession. Even more, where the oil crisis of the 1970s had unleashed plentiful loans for the larger and long-term projects of the centralized administrations of the Maghreb, in the 1980s, the day of reckoning gradually arrived. Both public and private banks required that the loans not only be serviced at rates that left few funds for alleviating internal stresses and strains, but that future external funding would be conditional on the restructuring of economies to fit IMF or similar liberal market prescriptions.

This is not a story exclusive to the Maghreb, as the retreat from the 1980s debt crises in Latin America has shown. What is interesting to note is how the Maghrebi states have adopted different management strategies since the mid-1980s. To similar crises, but with different sets of givens in terms of their external sources of revenue, the distribution of political and economic resources, and popular responses to change, the regimes of the Maghreb have adapted in different ways and, by and large, have survived. The Maghreb has seen no "Chilean exercise" in economic reform under military rule, for the military then to retire, as did General Augustino Pinochet, from the political scene. Nor have there been Mexican-style rescue packages for the Maghreb launched from Paris, Washington, or elsewhere.

Some attempt at political reform has accompanied most economic reforms in the Maghreb, whether this has been gradual and potentially successful as in Morocco, abrupt and violent as in Algeria, or piecemeal and quickly stifled as in Tunisia. There have been changes in presidents, from Habib Bourguiba to Zine El-Abidine Ben Ali in Tunisia in November 1987, and from Chadli Bendjedid through interim leaderships to Liamine Zeroual in Algeria. King Hassan of Morocco, belying all assessments of his health or predictions to the contrary, remains in power, on the throne to which he ascended in 1961. Some things change in the Maghreb while others are more illustrative of continuity, the two not necessarily being completely unlinked. Political change in Morocco, for example, may yet prove to be a successful example of transition to a constitutional monarchy, in which the main actors (or their heirs) will remain at the center of the political system. Nevertheless, at the end of the 1990s, just as at the beginning, the main political challenge across the region remains that of integrating younger generations into systems that have been comprised and organized in favor of the same groups, both military and civilian, since independence.[1]

A broader assessment of the dimensions of change would include all five members of the region's main organization, the Arab Maghreb Union (AMU). This chapter, however, will concentrate on the three Maghrebi states where responses to changing politics, economies, and societies have been the most marked and, in some senses, unavoidable. It is that sense of the "unavoidable" which distinguishes the three core Maghreb states of Morocco, Algeria, and Tunisia. For the other two member states of AMU, Mauritania and Libya, the particular juxtaposition of internal and external pressures faced by the other three have been different, or at least less present in state-level decision making.

Mauritania, to the southwest, belongs more in the context of sub-Saharan Africa, where assessments of economic and political bankruptcy often fail to materialize in the ways predicted, or where states and societies are too small for the international community to require them to deal with their debt through major reforms. Mauritania also lacks the population (and hence migratory) pressures of the more populous Maghrebi countries to provoke the kind of security reactions evident in much of Europe's policymaking toward migrants from North Africa, for example.

Libya, to the east of the Maghrebi heartland, is an anomaly for other reasons. On one hand, it has been largely excluded from the mainstream of international policymaking and interaction since the mid-1980s, for diplomatic reasons arising from Colonel Muammar Qadaffi's alleged sponsorship of international terrorism. On the other hand, Libya is less populated and wealthier per capita than its nearest neighbors, through its continued exploitation and export of hydrocarbons. Domestic Islamist pressures notwithstanding, Libya, like Mauritania, also does not pose the migrationary pressures so feared in Europe of the other Maghrebi states.

The Maghreb and Perceptions of Change

This section will focus on how the causes and effects of change in the Maghreb have been examined from both inside and outside the region and on how this analysis may develop further. Much of the literature points to similar causal factors to explain the processes that have led to change. Little of this analysis is, however, undertaken in a systematic way unless a particular methodology or theoretical approach is being called into play. Not infrequently (or particularly unnaturally), ways of perceiving developments in the Maghreb have differed according to the priorities and perspectives of individual analysts. Thus, for example, in addition to studying the proliferation of weapons of mass destruction and potential security regimes, studies concerned with security and stability in the broader Mediterranean region have tended to focus on regional manifestations of Islamism, or Islamist activism, and its relationship with Europe and the West.[2]

This security-studies approach is further refined by those whose main interest is the Islamist phenomenon perceived as a generic threat to (apparently) secular governments or as a series of sociopolitical opposition movements, whose spread across the Muslim world merits explanation. The regional focus of this approach is thus more likely to be on Algeria than on the other two states. The interstate or cross-boundary links that exist between individual Islamist movements also attract this kind of selective interest, where the primary concern is with assessing the cogency of a coordinated Islamist challenge to the stability of the Arab world and how to prevent or minimize its repercussions.[3] Work in this sphere, which started in earnest after the 1979 Iranian revolution, has also spawned apologists for Islamism, or at least those who, in trying to create a broader debate on Islamism, have been dubbed apologists. The work of François Burgat and John Esposito is often placed in this apologist camp, but it should not be forgotten that analysts and academics enjoy a good polemic, and "dealing with Islam," as Robert Satloff writes, "has provoked one of the few remaining debates on U.S. foreign policy."[4]

Approaches that do more justice to the cultural diversity and complexity of Maghrebi societies include studies of trans-Mediterranean migration. These situate what are often depicted as uncontrolled and novel flows of people, together with their potentially threatening cultures and ideas, in their proper historical context.[5] Some of the more recent theoretical approaches to security might serve to elucidate the cultural and social underpinnings of the tensions generated by migration issues within a new conceptual framework of "societal security." As yet, little empirical work has been undertaken specifically to put "societal security" to the test,[6] even though existing studies of migration and/or security issues might well be evaluated from this or similar perspectives. In other respects, international relations (IR) theories, when not more concerned with one another, prove difficult to employ in explaining relations within and beyond the Maghreb, not least because of their largely ethnocentric focus.[7] IR theories, moreover, have been slow to incorporate economic considerations along with their largely political concerns or to recognize "the imperative of multidisciplinarity in the understanding of change and outcomes," as Susan Strange has argued with some force.[8]

The new focus on globalization (although not, in all cases, as new as it looks with respect to interdependency theories of the 1960s) may facilitate incorporating both economics and politics into an explanatory model, but only if globalization is itself, as a concept, defined. As with Islamism, the polemical value of the globalization debate often has overtaken analytical precision, to the extent that "[i]deas of globalization are so broad, so diverse and so changeable that it sometimes seems possible to pronounce virtually anything on the subject."[9] As an approach that looks at the increasing role of transborder relations in shaping domestic developments of individual states, a globalization perspective may go some way toward explaining state transformation in the Maghreb. The value of approaches such as that put forward by Jan Aart Scholte is that they look at the changing functions and competencies of the modern state, as conventionally defined, to include the diminishing functionality of sovereignty and the decrease in governmental control over developments directly affecting the citizens of the state. All these factors have had impacts in the Maghreb as elsewhere and continue to affect the development of democracy, also pointed to by Scholte.[10]

A related and more direct approach to these issues might be found in an examination of the crisis of the state in the Maghreb. This does not mean that the state as an organizing concept has not taken root in the minds and actions both of governments and of their oppositions in the region. What it does mean is that there is still no clear separation between the apparatus of state (conventionally depicted as autonomous institutions in the West) and the regimes which dominate and work through these state institutions in a subjective and often self-perpetuating way. The crisis of the Algerian state is often referred to, but the fundamental lack of autonomous state structures in the Maghreb may be, as Bertrand Badie and others have suggested, part of a more general problem in the nonworld. The problem may be identified as the "imported state," or the nontransferability of the universalistic model of the state to societies not already sharing Western political cultures. As Anna Leander outlines Badie's views, "The logic that leads to adopting the state also indicates major problems in managing the ensuing change. Dependency on the West, difficulties in escaping the universalistic pretensions of the state, and the inclusion of imports in elite strategies hinder the development of real alternatives." According to Leander, "As the political center increasingly relies on and lives in an imported culture, it cuts itself off from the more traditional sectors of society." This sets in motion a growing vicious circle insofar as "[g]overnments pay off various groups and end up in a neo-patrimonial logic which blocks democratic change. This vicious circle is most visible in the absence of civil societies based on a division of public/private spheres, an individualization of social relations, citizenship, horizontal solidarities, and the spread of associations."[11]

Analysis along these lines would need to incorporate what Fred Halliday refers to in a wider Middle Eastern context as the "historical particularism" of each state, "according to which the specificities of the contemporary Middle East can only be comprehended in the light of the historical formation of the societies and politics of the region," even if the categories used to "grasp" this formation are universal.[12] Bertrand Badie's account would suggest, however, that there is a general tendency in Muslim political thought to distinguish between authority, or the expression of legitimacy, which is "in the hands of God," and the exercise of power, or expression of necessity, which is in human hands, "to maintain social order." This separation renders the conduct of political debate among citizens inconceivable and prone to violent explosion since, in the words of Leander, "Political opposition is directed against the political scene as such, whereas in the West, demands for political change aim for specific policies." Furthermore, "[p]olitical opposition explodes as the community (not the individual) considers the political power-holder illegitimate." The volatility of the situation is compounded by vertical solidarities (patronage, family, and region), which diminish "the potential role of trade unions and political parties in mediating and channelling political demands."[13]

There is plenty of scope here for analyzing the more violent aspects of change in Maghrebi states and societies, together with the uneven expression of this violence across the Maghreb. The successful melding of the symbols of both divine and secular power in the Moroccan monarchy, for example, has meant that King Hassan not only remains in touch with the traditional sectors of society (traditional, rural communities constituting, to a large extent, his strongest supporters), but that he also has undercut the legitimacy of the Islamists, who have to compete with a well-established and well-integrated precedent. In Algeria, the outbreak of violence can be perceived as having resulted from the absence of a clear or historically grounded expression of divine, or indeed secular, authority and legitimacy. In Tunisia (the state with the longest constitutional history of the three), the development since independence of a strong and centralized presidency has been both a strength and weakness, but it also has not been entirely exempt from violent opposition, as demonstrated by the Islamist-led protests of the 1980s. Whether any of these cases confounds or proves Badie's theory of the imported state would require a much closer reading of developments in recent years in order to evaluate whether or not the universal aims of the state model are adapting well to local realities. The element of choice (in other words: if not the state, what would the organizing principle of the modern Maghreb be?) also has to be considered.

The naturalness or not of the Western nation-state model in the Maghreb will also have more or less fortunate consequences for the future of democracy in the region. Ghassan Salamé's examination of the concept of *asabiyya* (the binding spirit of community, or esprit de corps, in Islamic tradition) may be further refined to take Halliday's "historical particularisms" into account in examining developments toward, or even away from, democracy. The whole debate about what constitutes democracy is, of course, largely defined in the West, and democratization is often required as a sign of modernity by policymakers. Salamé points to the dangers of trying to replace or match solidarities based on long-standing, community-based affiliations with notions of the individual (with his or her attendant duties and rights) and of the nation, where these obscure the inherent tensions between identification with the modern state and with the *asabiyya* of the preexisting community.

Both the nation and the individual have been central to the development of modern democracy in the West. The question remains: do these stages of modern state development have to be reached before one can begin to consider whether the "instrumental virtues" of democracy have taken root in the Maghreb?[14] Is there not also a danger (as exemplified by some variants of Islamism) that Maghrebi nations will reject the local validity of any models, given the conditioning of the history of the Maghreb by its proximity to Europe and the colonial presence of France and other European states in the region? As Salamé writes: "Islamism . . . is perhaps a reaction to this very specific situation which links as it differentiates Europe and the Islamic world. One attaches oneself to the absolute difference, that of faith, at the very moment that one feels particularly weak in the face of a neighbor who has become too strong."[15]

In pursuing these questions, what have been perhaps more enlightening and certainly less unidimensional than much of the focus on Islamism are accounts of the historical roots of change in the Maghreb. For explanatory purposes, the most useful studies are those that chart the evolution of political cultures from the precolonial, colonial, and protectorate eras together with their incorporation in or coexistence with more recent approaches to modernity. Predictably, accounts that take the specificity of Maghrebi states and societies into consideration largely have been written by nationals of the states in question, seeking—in the case of Algerians—for their own explanations as to where and how things went so wrong.[16] Given the relevance of the witness of academics and journalists who have lived, and tragically in some cases died, through so many of the profound changes of the 1980s and 1990s in Algeria, it is surprising how few of the relatively accessible French-language accounts have been fully incorporated into English-language analyses of political and social developments there.[17] This has become all the more salient an issue given the difficulties facing foreign researchers attempting to conduct any kind of empirical research in Algeria. This relativization of regional perspectives may well say something about what has been looked for within certain approaches—especially those undertaken from a security perspective or "Western policy" orientation— as well as the kind of answers that are likely to arise from their investigations.[18]

Islamism and Globalization: What Hope for Democracy?

To illustrate some of the above points, the remainder of this chapter will examine more closely what the general starting points, or perspectives, of Islamism and globalization have had to say in more specific terms about the Maghreb. Islamism as a prism through which to look at the Maghreb focuses more, but not exclusively, on internal developments; globalization, in constrast, examines externally generated impacts on domestic developments. The labels "Islamism" and "globalization" apply less to schools of thought than to vantage points from which to explore and explain developments in the Maghreb.

Charting the rise of Islamism in the Maghreb has been valuable in identifying trends, which were previously neglected in sociopolitical accounts of the region,[19] but it does not provide the whole story. The role of other political actors—for example, political parties and movements that are not Islamist (but not necessarily non-Islamic)—have been potentially neglected, and not only because of their limited electoral or popular appeal. Explanations of why Islamism has appeared to be such a strong alternative to current political systems or regimes too often emerge as descriptions of the strengths of individual movements or their ideologies, genesis, and organizational capacities. What these approaches do not explain is why other alternatives have failed to appeal to the same degree or win the popular support gained by Islamism. Comprehensive explanations may, in fact, need to be less circumstantial, or even teleological, than assessments of the strengths and weaknesses of Islamist movements alone. Much of the literature does pay attention to the notion of the state in the Maghreb, or to the connections between democracy and Islam in both theory and practice. However, the focus on Islam and Islamism per se tends to skew the analysis away from other sociocultural developments, which are as a result either marginalized, relativized, or even ignored.

The point is not so much that analysis of Islamist movements is limited or is determined by other ends—although in parallel with globalization, Islamism can appear at times to be almost all things to all people, as Martin Kramer observes.[20] More to the point is that the choice of Islamism as the main focus poses the main problem. Most North African writers (depending, of course, on their own sympathies and on their brief, if being asked to write for a Western audience) will incorporate observations about the growth of Islamism within a broader analysis of a given social and political crisis and/or change. The primary concerns of writers such as Ali El-Kenz or Samir Amin are with issues such as social justice, the rule of law, and the history and expression of cultural plurality, as well as with the more economically focused questions of the development paths taken in each Maghrebi state and the kind of economic and political choices facing the Maghreb.[21]

Islamism, however significant it may be in its immediate (or media-driven) sense, is only one in a spectrum of social and political issues facing the Maghreb. The whole question of Berber identity, for example, at the regional, national, and local levels, is both illustrative and indicative of the need to incorporate a broader set of disciplines, as advocated by Susan Strange, into an understanding of change and its effects in the Maghreb. The status of Berber culture and language has been challenged and repressed but never completely denied in the formation of the Algerian nation. In Tunisia, Berbers constitute a smaller proportion of society than in Algeria, where Tunisian national identity is more homogeneous but where Tunisian self-perception is nevertheless considerably influenced by Berber elements. In Morocco, variants of Berber culture coexist and intermingle with Arab identities in ways largely divorced from the overt politicization of the Kabyle *problématique* in Algeria. In this sphere as in others, such as the role of women, the questions of Islam and Islamism (however defined) cut across rather than define the parameters and contexts in which these issues are situated and evolve.

To paint a clearer picture of the specificities of political culture in the Maghreb, the work of anthropologists, such as David Hart, or sociologists, such as Mounia Bennani-Chraibi (to cite but two scholars who have worked on Morocco), must be more explicitly integrated into other kinds of research. Otherwise, the selective readings and interpretations of the thought and actions of various Islamist groups, above all in Algeria, are likely to continue to color external impressions of the Maghreb in Europe and North America above all. This misperception endangers not only accurate and multifaceted accounts of recent developments in the Maghreb; it also challenges the evolution of more-nuanced policy toward the region on the part of Western governments, with the most-direct consequences for trans-Mediterranean relations between southern Europe and the Maghreb.

Two dangers in this respect come immediately to mind. The first is that of too readily accepting and perceiving Islamists in and on their own terms, especially through analyzing their writings in order to assess what they would or would not do if they came to power.[22] Ideas and articulated intentions are important, but not as important as the context in which political actors operate. An analogy might be to say that what U.S. president George Bush had to say about his proposed fiscal policies ("read my lips . . .") before his election in 1988 did not tally with what he put forward after the election. Western politicians are not judged quite as sternly as Islamists in terms of the likely discrepancies between their words and deeds. The second danger is that of ignoring or underestimating the governments that Islamist opposition movements face. If the point of departure were not Islamism but the "use (and abuse) of violence," for example, then a different picture might emerge. The declared affiliations of political actors or their labeling as secular/Islamist would be less important than, say, an examination of their strategies of violence, the sources of violence within a given state's political culture, and alternatives to violence. Much of what has been written to inform policy toward Algeria depicts strains within the regime as secondary to the struggle with the equally internally strained Islamist opposition (if indeed different tendencies in "the ruling junta" are mentioned at all).[23] In other words, taking Islamism to be the key problem determines the structure and depth of analysis of other problems in Algeria's acute political, social, and economic crisis.

Globalization for most of the Maghreb means, first of all, closer regional interpenetration, if not integration, with Europe—not least because the majority of each state's trade (roughly 80 percent of exports and 70 percent of imports for Tunisia, for example) is already with its European neighbors. As most assessments of the EU's Euro-Mediterranean Partnership Initiative make clear, the opportunities presented by greater market access for the Maghrebi states within Europe is matched only by the far-reaching effects that deregulation and the ubiquitous *mise à niveau* of domestic industries will have on each state.[24] Some of the more detailed analyses of the effects of globalization concentrate on the economic effects and benefits to the Maghreb, arguing, for example, that free trade gives only the illusion of greater market access for most Mediterranean states, who have already enjoyed this (for their industrial products at least) over the last twenty years.[25] What is really at stake is the Maghreb's access to foreign direct investment (FDI) and the escape from marginalization on the fringes of a larger global market.

Besides the existing analyses of financial and trade flows, a future direction of research might explore fruitfully the impact on Maghrebi societies of a dwindling sense of choice in going down the globalized path. Official presentations of the Euro-Mediterranean Partnership Initiative depict it as a kind of "coming together" of the societies, states, and economies of the Mediterranean Basin to form a free trade area of benefit to all. The extent to which the engagement of the Maghrebi states in this policy reflects a real (as opposed to a symbolic) choice, however, begs for questions about possible alternatives if they had declined the invitation to enter into partnership with the EU or, like Libya, they had not been invited to join at all. As much as globalization in the Maghreb might be seen as an opportunity, or inevitability, it might be seen equally as (yet another) external imposition on states still not entirely secure in their foundations thirty-five to forty years after independence.

In light of this, it is probably as well that some of the less attractive aspects of globalization are unlikely to enjoy a wide audience in the Maghreb. David Rothkopf's defense of cultural imperialism, for example, is not far from the rallying calls of British imperialism or (closer to home for the societies of the Maghreb) the *mission civilisatrice* [civilizing mission] of nineteenth- and early twentieth-century France. "In an effort to be polite or politic," Rothkopf writes, "Americans should not deny the fact that of all the nations in the history of the world, theirs is the most just, the most tolerant, the most willing to constantly reassess and improve itself and the best model for the future."[26] Frequent and uncritical shorthand references to the "West" in much of the literature (including here!) too often conflate U.S. policies, interests, and values with those of Europe and other developed states into a single expression of "Western values," to which "non-Western" states and regions, such as the Maghreb, are expected to conform. The reality, however, is that forms of democracy and human values are as hotly disputed among Western societies themselves as they are within them or between the West and Islam.[27] The problem is that the disputes often appear less fundamental or serious to the outside world when modern democracies impose their own desires on how they are perceived. It is significant, for example, that the EU and the North Atlantic Treaty Organization (NATO) are seen from the outside as strongly unified organizations, but less consistently so from the inside. One should therefore not underestimate the effects of this externally projected unity on Maghrebis, who feel, on one hand, that they have little choice and, on the other, that Western models are inapplicable, irrelevant, or attainable for only a few of their fellow citizens, usually with support from outside.

Maghrebis may easily assume that when their governments espouse the challenges of integration into the global market, those governments are simply using another ploy to strengthen themselves at the expense of their citizens. In the midst of predictions that globalization will, in fact, weaken the state (whether it will or not is, of course, part of the polemic), this may seem an ironic conclusion to draw. It does, however, suggest that globalization may lend support to a growing divergence of interests between governments (allied with international banks, lending agencies, foreign companies, and foreign governments) and the citizenry of the Maghreb. It may also increase the intensity of the struggle between oppositions and nongovernmental actors seeking to reinforce the autonomy of the state and to limit the power of governments and the retrenched (and enriched) powers-that-be. If Maghrebis perceive the transfer of Western or "universal" values to be part of a process of divorcing state leaderships from any accountability to their citizens, then "democratization" may well come to be perceived in a rather more negative light within the region than it does to its Western proponents from outside.

It is also of relevance to assess what might be termed the "cultural robustness" of each society and political system in its ability to resist wholesale political imitations, or impositions, from outside. Each society and government will continue to need to find its own way of adapting to political and economic change. The prospects for gradual (as opposed to violent or dramatic) change, including the development of local democracy, may look distinctly more promising for Morocco, for example, than for either Algeria (suffering from cultural and political implosion) or Tunisia (in danger of aligning itself too closely with Greek and Spanish models, unfortunately of twenty years ago). Reaching assessments of the resilience of each society will require that questions of culture, and indeed civilization, are viewed in ways substantially different from those depicted in Samuel Huntington's model. Even if the latter's global characterization of cultural clashes has been widely condemned as oversimplified, the debate (another polemic) has in many ways captured its critics as much as its supporters in its predetermined parameters and focus for discussion.

Work in these and other areas has already taken on many forms in the academic literature. It is mostly the policy-oriented literature which needs to take the history and diversity of the Maghreb more into account—not only in looking for more comprehensive (and thus more convincing) explanations for change and crisis in the Maghreb, but also in adjusting the existing prisms of Islamism and globalization through which the region is analyzed and evaluated, and predictions about it are made. Democratic and accountable government in the Maghreb, for example, may assume a diversity of forms, just as it may frustrate any external policy designed to influence any state in one direction or another. It may be better, at the end of the day, to start by understanding change rather than by promoting it, whether in the interests of local, regional, international, or even "Western" security.

Notes

1. Rémy Leveau notes, for example, that the first results of a census conducted as long ago as September 1982 found that "nearly 70% of Moroccans were born after independence" (*Le sabre et le turban*, 99, n. 1).

2. "Europe" and "the West" are terms which are themselves, as Mohammed Arkoun points out, rarely subjected to any serious historical critique. Arkoun writes that the current debate on Islam and Europe suffers from the "political, social and even polemic limits of the short-run perspective (1970–1994)" which belies the much longer cultural history of the "presence of Muslims and Islam in Europe" ("Islam, Europe, Occident," 22–23). Arkoun's views are expounded at greater length in French in *L'Islam, moral et politique* and *Ouvertures sur l'Islam*.

3. It is nevertheless surprising as late as 1997 to see studies still inquiring whether Islamism is a unitary or multifaceted force. (See, for example, Pons, "L'Islam politique," 125–37.) In fairness to Pons, he swiftly concludes, as do many others, that there is no *Internationale* of radical movements, but there is one of the moderates, as represented by the Islamic League, the Islamic Council of Europe, and the International Islamic Federation (132, 130).

4. Satloff, "Islamism Seen from Washington," 100.

5. See, for example, Collinson, *Shore to Shore,* and the work of Yves Courbage, among others.

6. The reference here is to Weaver, Buzan, Kelstrup, and Lemaître (*Identity, Migration and the New Security Agenda*), who explore the concept of "societal security" at length. Chap. 7, by Barry Buzan and B. A. Roberson, examines the Middle East from this perspective, with some reference to the Maghrebi states.

7. See Halliday's critique of "postmodernity" in IR theory: "[M]ost of the claims about a new spatial and temporal world are at best metaphorical, at worst waffle, and often highly class-and place-bound ethnocentric indeed!" (*Rethinking International Relations,* 44).

8. Strange, *The Retreat of the State,* xv.

9. Scholte, "Global Capitalism and the State," 430.

10. Ibid., 440–52.

11. Leander, "Bertrand Badie," citing Badie, *L'état importé.*

12. Halliday, *Islam and the Myth of Confrontation,* 15.

13. All quotes are from Leander, "Bertrand Badie," 155.

14. Salamé, *Démocraties sans démocrates,* 16–17.

15. Ibid., 29.

16. Manceron, *Algérie;* Reporters sans Frontiéres, *Le drame algérien;* Goumeziane, *Le mal algérien;* Ignasse and Wallon, *Demain l'Algérie.*

17. Three recent edited volumes that include a majority of contributions from North Africans are Amin, *Le Maghreb;* Manceron, *Algérie;* and El-Kenz, *L'Algérie et la modernité* (also available in English, *The Challenge of Modernity).*

18. Generalizations, fortunately, always find their exceptions; in this case, Yacoubian's policy study on Algeria (*Algeria's Struggle for Democracy*) for the Council on Foreign Relations, in which she cites several Algerian sources. A more selective, "Islamist-driven," reading of Algerian works can be found in Fuller, *Algeria—The Next Fundamentalist State?*

19. The work of Jacques Berque, particularly in shaping concepts such as *l'Islam refuge* [Islam-sanctuary], nevertheless has long situated appeals to Islam within the context of political resistance and opposition in the Maghreb (see Berque, *Le Maghreb entre deux guerres).*

20. "One political scientist assures us that "the Islamist movements are basically social reform movements"; another expert tells us these are "political reform movements." Still another political scientist, a bit more cautious, tells a congressional committee that "whatever the ultimate aim of Islamist movements, their current function is a liberalizing one" (Kramer, *The Islamism Debate,* 162).

21. El-Kenz, *Algeria: The Challenge of Modernity;* Amin, *Le Maghreb.*

22. Stenberg, "The Revealed Word and the Struggle for Authority," 140–66.

23. Pierre and Quandt, *The Algeria Crisis;* Fuller, *Algeria—The Next Fundamentalist State?*

24. Confluences Méditerranée, *Le Maghreb face à la mondilisation;* Marks, "High Hopes and Low Motives."

25. Bensidoun and Chevallier, *Europe-Mediterranée,* 108.

26. Rothkopf, "In Praise of Cultural Imperialism?" 48–49.

27. See the debates between U.S. multiculturalists and hegemonists described by Gress, "The Subtext of Huntington's 'Clash,'" 285–87. One example of contested versions of "values" arose when the Italian press, the public, and the Pope protested, unsuccessfully, against the death penalty imposed on an American convicted of murder in 1985, who was subsequently executed by lethal injection in July 1997; see *Daily Telegraph* (London), July 25, 1997.

7.

MAGHREBI YOUTH: BETWEEN ALIENATION AND INTEGRATION

Mohamed Farid Azzi

Recent Maghrebi history has been marked by upheavals led by the young people, who burst onto the social and political stage and have continued to play a decisive role on that stage. All Maghrebi societies have experienced grave disturbances since the 1980s. The most striking example of those disturbances occurred in Algeria in October 1988.[1] Riots shook the country for three days and caused considerable human injury and property damage.

In Morocco, even earlier than in Algeria, the cycle of protest and rioting involved a majority of young people. Indeed, since its independence in 1956, Morocco has experienced violent protests involving large numbers of young people. After a short respite lasting from the mid- to late seventies,[2] the cycle of protests, which involved more than just young people, resumed. In June 1981,[3] riots in Casablanca resulted in the deaths of two hundred young protesters. The riots broke out after the government reduced food subsidies. Tunisia experienced similar disturbances. For instance, at the end of 1983, a violent uprising took place following an increase in the price of bread. The demonstrators attacked the state's institutions and the symbols of wealth. Scores of people died during the confrontation between the police and rioters.[4]

Youth movements have not always been limited to violence. For example, in the Algeria of the seventies, young people—especially students— were much involved in politics. They again became intensely involved during the short-lived period of democratization (1989–91). The youth constituted a significant proportion of the membership of the newly formed political parties and associations; many of the top positions in some major political parties were held by young leaders.[5] Therefore, it is not difficult to understand why young people reacted strongly to the interruption of the democratization process. The cancellation of the legislative election in January 1992 and the annulment of the results of the first round of elections have led to an open war between the state security forces and armed Islamist groups, the membership of which is dominated by persons between the ages of eighteen and thirty.[6] Although young people in Morocco and Tunisia have also alternated between participation and alienation, Algerian youth have suffered the most from alienation and marginalization.

The October 1988 events in Algeria and riots in Tunisia and Morocco have been examined in great detail. However, most of the analyses have focused almost solely on the most obvious aspects of the conflict, such as the army, the Islamists, and the political parties. Indeed, few studies have analyzed the factors affecting social change, leaving the youth of the Maghreb and their influence underanalyzed.

This chapter briefly examines some of the dimensions of the complex, multidimensional reality of Maghrebi youth and analyzes the socioeconomic conditions, which constituted the primary ingredients of the turmoil. This study is based on observation and on the primary findings of an opinion survey conducted in 1995 on social and demographic change in the urban milieu.[7]

Until the mid-1970s, the size and the youthfulness of the Maghrebi population were regarded as great assets, precious human capital necessary for social and economic development. Ambitious plans were undertaken to create the "man of tomorrow," the citizen of a modern nation. The "man of tomorrow" would evolve while modernizing society through culture, industrialization, and education. Young persons became the foundation of the postindependence modernization because of their numbers and because of the youthfulness of the political elite.[8]

Induced Social Change

A certain degree of "willfulness" (voluntarism) characterized the three Maghrebi states in their quest for modernization and social change. The will of the state to induce social change and to modernize society has determined, to a great degree, the destiny of a whole generation.

The willfulness of government policies was most pronounced in Algeria, where authorities sought to generate social and cultural change through rapid and planned economic development. Those authorities aimed to transform Algerians into "conscientious citizen[s] of a modern nation."[9] The concomitant objective of the government's policies was to eliminate tribal, patriarchal, and semifeudal structures of the old society.

An elite was entrusted with the task of modernizing society through a demiurgic state.[10] The industrialization launched in the early 1970s began the modernization. Industrialization was to fulfill such economic, social, and cultural goals as creating jobs, inculcating industrial cultural norms, and, eventually, producing consumer goods. Rapid industrialization (from 1967 to 1978) absorbed many workers. According to the technocratic elite, industrialization would acculturate the populace through the factory. The elite believed that the modern setting of the new place would instill new cultural values and norms in the workers, who, in turn, would diffuse the new culture into society at large. Studies by Algerian scholars on industrialization and industrial culture have shown, however, that the workers continued to conform to the traditional culture rather than to adapt to the industrial culture.[11] Those studies concluded that the acculturation within the factory did not engender the modern industrial worker, but rather another type of worker, whom they called the "majority worker" (*ouvrier majoritaire*).[12] Such a worker was young, of peasant origin, and attached to an Islamic cultural reference. Finally, industrialization failed to achieve its economic and acculturative missions.

In Tunisia, the voluntaristic approach apparent in the declared objectives of a vast program of social and cultural reforms and designed to prepare the Tunisian citizens for a better future set, as a priority, the change in culture. The main priority was to persuade the population to abandon traditional values and beliefs through a cultural and psychological revolution. Important reforms were implemented in order to modernize the society, emphasizing education, legal reforms, and the encouragement of new attitudes.

Education was to enhance social and cultural change. Indeed, in the last thirty years, the Maghreb has made considerable progress in expanding educational opportunities. In the mid-1970s, Algeria, for example, allocated as much as 30 percent of its national budget to education.[13] Tunisia and Morocco, too, devoted substantial portions of their national budgets to education. Because of the substantial investment in education, school enrollment swiftly increased: at the primary level, enrollment reached 99 percent in Algeria, 120 percent in Tunisia, and 69 percent in

Morocco (compared with 83 percent in 1980, which marks an important decrease). Secondary education also increased between 1980 and 1992 from 33 to 59 percent in Algeria, from 27 to 46 percent in Tunisia, and from 26 to 35 percent in Morocco. During the same period, college enrollment increased from 6.2 to 11.8 percent in Algeria and from 5.7 to 10.7 percent in Tunisia. In Morocco, however, while the ratio was increased at the same rate as the rates of the two neighboring countries during the 1970s and the 1980s, it has dropped significantly in the 1990s.

Upon independence, the new Maghrebi states opened the gates to secondary and college education nearly as widely as they opened those to primary education. The "democratization" of education was, in fact, carried out at the expense of efficiency and quality, resulting in a disparity between the system inputs and the technical and social requirements of economic development. Despite considerable achievements in education in the Maghreb, many shortcomings developed, as shown by the unjustifiably high illiteracy rate. Half of Morocco's adult population is illiterate, as is more than one-third of Algeria's and Tunisia's. Illiteracy in the Maghreb is more widespread among women than men; Morocco has the highest women's illiteracy rate.

Teachers are subjected to poor working conditions and do not enjoy high social status. In recent years in the Maghreb, education is no longer regarded as a means for social mobility as it had been regarded in the 1960s and 1970s; hence, it has lost much support, lowering the morale of teachers and students alike. This led the late Algerian president Mohammed Boudiaf to declare that "the educational system is disaster-stricken." Aside from the low quality of education, Maghrebi education has become a machine for exclusion. In Algeria, for example, although 27.64 percent of the total population is attending school, the passing rate for the baccalaureate examination has barely reached 20 percent in the last ten years, meaning that over three hundred thousand young persons are excluded from school every year.

Education also lies at the center of society's debate as well as its frustrations. The Algerian cultural and ideological elite argue about the educational system and the content of its programs. The modernist elite argue that the educational system has deviated from its original mission of molding citizens for the future: making them scientifically and technologically competent and culturally open to the universal values of the modern world. Instead, they argue, the system has become a pulpit for conservative forces, who have used the schools to instill their Islamo-Baathist ideologies, thus sowing the seeds of radical Islamism, which they helped transform into a major political and ideological force in the 1980s. The conservatives counter that schools have not done enough to enhance the authentic Algerian personality. Schools have instead introduced alien values, such as socialism, into society. A question was asked in that same survey about whether religious teaching in schools was sufficient or insufficient. As many as 50 percent of those under thirty (as compared with 40 percent of those over thirty) thought that the amount of religious teaching was insufficient.

In Algeria, the debate on the educational system also concerns Arabization, a much smaller issue in Tunisia and Morocco. In Algeria, the debate has become overideologized and politicized. As explained by an observer: "Arabization cannot be reduced to a linguistic problem only. It expresses clashes between opposed cultural and ideological trends."[14] Technical and linguistic constraints related to Arabization do, in fact, exist, but the criticism and the resistance of the francophone elite to its implementation obscure the issue of privileges and status. In reality, French is still the working language in most government services, especially in those related to the economy, whereas most college classes are conducted in Arabic. Arabization has accomplished two things: it has enabled a generation of young people to have direct access to the holy writings and their interpretations, and it simultaneously has marginalized those same young people from the administrative and economic spheres. The result has been an enormous frustration easily channeled by the Islamic opposition parties, who skillfully used the issue of Arabization to mobilize the monolingual generation.

The educational system is not the only cause of frustration and social exclusion of young people. A more precarious situation has prevailed in the employment sector. Industrialization was propitious for job creation; the unemployment rate had dropped from 22 to 18 percent between 1978 and 1984, but it rose to 25 percent in 1990 and to 28.1 percent in 1995. Because of the combined effects of the contracting economy and the implementation of stabilization and structural-adjustment programs, the number of unemployed reached 2,104,700 in 1995, as compared to 1,552,000 in 1992. About 80 percent of the unemployed are under thirty years of age. According to that last survey, only 7.3 percent of the unemployed have no education at all; 55.7 percent have primary and secondary education; 11.25 percent have professional training; and 4.4 percent are college graduates. Arabic degree holders are the most affected by unemployment.[15]

In Morocco, the rate of unemployment among urban youth was 30 percent in 1989, among whom 5 percent were university graduates and 47 percent had received secondary education; only 7.03 percent were illiterate.[16]

In Tunisia, unemployment among young people (ages fifteen to twenty-nine) reached 26 percent in 1989, representing 72 percent of the unemployed population.[17] As in Algeria and Morocco, more and more young unemployed Tunisians have secondary or college education. The statistics confirm the failure of the economic integration of the Maghrebi youth and their unmet growing demands.

Inadequate housing conditions are as crucial as the lack of jobs for the young. In fact, if they had a choice, many would prefer to have housing than to be employed. Overcrowded apartments (fifteen persons in two-room apartments in some populated areas) pose a grave problem because of the cultural code, which segregates men from women in domestic space. Despite efforts aimed at alleviating the housing shortage, construction cannot keep pace with growing demands. The housing deficit is estimated at 2 million units.

Parallel to rising unemployment and to the deterioration of the overall socioeconomic conditions of the lower and middle classes in the 1980s, an excessive concentration of wealth occurred. One observer noted: "In the midst of the present economic and managerial crisis, a few people succeeded in not only increasing their wealth but also in displaying it in the form of late model cars, new villas and new businesses."[18]

The convergence of such skewed socioeconomic conditions has contributed greatly to the wave of disturbances in the Maghreb since the mid-1980s, but those conditions themselves do not "justify" the depth or the intensity of the crises. The method by which those crises are subjectively interpreted instead explains the reaction of the social actors. Their perceptions and attitudes toward those whom they judge responsible for their frustrations and alienation have, to some extent, determined the method by which Maghrebis, especially the young, have manifested their discontent. In other words, sociological factors may broaden our understanding of the complex Maghrebi reality.

Young People: Deficient Socialization

The process of urbanization in the Maghreb, which started during colonial rule and accelerated after independence, has had disrupting effects. The authoritarian, but unfulfilled, modernization and the uncontrolled urbanization have greatly affected the pattern of traditional social life and its institutions of socialization in the Maghreb. The three Maghrebi countries adopted urban and housing policies, which have failed to integrate the large numbers moving into the cities. The consequences of those policies have resulted in social disintegration and social anomie.

In Algeria, social interaction and socialization processes in the cities took place and were regulated by social institutions, such as the family, peer groups, the neighborhood, or in the "native" quarters (*houma*). In fact, the *houma* is where most of a youth's social life takes place. Most Maghrebi cities are marked by the role that each quarter plays as a social unit with its own particular identity. During colonial times, those quarters served as refuges for the native population. After independence, and despite the massive arrival of newcomers from rural areas, those quarters continued their integrative role; however, because of rapid urbanization and continuous rural exodus during the 1960s and 1970s, peripheral new quarters mushroomed. To those new quarters the newcomers brought with them their lifestyles and often settled with or near their families and people from the same region. Most of the youths' activities and interactions, sports competition, music, and concerts take place in the quarter. The quarter thus serves as the community of belonging, the place where the individual is well integrated.

In view of the worsening socioeconomic conditions, the demographic pressure, and the withdrawal of the state (insufficient social services), the community no longer can function as a safety valve. Erosion of the social cohesion has thus occurred. In a fieldwork study on the famous quarter the Casbah of Algiers,[19] the author noted that the *houma* (quarter) is no longer a factor of urban integration. From a place of social harmony and solidarity, it has become a place of disorder, insecurity, and violence. Social links have weakened; vertical relations do not function anymore. The process of desocialization experienced by traditional groups has given way to new forms of sociability and new groups of young people. The street has become the cornerstone around which those groups revolve. The street is now the space within which informal political and economic activities and informal gatherings take place. In other words, the street is the same physical spatial entity, but it is less entrenched within the social network as the old quarter used to be. New forms of sociability have emerged, forming a network built essentially around the mosque.

The phenomenon of the "street" is common to all the Maghrebi countries. In Algeria, in particular, in the early 1980s, new social groups of young people appeared on the social scene. The better known are the *hittists*—those youngsters, without resources, who lean against walls all

day long. An Algerian politician has described them, rather contemptu-
ously, as "abandoned human beings, not attached to any social group,
not concerned by what is happening around them." Or worse yet:

> [I]f idleness is the mother of all vices, *hittism* is one step below. It
> is the total emptiness of soul. It is a look full of suspicion of others'
> luxurious cars, clothes. . . . [The hittist] is ready for any adventure,
> for he sincerely believes that he has been dispossessed. He, silently,
> execrates the state that did not employ him and will not accommo-
> date him. . . . He is not ready to integrate into society; on the con-
> trary, he is seeking ways to leave it or take revenge on it.[20]

Not all the socially marginalized young people stand against walls; a
large number are involved in the informal economy, known in Algeria as
trabendo (smuggling). Those involved in the *trabendo* show a high social
and economic dynamism; their activities have acquainted them with the
outside world, from France to Thailand. With little or no education, they
have learned how to manage their way through the complex international
trade and customs regulations. They have gained social status within their
quarters and families, for whom they have become young breadwinners,
thus displacing the role of the father or the older brother.

Like the *hittists*, the *trabendists* (smugglers), albeit for different reasons, resent the state. In their daily activities, they face continuous harassment from state agents, forced into bribery and corruption in order
to survive.

Among the social groups that have become visible in the 1980s is the
group of well-to-do young people known in Algeria as *tchi-tchi*. They are
the offspring of the *nomenklatura*, rich traders, and private industrialists
living in the shadow of the state. Their ostentatious lifestyle has sharp-
ened the sense of social inequality among the lower social groups.

Amid the profound social change which generated new social actors,
new ways of being, and (especially) a great number of unmet social demands, neither the state nor civil society has been able to structure those
new social groups or channel their demands into a peaceful process.

The traditional institutions and quarters have become obsolete and no
longer can fulfill aspirations or ease mounting frustrations. The Islamist
movement, however, has succeeded where the traditional institutions have
failed. The Islamist movement has also succeeded in the other Maghrebi
societies. The movement began in the mid-1970s on university campuses,
which provided the first cadres and activists for Islamist preachers. Ini-

tially, the leaders directed their efforts to the inner-city areas and peripheral quarters.

The new space of efficient sociability shifted from the street corner to the mosque, where, in addition to religious themes, matters related to professional, family, and even emotional life could be discussed and sometimes resolved. The key figure in the mosque was the imam, often self-proclaimed, who offered new models of behavior to young people and provided them with new reason, purpose, and ennobling myths.

The mushrooming of Islamist associations and parties further enhanced the social identity of the imams' young followers and bestowed upon them a sense of worthiness. The high mobilization of Islamist parties (particularly in Algeria in 1989–91) strengthened the sentiment of belonging to the community of the faithful, which overshadowed and replaced the traditional groups of solidarity, such as the family, kinship, neighborhoods, and sports clubs. The strength of the new order was demonstrated during the local and legislative elections (1990–91), in which FIS candidates outstripped others, even though the others were better rooted in their quarters and towns.

Some scholars believe that the Islamist movement has gained strength partly because some individuals' desire to escape from traditional communities has left no room for personal life.[21] The adoption of Islamist symbols and behavior by many young people has been interpreted as an attempt to break the patriarchal model. Youngsters suddenly gained new status and challenged the authority of the elders; for example, young women took the veil to escape the authoritarian male model. The young clearly found a response to their aspirations and expectations in the Islamist movement, which imparts a sense of worthiness to the marginalized young person. The movement made them discernible (beard, *qamis*) and useful (assisting the elderly and distributing aid). However, the new identity is paradoxical, because once the individuals are detached from their traditional milieus, they become members of a new community in which personal differences among the faithful are strictly prohibited.

Faced with social and cultural change, which coincided with major economic difficulties and important changes in the international environment, Maghrebi regimes undertook significant political and economic reforms. Those reforms, however, did not last long: they ended in Tunisia in 1989 and in Algeria in 1992, with the halt of the electoral process. The resulting violence and counterviolence that followed have forced society into a low profile. In Algeria, the youth responded differently and adopted opposite attitudes. Many formed or joined the armed groups to fight the regime, which they believe robbed them of their victory. Others returned to their original milieus, within which they sought protection and the means for survival. Given the continuous degradation of socioeconomic conditions (much worse than in 1988), the primary solidarity groups did not greatly help this group. A deep feeling of loneliness followed. The suicide rate rose—unusual in times of war, where the struggle for survival is supposed to give meaning to life. A considerable increase in psychiatric care and psychotropic drug consumption has also been reported. Some young people affirm that there are now two parties: "the party of the mosque" and "party of the drug."

Youth's Political Attitudes

Scholars and students alike often have emphasized two main features that characterize the political attitudes of Maghrebi youth: apathy and alienation. Although these attitudes might be considered a common denominator of the political orientation of young people in the Maghreb, some differences among countries should be qualified.

Algeria, until the late 1980s, lived under the rule of a single party and enjoyed a relatively stable political life. Many studies were undertaken to analyze Algeria's economic and political system, with emphasis on the economic changes, but little attention was paid to general public opinion or to political attitudes. No cumulative figures on political attitudes exist. Nonetheless, from the general political studies and participant observation, one can discern the pattern of political opinion and attitude in four periods.

The years that followed independence were marked by a close identification with the regime. Independence, newly won after a long revolutionary war, mobilized the population for government-oriented tasks. Following the military coup d'état in 1965, opposition and critics rose among the governing elite and extended to leftist student organizations. After the initial repression, the regime succeeded at the beginning of the 1970s in co-opting most of its opponents. The students were mobilized in economic and ideological campaigns, such as the agrarian revolution. The workers were involved in participatory management—for example, socialist self-management.

The first signs of a challenge to the political regime and antisystem political attitudes appeared in the late 1970s. Those culminated in April 1980 with the Berber uprising, during which serious disturbances shook the Kabylie region. The natives of that region demanded cultural emancipation and democratic rights; and Islamic activism appeared on university campuses. The reaction of the political regime was repression and co-optation.

The most politically alienated social groups among the youth expressed themselves by rioting many times during the 1980s, culminating in the general revolt of October 1988. The political changes that occurred between 1989 and 1991 prompted political participation, symbolized by such manifestations as a growing number of civic associations, political parties, and high turnouts in various elections.

More recently, and conducted during a time of intense political violence and great uncertainty, a survey in 1995 revealed a low level of personal involvement in political activities and public life in general. A mere 6 percent of the respondents in the survey claimed that they belonged to an association of any kind, and only 13 percent participated in some type of public-service work.

In spite of the proliferation of associations and political parties since 1989, Algerian men and women seem to have returned to political passivity and apathy. The violence of armed groups and the legal constraints imposed by the regime on politics (a ban on demonstrations, a state of emergency) discouraged any participation.

In Morocco, antiestablishment grievances and political alienation of its young people date back to the 1960s. The period between 1960 and 1972 was punctuated by confrontations between the opposition and the regime. In those confrontations, the youth, especially students, played leading roles. Surveys taken during that period showed that many Moroccan students exhibited strong refractory feelings, as demonstrated by the riots in Casablanca in 1965, during which hundreds were killed. Unrest and rioting have continued until the present. Unlike the Algerian regime, which succeeded in mobilizing the population around economic and social policies in favor of the masses at large, especially in the 1970s, the Moroccan monarchy undertook no significant social or economic policies in favor of the populace. This partly explains Moroccan young people's relative lack of participation in politics.

This apparent indifference did not mean that young people were depoliticized; on the contrary, they tended to be well informed and highly attentive to politics but unwilling to participate in political life. The alienation of so many young people results from their attitudes toward the politics of the country. Moroccan youth, for example, fear politics because of a traditional reverence for the *Makhzen*. In Algeria, however, "doing politics" or talking about it is no longer taboo, perhaps because of the different histories of state building and dissimilarities in the legitimizing mechanisms of political power in the two countries. In Morocco, politics is considered to be beyond the sphere of ordinary citizens. Even among those few who show some interest in politics, much skepticism exists; politics is considered to be reserved for the governing elite, who strive to satisfy their own interests in the name of the people. As a young Moroccan stated, "He [the king] bought off all of them; once you are in the parliament, you are bought off. He offers you a villa or a farm, you will say, 'Long live my lord,' and that's it. This is the truth."[22]

The governing elite is thus stigmatized through the disrepute of the political institutions, which are conceived of as private clubs. That disrepute could explain the lack of interest in politics and public affairs of the majority of young people. A Moroccan researcher conducted a survey in which only 25 percent of those interviewed expressed some interest in politics.[23] Almost the same proportion of Algerian young people expressed the same attitude: In response to the question "How do you perceive politics?" a mere 30 percent felt they understood the subject.

Antiregime feelings are also widespread among Algerian youth. Only 38 percent held positive views on the performance of the regime, and 51 percent of interviewees believed that the regime rarely or never cared about the needs of the citizens. Nowadays, the majority of Algerian respondents are more concerned about seeing civil peace restored than anything else. They rank peace as the top priority toward which the government should be working. The concern for peace was confirmed in the presidential election of November 1995. Indeed, an unexpectedly high percentage (75) of voters participated in the election. Clearly, the message of the voters was a call for peace and a rejection of violence. Here, too, age accounted for only a slight difference: 42 percent of young people, as compared to 44 percent of those over thirty years, made the restoration of peace their top priority.

Tunisia has experienced a similar process of political alienation among its young, especially during the 1970s and the 1980s. Unlike Morocco, the 1960s in Tunisia were a decade of relative political stability and social peace. During the 1960s, an ambitious program of modernization of the country was implemented. Modernization had the support of a large portion of the population, particularly among the educated youth. Many studies revealed positive political attitudes among Tunisian youth,[24] particularly the "university-educated fringe who were politically confident and ascending and disclosed positive orientations towards the regime."[25]

The goodwill of the educated young was, however, short lived, because economic reforms resulted in changes in political attitudes. Social unrest occurred in the 1980s; in late 1983, the unrest included widespread, bloody rioting in Tunisian cities. Reporters and analysts of Tunisian politics pointed to the growing alienation of the society as a whole, especially the young. That alienation partly resulted from radical leftist movements of the 1970s and early 1980s, in which the workers' and students' unions played an important role. Discontent among most social groups grew in the mid-1980s and the early 1990s. Islamist groups, which found support among the educated fringe of society, voiced society's grievances.[26]

Antiregime feelings, political alienation, and Islamist sympathies best characterize the attitudes of most Maghrebi youth during the last fifteen years. A new political culture among the politically alienated youth has emerged and expanded. It has been expressed in Islamist ideologies, and those ideologies have won their widest support in Algeria.

Maghrebi young people who feel alienated from politics and do not share the political culture have perceptions and values regarding society and politics. Their beliefs highlight some values and attitudes, and reshape and redefine some others. The Algerian young people interviewed in 1995, in a context of political violence and economic hardship, emphasized values and aspirations such as social peace, solidarity, social justice, and strong political leadership. Other values, such as democracy and pluralism, do not seem to constitute a high priority. Only 18 percent of respondents answered the following question affirmatively: "Should the establishment and development of democratic institutions be an immediate task for the government to be concerned with?" In the last legislative elections, held in June 1997, the democratic parties registered a low 12 percent, confirming the low priority assigned to democratization.

To ordinary Algerians, democracy is often equated with anarchy; it is partly blamed for what has become of the country. The chaotic political liberalization following the 1988 riots led to the burgeoning of a myriad of political parties, but these parties operated without well-established rules of the political game and witnessed grave events such as the civilian disobedience organized by the FIS in May and June of 1991. The resulting violence following the interruption of political liberalization in 1992 convinced many ordinary Algerians that democracy was not suitable for society. Democracy is the *boulitique,* the Algerian argot for "dirty politics" or "trickery," which the government uses to stay in power.

In the opinion survey mentioned earlier, 50.2 percent rejected multipartyism; nonetheless, though the respondents do not lend much credit to democratic values and though some reject pluralism, their responses ought to be qualified. Given the context in which the political reforms were implemented, one can understand why the respondents opposed democracy. However, when asked which political system best serves the interests of its citizens, over 65 percent named Western democratic regimes; France ranked at the top with 39.7 percent, the United States with 14.3 percent.

The age variable seems to make some difference. Those over thirty preferred France (41 percent); only 11.2 percent favored the United States. The youngest generation (those under thirty) scored 36 percent and 21.5 percent, respectively. The only non-Western country that interviewees preferred was Saudi Arabia (12 percent). Do the choices of the respondents mean an inclination toward democratic political systems, or do they denote an attraction to a state of welfare and supposed or real well-being of the citizens of those countries? Further research will answer the questions.

In Algeria today, other political values are expected from the government: moral integrity and a sense of justice. Tales of widespread corruption and deep-seated social injustice have destroyed those values in the government as far as Algerians are concerned. Now they want political reform and strong leadership.

The 1980s were, in the eyes of Algerians, a "black decade," in which politics served private interests and rival clans weakened the state. Chadli Bendjedid personified that decade. Although no public-opinion survey was taken then to account for public attitudes and political culture, the popularity of political jokes and metaphors clearly reflects the mood of the time.

The need for strong leadership is reflected in the interviewees' answer to the question: "Who were the two personalities who marked the history of the country?" The Emir Abdelkader and President Houari Boumediene were often cited, the former for his long-armed resistance against the French, the latter for his efforts to build a modern Algeria. Although Chadli's period was relatively more relaxed in terms of access to consumer goods and freedom to travel, nobody was nostalgic about his governance. What counted was the sense of justice, strength, and national pride that most Algerians attributed to Boumediene.

Some basic cultural traits and values persist and characterize Algerian political culture. Egalitarianism is one of those values; it is rooted in the long struggle against colonization and amplified by the official populist ideology since independence. The value of egalitarianism has also compromised the legitimacy of wealth and authority. The October 1988 riots, for example, were not so much hunger riots as they were demands for social justice. The youths' feelings that they had been deprived of their rights to enjoy their part of the national wealth motivated their violent rejection of the political system and of the governing elite. Among Algerians, there is a strong conviction that their country is immensely rich but that corruption and incompetence among its leaders have made the country poor.

The reference to the 1970s and to the leaders of that decade denotes in the youths' political culture nostalgia for a welfare state and for nationalistic ideals. The score of the "nationalist" parties (50 percent of the votes) in the June 1997 election has also confirmed their nostalgia.

In the qualitative study on Morocco mentioned earlier, one may detect some attitudes among the Moroccan youth similar to those among their Algerian peers concerning expectation and political views. In Morocco, too, Western regimes are looked upon as the best in serving the interests of their citizens. What is most valued in those regimes are, on one hand, their economic development and their strength and, on the other hand, the social justice achieved through the welfare state, which provides all kinds of social assistance, such as social security and unemployment benefits. Also emphasized were the sense of civic responsibility and the respect for human rights that characterize Western societies. France is often mentioned as the model that best represents those rights.

Like their Algerian and Tunisian counterparts, young Moroccans stress the value of social justice and egalitarianism. That emphasis seems to be one of the most common feelings among Maghrebi people in general, perhaps explained by the widening gap between the rich and the poor, egalitarian traditions which uphold a long struggle against foreign occupation, and the populist promises formulated at independence. Morocco is the Maghrebi country in which inequalities are the most striking, where misery cohabits with opulence, and where high walls separate sprawling, overpopulated shantytowns from wealthy districts. The gap between the poor and the rich has also been widening in Algeria, especially during the last decade. In the Algerian opinion survey discussed earlier, 82 percent of the respondents thought that such a gap between the rich and the poor was widening. In Algeria, a populist, egalitarian ideology coupled with a redistribution policy has greatly contributed to the sharpening perception of inequality and thereby the sense of injustice that arose in the 1980s. The violence prevailing in Algeria for almost a decade may be explained partly by idealistic aspirations of egalitarianism and social justice.

As an alternative to an unjust state, Maghrebi youth have espoused democratic or Islamist values and attitudes. Democracy and Islam do represent to a majority of young people the ideals of social justice. Those ideals are reinterpreted and given additional meanings to suit expectations of the young and to express their frustrations. Democracy, Islam, and respect for human rights are seen as lacking in the Maghreb.

Conclusion

Significant and rapid change has occurred in the Maghreb during the last three decades. That change has resulted from state-led development based on mass education, urbanization, and the institutionalization of a salaried society. The first two decades seemed to favor the population in general, and the young generation in particular, as far as their integration in society was concerned. The last three decades were times of ascending social mobility and political mobilization, at least for Algeria and Tunisia.

Mounting economic difficulties, persistently high birth rates (at least up to the mid-1980s), a hindrance to social and professional mobility, the lack of significant political reforms, and unmet social demands have resulted in the marginalization of many youth. Young people periodically express their alienation and their anger by descending into the streets, destroying on their way what they believe are the sources of their alienation.

When Maghrebi youth are not rioting, they are negotiating the terms of their integration into society. Their economic integration has followed a tortuous path. They use all available resources: the family, the state, and the informal economy. They also negotiate their cultural integration through syncretism and some patching up of models. The attitudes adopted by young people who try to reconcile a pragmatism and a normative order have resulted in tensions when they were denied participation in the mass-consumer society. The integration of the Maghrebi youth has been particularly difficult at the political level.

The dilemma that faces Maghrebi governments is the convergence of differing demands of different natures. On one hand, Maghrebi governments confront socioeconomic grievances; on the other, they are pressed by demands for political participation and more government accountability. The socioeconomic demands can be partly met only if resources are efficiently managed—presupposing, among other things, institutions of control and an accountable government.

Economic reforms have been instituted without any accompanying social policies, posing dire consequences on vulnerable people. Too much repression has been used to stifle demands of the youth without any effort to reform politics or to integrate young people into society. Much is to be feared; the reasons for discontent and violence still exist, and if no genuine effort is made to resolve them, violence and rioting will continue to be the only means of expression left to the young.

Notes

The author would like to express his deepest gratitude to Zeddic Lanham, professor of English at Thunderbird, and Yahia H. Zoubir for the thorough editorial revisions of this chapter.

1. Other riots involving mainly young people occurred in Oran in 1982 and in Constantine in 1986.

2. Morocco experienced a period of relative stability from the mid-1970s to the beginning of the 1980s. This was due mainly to the high national mobilization for Western Sahara.

3. Serious disturbances and riots shook Morocco before and after the 1981 riots.

4. Tessler, "Youth in the Maghrib," 71.

5. The average age of the local Islamist party's cadres was thirty-two. See Mohamed F. Azzi, "Itinerary of the FIS Cadres," unpublished paper, 1992.

6. Official statement by chief of police, reported in *El-Watan* (Algiers), October 19, 1996.

7. Opinion survey conducted jointly by the American Institute of Maghrebi Studies (AIMS) and the University of Oran.

8. Upon independence, most of Algeria's influential leaders, such as Houari Boumediene and Abdelaziz Bouteflika, were under thirty.

9. *Charte Nationale, 1976.*

10. de Villers, *L'état démiurge.*

11. Guerrid, *L'Algérie: L'une et l'autre société*; El-Kenz, *L'Algérie et la modernité.*

12. Guerrid, *L'Algérie.*

13. Bennoune, *The Making of Contemporary Algeria.*

14. Grandguillaume, "Arabisation et démagogie en Algérie," 3.

15. Statistics on unemployment in Algeria are drawn from Benachenou, "Inflation et chômage en Algérie."

16. Abzahad, "Activité et chômage des jeunes citadins au Maroc," 486.

17. Gharssali, "Les jeunes de 15 à 29 ans en Tunisie."

18. Tessler, "The Origins of Popular Support for Islamist Movements."

19. Verges, "La Casbah d'Alger."

20. From a flyer describing the program of the Party for Algerian Renewal (PRA).

21. Leveau, *L'Algérie dans la guerre.*

22. Bennani, "Les représentations du monde des jeunes marocains."

23. Ibid.

24. Tessler, "Regime Orientation and Participant Citizenship in Developing Countries."

25. Ibid.

26. Zghal, "The New Strategy of the Movement of the Islamic Way."

8.

HUMAN RIGHTS IN THE MAGHREB

Youcef Bouandel

Human rights came to prominence in the Maghreb during the second half of the 1980s. Human-rights groups in Algeria, Morocco, and Tunisia have emerged to challenge the political systems and have put human rights firmly in the political discourse of governments, which, in turn, refer to international standards of human rights. They incorporated them into their national institutions, which indicated that perhaps further developments were on the horizon.[1] Similar changes also took place in Libya. Indeed, Colonel Qadaffi released political prisoners and, in a series of speeches in March 1988, suggested a number of political reforms. He even pledged to "make Libya a place where human rights are respected."[2]

Evaluating the status of human rights has proven elusive in the Maghrebi countries because those countries are undergoing significant transformations. In Algeria, ever since the electoral process was brought to a halt in January 1992, the country has suffered civil unrest. Information about Libya, because of the international embargo, may not necessarily paint an accurate picture.[3] In Morocco, the reforms undertaken by the king in the early 1990s have not yet clearly developed.[4] Tunisia is the least complex to evaluate: in spite of some reforms introduced by President Zine El-Abidine Ben Ali when he seized power in 1987, the regime has reverted to the old days of Habib Bourguiba.

This chapter deals with human rights in the Maghrebi states. It includes a brief discussion of human rights from the time of independence, but it primarily focuses on the period since the late 1980s. That period represents the start of the gradual, but incomplete, changes in the political landscape of the Maghreb. However, one may argue that the Maghrebi states recognized human rights because those states sought "legitimacy," but that their official pledges to respect human rights have not yet been put widely into practice. In particular, this chapter concentrates on how human rights have affected the domestic politics of those states. It discusses the question of whether Maghrebi states can establish democratic societies without the legislation, institutions, and mechanisms that promote human rights, according to the standards set by international instruments. The chapter, while acknowledging the role of local human-rights organizations, concentrates primarily on the changes that Maghrebi states have introduced in the human-rights field. This chapter begins with a general discussion of the politics of human rights. After a review of the political landscape of the Maghreb, human rights in the region will be examined. The chapter concludes with a general evaluation of human rights in the Maghreb and the future prospects for human rights in the countries of the Maghreb.

The Politics of Human Rights

The issue of human rights is relatively new in international politics. It has attracted much attention since the end of the Second World War. Apart from the Geneva conventions, which apply only in times of war, no single agreement qualified how states could treat their citizens. The first international document to do so was the Universal Declaration of Human Rights (UDHR), adopted by the General Assembly of the United Nations on December 10, 1948. A nonbinding agreement, it merely set a "common standard of achievement." The declaration contains two sets of rights: civil and political, on one hand, and economic, social, and cultural, on the other. However, differences arose between liberal democracies and the former communist countries when the declaration was to become legally binding. While the West emphasized civil and political rights, the former communist states insisted on economic and social rights. Those differences resulted in the adoption, in 1966, of two separate international instruments: the International Covenant on Civil and Political Rights (ICCPR) and the International Covenant on Economic, Social and Cultural Rights (ICESCR). They came into force in 1976, each ratified by thirty-five states.

Since those agreements, human rights have moved higher on the political agenda, as more individuals and organizations have become concerned with them. Amnesty International and Human Rights Watch are examples of organizations that have devoted their efforts to monitoring and promoting respect for human rights. For example, the provision of Article 28 of the ICCPR calls for the establishment of a Human Rights Committee (HRC), which came into effect in January 1977. Its function is to monitor the states that signed the covenant in order to determine whether they have been fulfilling their international obligations. More recently, some governments, such as those of the Netherlands, Norway, and the United States, have linked their development aid to respect for human rights. For example, in 1973 the U.S. Congress recommended that human-rights records be linked to development aid, and in 1975 the linkage between the two became mandatory. As a result, the United States produces annual assessments in the form of the *Country Report on Human Rights*. The U.S. Department of State has published the reports regularly since 1976.[5] The link between economic aid and foreign investment has become more significant since the end of the Cold War in the late 1980s. Human rights, economic aid, and the climate for foreign investment are interdependent, thereby motivating nations to assign a high priority to human rights. The Maghrebi countries, which now must find new ways to attract foreign resources for growth and development, no longer can ignore human rights.

Research on human rights has been divided into two points of view. The first treats human rights as universal and therefore undeniable to anybody, regardless of any other consideration. The other point of view stresses diversity and difference, arguing that human rights are social phenomena and are therefore influenced by the environment in which they exist.[6] The relationship between human rights and Islam has, for instance, become significant and has been greatly debated.[7] While some argue that Islamic culture is alien to human rights,[8] others insist that "participation by the Islamists in . . . elections is a testimony to their willingness to abide by the rules of the democratic process."[9]

The Maghreb: A Political Landscape

Despite the differences in the forms of government in the Maghreb, the similarities are the most striking. All countries are centrally governed, and power (except in Algeria to a lesser extent) is concentrated in the hands of one person.[10] Maghrebi constitutions provide for the separation of powers (except in Libya), but that separation has yet to be put into practice. The legitimacy of the governments differs according to their systems of government. In Morocco, legitimacy stems from the king and the privileged position he occupies in Moroccan society—not only as the chief executive but as a spiritual leader.[11] As "the Commander of the Faithful," he provides unity, continuity, and stability. In Tunisia after independence and in Algeria after the victory of the nationalists, single parties took power. In both countries, the legitimacy of the system revolved around the president and historical precedent. In Tunisia, Bourguiba became indistinguishable from the state. He ran the country, and his grip on political power was reinforced by a 1974 decision to make him president for life. When asked about Tunisia's political system, he reportedly exploded, "What system? I am the System."[12] In Algeria, the one-party system drew its legitimacy from the war for independence. In Libya, since the coup d'état in 1969, the legitimacy of the system has centered around Qadaffi.

In Morocco, because of the apparent consensus on the "untouchable trinity" (country, monarchy, and the sanctity of Islam), the political system appears to be more open than those of Algeria and Tunisia. The constitution calls for a pluralist and competitive political system. Despite the fact that parties loyal to the palace have formed the government, opposition (however limited) has existed longer than it has in the other Maghrebi states, and ministries have been filled with candidates drawn from different political affiliations. The Algerian and Tunisian governments share the same characteristics. Soon after independence, nationalist leaders outlawed opposition parties. Parties were carefully allowed to return to political life in Tunisia during the early 1980s, as they were also in Algeria—notably the Parti d'Avant-Garde Socialiste (PAGS), which served some of the government's interests. The governments, however, in reality established one-party systems. In Libya, political parties simply have been banned. The banning of opposition parties also was accompanied by an abrogation of civil and political rights. According to the laws and practices governing the formation of associations in Algeria, Morocco, and Tunisia, citizens wishing to form an association usually submit a written request to the ministry of interior. Only after the ministry's approval of the request does that association acquire legal status. The governments or the ruling parties also commonly interfere with trade unions and student movements, thus impeding the emergence of an unfettered civil society.

For their survival, the four political systems have relied heavily upon a security apparatus. The four governments have adopted similar strategies for eliminating opposition, including assassinations. Those who did not share the regimes' views were, at best, excluded from political participation and, at worst, either exiled or eliminated.[13] Maghrebi governments also have been notorious for their heavy-handed reaction to any demonstrations against them. The harsh suppression of the students' demonstrations throughout the 1980s in Morocco, of the "Berber Spring" in 1980, the October 1988 uprisings in Algeria, and the 1978 workers' strikes in Tunisia provide good examples of governmental practices.

Human Rights in the Maghreb

In spite of governmental repression, all Maghrebi governments since the early 1970s have faced steady, albeit limited, opposition. With growing demands for respect for human rights and the governments' adoption of this rhetoric, a more autonomous civil society has emerged. Apart from Libya, human-rights organizations and Amnesty International's sections are now established in all the countries in the region.[14]

An assessment of human rights in Maghrebi countries suggests that, although the circumstances developed differently and for distinctly different reasons since the mid-1980s, those countries share, nonetheless, the same characteristics: they have experienced significant changes in their politics of human rights; they have all signed the ICCPR and the United Nations Convention against Torture and Other Cruel and Inhuman and Degrading Treatment and Punishment. The governments of Algeria, Tunisia, and Morocco have responded by creating official organizations to "monitor" and "protect" human rights. More important perhaps, those organizations have provided a facade for international respectability. Except for the government of Morocco, where the changes have occurred more recently, commitments to human rights have been short lived because concessions to democratic principles and human rights have opened the political space to the already strong Islamist movement. This trend has been especially pronounced in Algeria and Tunisia, strongly challenging the regimes. The Islamist movement has also been strengthened by the weakness and fragmentation of the democratic parties.

Maghrebi states have responded differently to the Islamist challenge.[15] Because of its political culture and the king's position as a religious leader, Morocco has thus far been the least threatened. However, citizens in the Maghrebi states have not yet demonstrated the ability to change their governments or their leadership,[16] despite constitutional provisions for doing so.

Algeria: The Domestic Factor

The riots of October 1988,[17] in which hundreds of young Algerians were killed, marked a turning point in the history of independent Algeria. Those who were detained and tortured had their cases taken up by human-rights organizations which publicized their treatment.[18] When political reforms were initiated in 1988–89, human rights became an important element of those reforms. Indeed, Algeria's record between 1989 and 1991, while new, clearly demonstrated respect for the principles of individual liberty.[19] In those years, political reforms were introduced; plans for economic liberalization were developed; and, most importantly, challenge to the old political elite grew when the political opportunities were extended to previously excluded groups. Progress in the protection of human rights was, as a result, the most positive effect of reforms in the country's regime.[20]

The reforms, which began with a new constitution in 1989, resulted in the advent of a more autonomous civil society. Political parties were legalized; independently owned newspapers began circulation; local, regional, and legislative elections were held; and independent human-rights organizations acquired legal status. Although the legalization of those organizations took place in 1989, the seeds for the movement date back to the mid-1980s.[21] However, as Gorbachev once observed: "There can be no observance of law without democracy . . . [and] democracy cannot exist and develop without the rule of law."[22] The Algerian authorities, too, paid particular attention to the development of the rule of law. While the 1989 constitution sanctioned the independence of the judiciary, a code adopted on December 12, 1989,[23] not only confirmed its independence, but introduced mechanisms to guarantee that independence.

The political process of creating the rule of law, however, ended when the authorities nullified the election results in January 1992.[24] Despite public promises by President Mohammed Boudiaf (January–June 1992) not to tolerate any physical or mental abuses, the government has since violated human rights on a large scale. The Islamic Salvation Front (FIS), poised to win a majority, was banned, and thousands of its members and supporters were confined in camps in the Sahara. A state of emergency was declared, and political violence became a daily event. The Islamist party's supporters resorted to violence and terrorist attacks, committing indescribable atrocities. In order to protect citizens, especially in remote areas, the government responded by creating units of self-defense. The ministry of human rights, despite its importance in principle and its ineffectiveness in practice, was replaced by l'Observatoire National des Droits de l'Homme (the national overseer for human rights, ONDH), an "independent" twenty-six-member body whose role was to promote human rights and investigate any abuses.[25]

The increasing violence resulted in the daily violation of human rights.

The violence has claimed over sixty thousand lives, according to conservative estimates; the vast majority of those killed have been civilians. The daily, indiscriminate massacres which prevail in many parts of the country, especially around Algiers, represent a massive case of cruel and inhuman treatment, as the psychological condition of much of Algerian society bears witness. In addition, the tactics used by the security forces as they pursue "terrorists" have resulted in continuous arbitrary interference with family and home and in a complete disregard for the internationally recognized human-rights codes to which the Algerian government has committed itself.

The provision of Article 4 of the ICCPR allows states who are party to the covenant to derogate from the provision of the covenant by suspending some rights in a state of emergency, but the covenant also states that some rights cannot be taken away, regardless of the situation. Algeria, however, because of the state of emergency, has systematically violated human rights despite its commitment to the ICCPR.[26]

The most significant violation of human rights was the adoption, on October 1, 1992, of Decree 92-03, which relates to the struggle against "subversion and terrorism."[27] That decree, which was eventually incorporated into permanent legislation in February 1995,[28] compromises the independence of the Algerian judicial system.[29] The law broadens the definition of terrorist acts to include those acts against state security and private property. The law also called for the creation of three special courts, dissolved in 1995, to try secretly and speedily those convicted of "terrorist" acts. Most importantly perhaps, the law rejects the principles enshrined in human-rights agreements, because sentences for all acts of terrorism are double those called for by the penal code, and the death sentence was imposed on those who had already been sentenced to life. In addition, not only did the law of February 1995 lower the age of criminal responsibility to sixteen, it also increased the *garde à vue* detention from forty-eight hours to twelve days, and the lengthened detention was also applied retroactively. Another provision of the February 1995 legislation allowed any cases awaiting trial to be transferred to special courts. In sharp contrast to Article 15 (1) of the ICCPR,[30] those then tried in the special courts could be punished, according to the harsher sentences, regardless of whether "their crimes" had been committed before the legislation or after it. In summary, the legislation of February 1995 gave carte blanche to government forces in their pursuit of terrorists. Torture, "disappearances," and inhuman treatment have since become widespread and have not been thoroughly investigated. The massacre in the Serkadji prison on February

21, 1995, provides the best example of the unrestricted power of the government.[31]

The legislation also impedes lawyers in representing their clients. Lawyers are not informed where their clients are being held, and they are not given enough time to prepare for their clients' defense. In fact, Articles 24 and 31 empower judges to expel lawyers from the special courts, and they may be suspended from practicing for as long as one year. Because of such intimidation, lawyers have been reluctant to argue before the special courts. Mustapha Bouchachi, a human-rights lawyer, felt that the "law was absent" and that those policies were created in order to compel lawyers "to adopt a particular stand."[32]

Freedom of the press is the second most significant victim of the February 1995 legislation. No independent TV and radio stations exist, so the government has been able to control the information. Newspapers are also restricted because the government controls newsprint and printing presses. The government also has applied economic pressure on newspapers that espouse opinions different from its own. The government allocates advertising, so some newspapers could easily and quickly fail if they fall into disfavor. Newspapers in Algeria therefore suffer a tripartite censorship. First, journalists censor themselves in order to conform to the "official line" and to avoid intimidation. Second, the editors prohibit any stories (especially those related to security matters) that did not originate from the state-controlled Algérie Presse Service (APS). Third, the newspapers have established "reading committees" to ensure that whatever is published conforms to the official account.[33] The government has confiscated newspaper companies or suspended the publication of many newspapers that have failed to conform to official guidelines; for example, *Le Matin* failed to appear on the newsstands in March 1996 because it would have contained a report on human rights in the country.[34] *La Nation,* a weekly newspaper that had been suspended on several occasions due to its critical stance against the regime, has virtually been banned since mid-1996.

Tunisia: Short-term Interest

The change in Tunisia's politics of human rights came with the change in the country's leadership. Zine El-Abidine Ben Ali, architect of a medico-constitutional coup, deposed Bourguiba on November 7, 1987.[35] Without any popular base, he espoused human rights in an attempt to broaden his support. The last year of Bourguiba's rule was chaotic, with frequent government reshuffling and increased repression of Islamist activists, clearly necessitating a change of leadership and new rhetoric about human rights. The Ben Ali regime released political prisoners, invited those exiled to return to the country, abolished the state security court, and restricted the presidency to three five-year terms. Most importantly, Ben Ali committed himself to negotiating with all opposition forces, without exception, and called for the drawing of a "national pact" to define the direction of the Tunisian system. Rachid Ghannouchi, leader of the Islamist movement, initially praised the new president and delegated one of his subordinates to take part in the drawing of that pact. According to the new law on associations, the ministry of interior was required to consider applications by political parties and organizations within three months of receiving the application.[36]

Despite the changes and cabinet appointments for two founding members of the Tunisian human-rights organization, the president's commitment to human rights soon became questionable. In an attempt to comply with the law, which called for the separation of religion and politics, the Mouvement de la Tendance Islamique changed its name to Nahda, and its requests for recognition have been repeatedly turned down. The honeymoon lasted only until 1989. The government has steadily restricted human rights in Tunisia since 1990, suggesting a great gulf between Ben Ali's statements and the behavior of his government.

The enthusiasm that accompanied the "national pact" soon faded, and the first test of the president's reforms came in April 1989, when elections were held. The president, who ran unopposed, won 99.27 percent of the votes cast. His party, the Rassemblement Constitutionnel Démocratique (RCD), won an overwhelming majority of the seats in the National Assembly.[37] Although Nahda was not legalized, Islamists running as independents proved a formidable political force. They won 13 percent of the vote for the National Assembly, with an impressive 30 percent in the capital, Tunis.[38] A month later, Ghannouchi went into exile and repression of Islamists began in earnest.

Denouncing the threat to human rights posed by religious fundamentalism, Ben Ali's regime has treated the Islamists harshly. In 1991, given the success of the FIS in neighboring Algeria, repression grew. According to Amnesty International, more than eight thousand people were arrested,[39] and by 1992 the majority of Nahda activists, including women sympathizers, were silenced, exiled, or imprisoned. The nonrecognition of this "party" and its virtual elimination can be considered as an elimination of any significant opposition, because legal opposition parties are either fragmented or weak.

The regime, whose security forces quadrupled, turned its repression against activists in the Communist party (PCOT), the remaining "most outspoken opposition party in its criticism of Tunisian government policy and repression."[40] However, aware of the scrutiny of human rights by aid donors and trading partners, Ben Ali created the post of presidential advisor in charge of human rights. He also offered not to "present candidates during the legislative by-elections in October [1991], which would guarantee the opposition at least nine seats in the 141-seat Chamber of Deputies."[41]

In a further attempt to tighten Ben Ali's grip on Tunisia's political life and to reduce criticism by Tunisian human-rights organizations, the National Assembly amended the law on associations "in March 1992 in such a way that individuals occupying positions of responsibility in political parties may not at the same time belong to organizations or associations considered to have a general nature."[42] The Tunisian League of Human Rights was temporarily dissolved in May for not amending its rules to correspond with the change in the law. When it resumed work in 1994, however, it conformed further to the government's orders.

Because of widespread disillusionment with the previous changes, a new set of reforms was introduced in 1994. The reforms increased the size of the National Assembly to 163 seats: 144 seats to be contested, according to the winner-takes-all formula, while the remaining 19 seats would be divided among other parties according to their share of the popular vote. The reforms guaranteed "opposition parties" representation.[43] Ben Ali's RCD won 144 seats in the National Assembly; the other 19 seats were divided among four parties. The party also won, in May 1995, 4,084 out of 4,090 seats in the municipal elections.[44] Ben Ali, again running unopposed during the March 1994 presidential election, improved on his first performance by securing 99.91 percent of the votes cast, a record in the Arab world.[45]

The press has suffered the most from Ben Ali's control of Tunisia's political life. Similar to the practice in Algeria, the Tunisian government uses its allocation of advertising to silence newspapers. Censorship of foreign newspapers, especially *Le Monde,* and harassment of journalists have been common practice since 1994.[46]

The situation in Tunisia suggests that *plus ça change, plus c'est la même chose* (the more things change, the more things stay the same). Ben Ali's reforms have amounted to nothing more than a tactical move to secure support throughout the country, because initially human-rights supporters, as well as the Islamists, were quick to support his actions. Clearly, his adoption of the human-rights vocabulary, the change in the law on associations, and the appointment of two human-rights activists to his cabinet were aimed at weakening the human-rights organization by undermining its unity. The new policies also served to identify where real opposition came from, so that it could be more easily neutralized. Using the threat of Islamic fundamentalism as an excuse, the government has engaged systematically in tactics to silence any form of opposition.

Morocco: The International Effect

While historically abysmal, Morocco's human-rights record began to receive worldwide attention only in the late 1980s. The systematic use of force, torture, and "disappearance" to maintain political control dates back to the 1960s. In Morocco, unlike the governments of Algeria and Tunisia, the king took decisive steps toward improving the exercise of human rights in order to avoid criticism. Domestic groups and independent international organizations, such as Amnesty International, played an increasingly prominent role in publicizing human-rights abuses and in raising people's awareness of those abuses.[47] As a result, Morocco set up a "Committee for Dialogue with Amnesty International" to find ways of improving the overall situation. More important, perhaps, was the publication, in France, of a book detailing the large-scale, human-rights abuses in Morocco.[48] The book received enormous publicity, and it decisively strengthened the human-rights movement in Morocco. Morocco's traditional supporters, especially France, began to pressure the king to allow the exercise of human rights, and, since 1990, he has done so, a situation described as the "boomerang effect."[49] The international publicity arising from the exchange of information between national and international organizations has directly affected Moroccan policies on human rights.

The year 1990 was therefore a significant year. In an attempt to show his commitments to human rights, the king announced that a Human Rights Advisory Council, an independent body with thirty-six members, was to be established. The dependence of the council on the royal palace for its budget, however, casts doubts on its independence. Perhaps the most important development in 1990 was the beginning of discussion of some of Morocco's taboo subjects. In December, the existence of the infamous Tazmamart prison was raised in the national parliament, thus breaking a long tradition of silence and cover-up.[50] That debate motivated the king to take further measures on human rights. He declared 1991 "Human-rights Year." The Tazmamart prison was closed down. "Over 30 people who had been held in detention since their 'disappearance' 19 years before" were released;[51] furthermore, "members of the Istiqlal party raised the issue of constitutional reforms and argued that the current constitution did not permit installation of real democracy."[52]

In September 1992, a new constitution was proposed by the king and submitted to a referendum without debate. The constitution enlarges the powers of the parliament and places constraints on the monarch. He no longer can dissolve the parliament, for example, and is obliged to choose a prime minister from among the elected majority.[53] After the parliamentary elections of June 1993, the king, in yet another gesture, appointed a minister for human rights.

In spite of the constitutional changes, Morocco's respect for human rights, while relatively better than that of the other Maghrebi states, is still limited. The judiciary is corrupt and subject to interference. It is, for instance, illegal to criticize the king and the royal family. The government is still denying knowledge of the "disappeared"; however, the most significant criticism of Morocco's human-rights record has to be its reluctance to hold a referendum on the future of the Western Sahara. Despite its initial acceptance and its ratification of the ICCPR, which provides for self-determination, Morocco not only has yet to fulfill its obligations, but it continues to violate the rights of the Sahrawi people.[54]

Libya: Qadaffi's Change of Heart

The human-rights situation in Libya is appalling. Freedoms of speech and of association do not exist. Libyan jails hold over five hundred political prisoners, including long-term inmates subject to dreadful prison conditions and abuse.[55] In the late 1980s, however, Qadaffi espoused the human-rights rhetoric. He initiated a series of reforms to improve the country's human-rights record.[56] "The Great Green Document on Human Rights in the Era of the Masses" was adopted by the General People's Congress in June 1988; a number of reforms aimed at improving judicial procedures. It called for fair trials, outlawed any degrading and inhuman punishment, and called for restricting the death penalty with a view to its eventual abolition. However, those reforms remain limited and have certainly not inaugurated wider reforms.

Despite the fact that Qadaffi consistently wraps himself in the banner of Islam, he encounters opposition from Islamists and has suppressed their activities. His regime, perhaps in an attempt to appease the Islamists and to be seen as the guardian of Islam, seems to have abandoned all its earlier commitments to human rights. In a televised speech in June 1993, for example, he called for the introduction of some laws based on Islamic principles, such as amputation and flogging as judicial punishments, and for "widening the scope of the death penalty."[57]

Conclusion

Contemporary events in the Maghreb, where multiparty elections have taken place, demonstrate that respect for human rights has yet to be institutionalized. Human-rights rhetoric provides legitimacy to the rulers of Maghrebi nations and serves their immediate interests.

Morocco, perhaps because of a lack of a strong Islamist movement, is the only country in the region whose human-rights record showed some improvements; however, those modest advances could be halted at any time. Algeria is trying to resume the democratic process while coping with a severe political crisis. Tunisia has yet to improve its human-rights record; ideally, international pressure will, as in Morocco, lead to some improvement. Libya's record is deplorable; United Nations sanctions have strengthened the Qadaffi regime domestically rather than weakened it. It is doubtful, however, whether lifting the sanctions would lead to any progress, because the regime faces growing domestic opposition. (See chapter 5.)

Notes

I am grateful to the University of Lincolnshire and Humberside for its financial assistance, and to Yahia H. Zoubir and A. Lewis for their comments on earlier drafts.

1. Waltz, *Human Rights and Reform.* Unlike the approach I have pursued in this chapter, Waltz's treatment focuses on the role of the local human rights organizations in the Maghreb.

2. Amnesty International, *Libya: Amnesty's Prisoner Concern in the Light of Recent Legal Reforms,* 1.

3. In its entry for Libya, the U.S. State Department Report of 1996 stated that information on human rights in this country was limited. Amnesty International, for instance, last visited Libya in 1988.

4. El-Alaoui, "La monarchie marocaine tentée par la réforme."

5. The European Union, in its revisions of the Lomé Convention in 1995, insisted on the human-rights clause.

6. Donnelly, "Cultural Relativism and Human Rights," 400–419.

7. Mayer, *Islam and Human Rights.*

8. El-Din Hassan, "Towards Inclusive Strategies for Human-Rights Enforcement in the Arab World," 171–89.

9. Al-Ghannouchi, "Towards Inclusive Strategies for Human Rights Enforcement in the Arab World—A Response," 190–94.

10. Power in Algeria is still concentrated in the hands of the military.

11. Waltz, *Human Rights and Reform;* Dwyer, *Arab Voices.*

12. Waltz, *Human Rights and Reform,* 50.

13. The assassinations of historic figures, such as the Moroccan Mehdi Ben Barka (1965), the Tunisian Salah Ben Youssef (1965), and the Algerian Krim Belkacem (1970) are the best illustrations.

14. An account of the emergence of human-rights organizations in the Maghreb can be found in Waltz, *Human Rights and Reform,* chap. 7.

15. de Barrin, "Les différentes réponses des pays maghrébins à la menace islamiste."

16. Despite the free presidential election held in Algeria in November 1995, in which four candidates stood, Liamine Zeroual, the military candidate and president of the state, clearly had the advantage.

17. Boukhoubza, *Octobre 88—Evolution ou rupture?*

18. Comité National Contre la Torture, *Cahier noir d'Octobre.*

19. In a series of interviews conducted by the author in 1991, a policeman stressed that "getting a confession was easy. Now they talk about human rights."

20. Torture, for example, was almost eradicated in Algeria between 1989 and 1991, and in an attempt to show its commitment to human rights, Chadli's regime appointed a minister delegate for human rights, elevated to ministerial status in June 1991.

21. Chaker, "Les droits de l'homme sont-ils mûrs en Algérie?" 489–503.

22. Mikhail Gorbachev, *Perestroika: New Thinking for Our Country and the World,* 105.

23. Chambati, "Une justice sous pressions."

24. For an interesting discussion, see Yahia H. Zoubir, "Stalled Democratization of an Authoritarian Regime: The Case of Algeria," 109–39.

25. The authorities abolished the ministry of human rights because its role and position could not be reconciled: it could not be part of the government while criticizing that very same government for any abuses. Instead, the authorities created the ONDH, which has, nevertheless, been accused of being proregime. Despite the widespread use of torture, ONDH's director acknowledged that they received only fifteen complaints alleging ill treatment. For details see *L'Opinion* (Algiers), November 23, 1993.

26. Amnesty International, *Algeria: Deteriorating Human Rights under the State of Emergency.*

27. Chambati, "Une justice sous pressions," n. 23.

28. Amnesty International, *Amnesty International Report,* 72.

29. According to Mahmoud Khelili, a human-rights lawyer, this law is unconstitutional. *L'Evénement* (Algiers), March 28–April 3, 1993.

30. "No one shall be held guilty of any criminal offense on account of any act

of omission, which did not constitute a criminal offense, under national law or international law, at the time when it was committed. Nor shall a heavier penalty be imposed than the one that was applicable at the time when the criminal offense was committed."

31. On the night of February 1, 1995, 105 detainees, including political prisoners, and four prison guards were killed by government forces for allegedly trying to escape from Serkadji, in central Algiers—one of the most secure prisons in the country. For details, see Ait-Embarek, *L'Algérie en murmure. Un cahier sur la torture.*

32. *La Nation* (Algiers), April 11–17, 1995.

33. Algerian journalists have confirmed these to the author on a research trip to Paris, April 1996. It seems, however, that those committees were disbanded in January 1998.

34. The report was published in *Le Monde Diplomatique,* March 1996.

35. Article 57 of the constitution provides that the prime minister should assume power if the president is incapacitated.

36. Dwyer, *Arab Voices,* 155.

37. Ibrahimi, "Les libertés envolées de la Tunisie."

38. de Barrin, "Les différentes réponses des pays maghrébins à la menace islamiste," n. 15.

39. Amnesty International, *Tunisia. Women Victims of Harassment, Torture and Imprisonment.*

40. Ibid., 3.

41. Freedom House, *Freedom in the World 1991–92,* 445.

42. Amnesty International, *Amnesty International Report,* 1993, 116.

43. Waltz, *Human Rights and Reform,* 59–60.

44. Amnesty International, *Amnesty International Report,* 1996, 229.

45. Ibrahimi, "Les libertés envolées de la Tunisie."

46. Ramonet, "Main de fer en Tunisie"; Boucher, "La société tunisienne privée de parole."

47. Amnesty International, *Morocco: Human Rights Violations in* Garde à Vue *Detention.*

48. Perrault, *Notre ami le roi.*

49. I have borrowed the "boomerang effect" concept from Sieglinde Granzer, "Norms, International Institutions, and Domestic Change: Human Rights in Tunisia and Morocco." Paper presented at the 37th annual convention of the International Studies Association (ISA), Toronto/Canada, March 18–22, 1997.

50. The Tazmamart prison, which until 1990 did not figure on any list of prisons in Morocco, has housed many of those who "disappeared." It is only after a letter was smuggled out of prison and government officials lobbied that its existence was admitted. For details, see Amnesty International, *Morocco: Breaking the Wall of Silence.*

51. *Amnesty International Newsletter,* November 18, 1993.

52. Waltz, *Human Rights and Reform,* 116.

53. Korn, "The Middle East: Islam vs. the Established Order," 42.

54. U.S. Department of State's reports on human rights for 1996 for Morocco and Western Sahara, published in January 1997.

55. Amnesty International, *Libya: Further Information on Political Detention.*

56. Amnesty International, *Libya: Amnesty's Prisoner Concern in the Light of Recent Legal Reforms.*

57. Amnesty International, AI Index MDE 19/WU 02/93.

9.

COMMITMENT AND CRITIQUE: FRANCOPHONE INTELLECTUALS IN THE MAGHREB

Patricia Geesey

The French language came to the Maghreb by way of the French colonial presence. As in the previous struggle for independence in North Africa, the French language still serves as a means of expression for numerous intellectuals who offer independent analyses and critiques of their societies.[1] For some, writing in French is a necessity originating in their personal situations of having been educated and having come of age in the colonial era (for example, Mohammed Dib, Assia Djebar, Abdelkébir Khatibi, and Driss Chraïbi); for others, French is the preferred language for a variety of personal, political, and ideological reasons (for example, Tahar Djaout, Tahar Ben Jelloun, and Rachid Mimouni). During the struggle for independence against France, intellectuals and militants in all three nations of the Maghreb used French to develop their platforms and express their demands for sovereignty. As Amin Khan points out, during Algeria's war of independence (1954–1962), all FLN documents, including the famous November 1, 1954, proclamation, were drafted in French.[2] Clearly, the French language may be associated with a tradition of voicing political and social protest, whether through fictional narrative or prose essay. Yet today, the French language (and those intellectuals who use it) in the Maghreb suffer from negative perceptions. For Algeria, as will be discussed in greater detail later in this essay, the antagonism between the proponents of Arabic and French and the position of these two languages in the debate on national identity have reached a paroxysm of tragic dimensions. In Tunisia and Morocco, the continued use of French by many well-known intellectuals leads to simmering animosity and jealous sniping in literary and cultural journals, but it stops short of open violence. Indeed, for many Maghrebi intellectuals who express themselves in French, the tensions between francophone and arabophone intellectuals are usually partially blamed on the very problematic notion of *la francophonie*.

The term *francophone* indicates "of, or in the French language," while *francophonie* has a much more ambivalent status. Virtually all French-language intellectuals of the Maghreb explicitly reject the term *francophonie* because of this word's close association with the French government's attempts to unite former French colonies into a loose organization of economic, cultural, and technological exchanges and dialogues. The creation of the *espace francophone* was justified by the fact that the French language in these now independent nations is the secondary (or even in some cases, the "official") language. Tahar Ben Jelloun, often condemned by literary critics and fellow writers in the Maghreb for his alleged complicity in promoting the values of francophonia, tirelessly expresses his opposition to the French government's heavy-handed approach to promoting the French language in former colonies, often to the detriment of those intellectuals who use French but do not wish to be associated with the policies of francophonia. In his brief essay "Le français tel qu'on le rêve," Ben Jelloun points out that "today, francophonia can only have meaning in a definitive rupture with its historic and political origins, which are colonialism and paternalism."[3] Ben Jelloun's remarks reveal that intellectuals in the Maghreb who use French do not see themselves as heirs to the region's colonial past. Like Ben Jelloun, many Maghrebi intellectuals believe that in the postcolonial context, a new status of francophone writers must be recognized: committed writers who bear witness to social change in their societies.

The Moroccan novelist and sociologist Abdelkébir Khatibi defines the role of the Maghrebi intellectual as one in which the culturally diverse heritage of the Maghreb, what he refers to as "un carrefour de cultures" (a crossroads of cultures), must be assumed. Khatibi also insists that the intellectual must be a committed "intermediary between men of action and those dominated by them." Khatibi stresses the three functions he considers essential for the intellectual to fulfill: a technical or pedagogical function, a social function, and an ethical function. Khatibi underscores the vital element of freedom of conscience that is required for all aspects of the intellectual's role in society. He observes that in the Maghreb, the intellectual must be "a bearer of a continuous freedom of thought. Without this freedom, what would become of the intellectual? What would become of him as an active agent of civil society?[4] Clearly, for Khatibi, the task of North African intellectuals is to be critically and meaningfully engaged with the whole of their society.

In his preface to Abdellah Labdaoui's study, *Les nouveaux intellectuels arabes,* Yves Schemeil observes that since Maghrebi intellectuals are *not* writing exclusively for their own compatriots, and given the fact that they might write in a language that is not the lingua franca of their nation, their situation is, in fact, "a freedom more than a constraint." By using another language, Schemeil remarks, intellectuals in the Maghreb "free themselves from social pressures, whether private or public ones."[5] Schemeil suggests, therefore, that the use of French actually allows the Maghrebi intellectual greater freedom to critique society and its institutions.

Algeria

The Algerian civil crisis has directed a tragic spotlight on the situation of Algerian intellectuals, both francophone and arabophone. Included in the tens of thousands of civilian victims are several hundred "intellectuals." For Lahouari Addi and François Burgat, the term "francophone intellectual" seems to include both published authors and government technocrats (also referred to as "the elite" in their essays), who use French in the context of their work.[6] There exists among Western observers of the Algerian crisis a perception that francophone intellectuals have paid a higher price in the violence than any other group of civilians.[7] While this fact cannot be supported by the real statistics, it is possible to note that the widely reported killings of intellectuals and numerous journalists (who worked for *both* French and Arabic, and/or state-sponsored *and* independent newspapers) have led observers in Algeria and France to speak of "un terrorisme intellectocide."[8] The francophone novelist Rachid Mimouni raised the alarm in an essay published in *Le Monde* in May of 1994 that the Islamist-inspired militants had decided upon a course of action that would effectively "décerveler" ("de-brain") the Algerian nation. As Mimouni writes in his impassioned article: "C'est la première fois dans l'histoire qu'on voit un mouvement terroriste se proposer d'éradiquer toute l'intelligentsia d'un pays, comme s'il s'agissait d'une mauvaise herbe ou d'une maladie. Le projet consiste à décerveler le pays"[9]

(It is the first time in history that we see a terrorist movement proposing to eradicate the entire intelligentsia of a nation, as if it were a question of weeds or an illness. The project consists of "de-braining" the nation).

Since Tahar Djaout and others have fallen victim to the senseless violence that has claimed so many lives in the country, Algerian and Maghrebi scholars, journalists, and novelists have examined the place of francophone intellectuals in Algerian society. They have attempted to understand how it has become possible for a group to be so singularly targeted because of what they write and how they think.[10] In his brief essay entitled "Intellectuels à titre posthume," Abdelmalek Sayad describes Algerian intellectuals as individuals who have made "the choice to live, to act, to work, and above all to think independently, on the margins, and if necessary, against what is ordinarily done, said, and thought." Sayad notes that, in most nations, "going against the grain" of accepted positions and dogma would be tolerated. But in the unique political and historical context of Algeria, "being an exception," as Sayad notes, "is an act that is tolerated only with difficulty." For Sayad, the intellectual who stands apart, who thinks and writes "against the grain," "is the one who *disturbs* by the effort he makes in all areas of his activity and sometimes by his very existence."[11]

In his essay "Les intellectuels qu'on assassine," Lahouari Addi offers his own theory as to "how has Algeria managed to become indifferent to the murder of its intellectuals."[12] Although "indifferent" is perhaps too strong a word to use, it remains nonetheless important to examine the Algerian situation in order to understand how French-language intellectuals are perceived by the members of their own society. For Addi, quite simply, francophone intellectuals are seen as belonging to a privileged, French-speaking (military-governmental) elite who has maintained a firm hold on power, money, and social prestige in Algeria since independence. Yves Lacoste makes a more thorough analysis of the situation of francophone intellectuals in Algeria in his essay "Les causes spécifiques du drame algérien" (1995). Lacoste emphasizes the way in which Islamist party officials and their supporters (with the complicity of members of the FLN) have manipulated public discourse in such a way as to claim that in Algeria there exist two kinds of Muslims: "les bons et les mauvais." In public political debates, introducing the divisive notion of "good and bad" or "real or inauthentic" Algerians and/or Muslims has led to the scapegoating of francophone "elites" and intellectuals who, in the eyes of Algeria's disenfranchised (and largely monolingual) citizens, benefit from greater privileges thanks to the former's contacts with French and Western society.[13]

Before his assassination ostensibly at the hands of Islamic fundamentalist militants, Tahar Djaout published four novels and three collections of poems. Djaout also worked as a journalist covering the cultural and literary scenes of Algeria and the Maghreb for *El Moudjahid* and then, for a ten-year period, *Algérie-Actualité*. The limited liberalization of the press in 1989 enabled Djaout along with two other journalists to start an independent French-language publication called *Ruptures*. During his lifetime, he worked tirelessly to denounce extremism and injustices carried out against the Algerian people. For Djaout, "commitment" meant being engaged only through total freedom in order to advance the cause of "certain values that are considered primordial." Djaout made it clear which principles and values he wished to be associated with: secularism, democracy, justice, freedom of expression, and the inalienable human rights of men and women. He defined "the committed intellectual" as being a person who tries to "question and to make sense of the world through the tools of his intelligence and knowledge." Djaout explained that intellectuals who conduct themselves with a certain "discretion" (that is, avoiding the political limelight and relying on the quality and insight of their works) have a more meaningful influence on their society. Yet again, Djaout reiterates that the Algerian intellectual can be of service only if he or she acts in total independence from political pressures. He noted, "It is clear that making sense of society can only successfully be carried out when one is cut loose from all taboos and all burdens of the tribe . . . of the different tribes who want to exert their control over us. I think that only an independent intellectual can overcome the taboos, the hurdles that are constantly put in his path."[14]

Just several days before his assassination on May 26, 1993, Djaout published an editorial in *Ruptures,* and this incisive analysis of the political stalemate of spring 1993 is believed to have provoked his enemies. Entitled "La famille qui avance et la famille qui recule," this piece soundly denounces the complicity of the HCE (the emergency executive council ruling Algeria in the aftermath of the 1992 coup), in bringing about the present state of affairs in which religion and politics had become so impossibly intertwined in Algerian society. In this essay, Djaout effectively challenges the regime to establish fully a democratic and secular government in Algeria. Nothing less, he believes, can pull Algeria back from the edge of the abyss where the nation had positioned itself at that point in 1993. In his editorial, he presents Algeria's basic dilemma as he saw it: the factions may be grouped into two "families" of ideas. According to Djaout, in Algeria "there are really only two families: the family who advances and the family who falls behind."[15] Progress and advancement, in Djaout's view, could be achieved only if Algeria took the side of democratic secularism. The time for hard choices had arrived for Algeria, and in his work with *Ruptures* Djaout challenged the powers that be to act with Algeria's future in mind.

Whereas Tahar Djaout restricted his critiques of factions struggling for power to the columns of *Ruptures,* two other Algerian intellectuals with international reputations have published treatises in France that are extremely critical not only of the FIS and the armed Islamist-based groups but also of the regime that has ruled Algeria since 1962. The French media have sought out both Rachid Mimouni and Rachid Boudjedra for interviews largely because of their previous reputations as acclaimed novelists. The media attention they receive increased after the publication of their anti-Islamist essays *De la barbarie en général et de l'intégrisme en particulier* (Mimouni) and *FIS de la haine* (Boudjedra). Before his death from hepatitis in exile in February 1995, Mimouni, like Boudjedra, gave numerous interviews to European journalists regarding the Algerian situation. This caused François Burgat to refer none too subtly to them as "les plus médiatisés des analystes"(the most mediatized of analysts).[16] Rachid Boudjedra, in recent years, has become a favorite guest on French talk shows and news programs about Algeria; he has also appeared in the pages of *Le Nouvel Observateur* under such startling headlines as "Pas de compromis avec les égorgeurs" and "Celui qui affronte l'Islamisme à mots nus."[17] Even before his increased notoriety since the publication of *FIS de la haine,* Boudjedra has been a controversial personality in Algerian belles lettres.

According to literary scholar Hafid Gafaïti, Boudjedra is "an unusual person who provokes the most diverse reactions, ranging from the most passionate attachment to the most virulent hostility."[18] At present, Boudjedra lives clandestinely, moving between Algeria and France. He has told French journalists that he has received death threats from Islamic groups since 1983, the year in which an Arabic version of *L'insolation* appeared. Boudjedra also describes having survived an assassination attempt mounted by the FIS and the GIA; he is always armed and carries cyanide capsules with him wherever he goes in case he is captured by his enemies. If Boudjedra's name had already appeared on "hit lists" in 1983, then it is not surprising that his controversial work *FIS de la haine* provoked even greater hostility. Boudjedra's polemical and vitriolic essay is frank in its condemnation of the FLN regime, and the FIS and their armed offshoot, the GIA. The language he uses in *FIS de la haine* to describe Islamic militants is vehement, referring, for example, to "a green fascism."[19] For Boudjedra, the followers of the FIS are "les fous de Dieu" (the madmen of God), "card-carrying killers," "backward simpletons," and "rabid rats."[20] In interviews, Boudjedra likens the FIS to Nazis and the GIA to the SS. Furthermore, in his view, adherents to the FIS platform are "incultes" (ignorant) and "complexés de la modernité" (modernity-phobes).[21]

In *FIS de la haine,* Boudjedra also takes a critical stance toward the FLN, which he blames for allowing the FIS to rise to power in the first place, hence the title he has chosen for his treatise—*FIS,* a homophone of *fils* (son) of hatred. Additionally, Boudjedra blames the French government for sustaining a corrupt government and helping to maintain Algeria's cultural and economic dependency on its former colonial master.[22] The author also severely criticizes Algeria's own intellectuals, especially those who have exploited the privileges of francophonia at the expense of making a real contribution to the vitality of Algerian culture and literature.[23] In short, Boudjedra examines the origins of the civil crisis in 1992 and arrives at the conclusion that everyone is collectively responsible for the rise of the FIS and the advent of sectarian and civil violence. Everyone is partially to blame, Boudjedra believes, because as a nation, Algeria has not successfully assumed its own "share of tradition" and "its share of modernity." In *FIS de la haine,* Boudjedra notes that only a collective "social psychoanalysis," one that will allow Algeria to come to terms with its repressed truths and identities, will enable the nation to "emerge from its mental chaos."[24] In the postscript Boudjedra includes in the second printing of his essay, he makes a plea for the Algerian people to demand and to continue the fight for their right to a freely elected, democratic government—one that will guarantee political freedoms and religious tolerance, as well as a government that will promote "un respect pour des multiples langues et cultures qui sont le patrimoine essentiel de tout le peuple algérien"[25] (a respect for the multiple languages and cultures that are the essential heritage of the Algerian people).

Rachid Mimouni, along with Tahar Djaout, has often been considered one of the finest representatives of the "second generation" of French-language Algerian novelists. Already ill and under death threats from factions fighting in Algeria, Mimouni went into exile in Morocco in January 1994. Boudjedra dedicates his collection of essays *Lettres algériennes* to the memory of Mimouni, whose "body was unearthed and mutilated the day after his funeral by the fundamentalist hoard whose barbarity and insanity aroused only sorrow and compassion in Mimouni."[26] The tone of Mimouni's *De la barbarie,* while noticeably less vitriolic than the essay written by Boudjedra, nevertheless reaches many of the same conclusions about the rise of the Islamist movement.

In *De la barbarie,* Mimouni reflects at length upon the historical role that Algerian intellectuals have played in their society. His observations are blunt: Algerian intellectuals have missed their rendezvous with history on every occasion. According to Mimouni, if there is apparently little sympathy in Algeria today for the plight of intellectuals who are assassinated in their offices and in the parking lots of their buildings, it is because the citizens of Algeria have not forgotten how intellectuals have altered their ideological positions for their own benefit.[27] In the postindependence decades, Mimouni admits that some Algerian intellectuals who sought to express views contrary to the regime were effectively silenced by government threats and censure.[28] Mimouni is, above all, critical toward Algerian intellectuals who have curried favor either with the FLN government or with the representatives of "la francophonie" at European embassies. For Mimouni, the most unforgivable tendency of some Algerian intellectuals has been their demonstrated "lack of combativeness." Supporters of the Islamist movement are to be admired, observes Mimouni, because they had the courage to go out in the streets and confront the army face to face. Mimouni scolds his fellow Algerian intellectuals who reason in bad faith: they reproach the government for the coup, yet it is this very action that prevented many of them from becoming victims of the fate reserved for them by Islamic radicals.[29] In short, Mimouni's treatise is blunt in its criticism of those Algerian intellectuals who have not shown themselves to be capable of assuming a constructive and engaged role in their society. Indeed, Mimouni reveals his great pessimism regarding the future of democracy in Algeria, because so many figures who should be an example and assume an active role are paralyzed by hesitation and compromised by past errors of judgment.

Morocco

In Morocco, the dilemmas surrounding the continued use of French and the institutionalization of Arabization programs have not provoked the same intense reaction as in Algeria. Morocco instituted Arabization programs somewhat later and more gradually than Algeria; furthermore, Morocco's colonial relationship with France was not as long or as profound as Algeria's. However, this is not to suggest that francophone intellectuals in Morocco have been immune from controversy. Moroccan

French-language writers came to international attention with the publication of Driss Chraïbi's *Le passé simple* in 1954. This novel, published when Morocco was engaged in the struggle to free itself from the French protectorate, condemned both French colonial exploitation and the fossilized and patriarchal Moroccan bourgeoisie. Chraïbi was vilified as a traitor to his people for writing a work that negatively portrayed indigenous Moroccan values and practices. The novel is especially harsh in its depiction of the family patriarch, a man who abuses the authority vested in him by cultural and religious tradition. Since the 1950s, Chraïbi and other Moroccan francophone intellectuals have produced works of fiction and nonfiction in which the centuries-old foundations of Moroccan cultural, political, and religious institutions are reexamined and critiqued.

The most internationally recognized Moroccan French-language intellectual is Tahar Ben Jelloun. He has been the subject of controversy because of what he writes and because his works find a larger audience abroad than in Morocco. Educated in Morocco and in France as a doctor of psychiatry, Ben Jelloun began his literary career as a poet and novelist at the start of the 1970s. With eleven novels, three volumes of poetry, one autobiographical essay, two short-story collections, and a drama to his credit, Ben Jelloun might well be the most prolific Maghrebi francophone novelist. Ben Jelloun's immense success in Europe, in the Maghreb, and even in North America has not been without its price. The very nature of Ben Jelloun's success in academic and popular circles has attracted a range of attitudes toward the novelist himself and the opinions and causes he discusses.

Ben Jelloun's first work of fiction, *Harrouda,* introduced a theme that constantly reappears in his writings: the status of women in Arab-Muslim societies. Ben Jelloun is a committed writer in that he exposes to critical scrutiny certain elements of Morocco's postcolonial order. By focusing in his fiction on marginalized members of Morocco's society, Ben Jelloun introduces a critique of the power structures in place. Ben Jelloun remarks that the large place women occupy in his fiction is due to his belief that change in the Maghreb will come about through the actions and engagements of women. In an interview with Thomas Spear, Ben Jelloun explains that he is not an "engaged" writer in the Sartrian sense. For Ben Jelloun, the literary or poetic quality of the writing must always transcend the political message that an author weaves into the text.[30]

In their work *The Ambiguous Compromise: Language, Literature and National Identity in Algeria and Morocco,* Jacqueline Kaye and Abdelhamid Zoubir reserve some of their harshest criticism for Tahar

Ben Jelloun. In Kaye and Zoubir's analysis, Ben Jelloun is guilty of writing "self-orientalizing texts."[31] They claim this because Ben Jelloun's novels portray gender relations in the Maghreb as retrograde and his fiction focuses attention on traditional attitudes and practices that are demeaning to women. In Ben Jelloun's writings, one also finds criticism of institutionalized political corruption and religious hypocrisy. In short, Ben Jelloun draws attention to those aspects of Moroccan society which he feels need radical change. The authors of *The Ambiguous Compromise* describe Ben Jelloun's literary production as being "locked within a discourse of Moroccan degradation and humiliation that makes the authentic elements of Moroccan culture irretrievable."[32] Kaye and Zoubir are critical toward a literary trend which they feel encourages orientalist fantasies of a cruel civilization in which men's sexual brutality is sanctioned by religious decree. By focusing exclusively on how he portrays women in his texts, Ben Jelloun's harshest critics often ignore the frequent criticism of political corruption and religious hypocrisy that is to be found in his fiction.

Ben Jelloun's novel *L'homme rompu* is a fine example of his narrative style and political and social concerns. This novel is a moral and political fable about postcolonial Morocco. It is the story of a bureaucrat, an engineer by training, named Mourad, who is responsible for approving new building projects. For years, he makes it a matter of principle to refuse the bribes that have come his way, until one fateful day when he yields to temptation. From that day forward, his life is a nightmare of guilt, moral compromise, and regret. Bureaucrats all around Mourad are getting rich by exploiting their position. His superior advises him to choose the reasonable path and to stop being an obstacle to the smooth functioning of the bribery system, which the bureau chief refers to as "une économie parallèle." Corrupt bureaucrats justify their wrongdoing by noting that the corruption goes all the way to the top; in fact, according to Mourad's superior, helping oneself to a decent compensation package is actually the way the state *wants* the system to function. In this way, he reasons, official salaries may remain low.[33]

In *L'homme rompu*, Ben Jelloun directly refers to many of the ills that make life difficult for the middle class in present-day Morocco: housing shortages, inadequate public transportation, poor medical facilities, overcrowded universities, no real freedom of the press, and a government that does not guarantee the personal security and freedom of its citizens. This moral fable has an equivocal ending. After nearly having a nervous breakdown from guilt at having accepted his first bribe, Mourad is then hopelessly caught in the spiral of corruption, through his own initial weakness and the complicity of his superiors and the police. The novel ends with Mourad almost meekly assuming his place in the never-ending circle of personal gain and corruption. The novel's last line is "Welcome into the tribe,"[34] uttered by his coworker and expert graft artist, Haj Hamid. *L'homme rompu* is both an entertaining work of fiction and a caustic indictment on the political and social realities of modern Morocco. Ben Jelloun's international status offers him a somewhat greater degree of immunity from the vicissitudes of the Moroccan literary establishment. Normally a novel such as *L'homme rompu* would not be allowed to be displayed or sold in bookstores in Morocco. The only censure that effectively works against Ben Jelloun at this point in his career is an economic one. He regularly publishes with Le Seuil, in Paris, and the cost of his novels, when imported to Morocco, is prohibitive for many people, thereby effecting a censure that is "economic" if not political.

Tunisia

Francophone Tunisian literature was heralded by the publication of Albert Memmi's *La statue de sel* (1953). For some critics, Memmi's luminous career as a novelist and essayist often has overshadowed much of the subsequent literary development in Tunisia. For critic Tahar Bekri, it is only in the decade of the 1980s that French-language Tunisian writing will "confirm its dynamic presence."[35] In 1982, Hélé Béji published her ground-breaking analysis of decolonization and the Tunisian postcolonial order, entitled *Le désenchantement national: Essai sur la décolonisation.* Starting from the euphoria of independence under Habib Bourguiba in 1956 and leading up to the decided absence of real democracy and freedom of expression in Tunisia of the 1980s, Béji's study asks the question, "Why has our national political universe become so closed, so crushing?"[36] To arrive at an answer to this question, Béji examines the concept of "national consciousness" and the manipulations of nationalist sentiment that were the hallmark of the Bourguiba administration. *Le désenchantement national* also focuses on a subject that has continued to preoccupy Béji's research: cultural identities and the legitimizing, political uses that are made of identity and religion in the Maghreb. The author states that she wrote the book because she learned that "the enemy was on the inside. It is not the West."[37] Béji's most recent publication, *L'imposture culturelle,* expands and updates this inquiry in a Maghreb that has experienced increasing strife over the questions of cultural and religious affiliations.

In this particular work, Béji condemns both the Orient and Occident, which have made culture in its most abstract form the preeminent consideration for all human interaction. It is because of humanity's current obsession with essentializing and relativizing all cultures, Béji believes, that fanaticism and fundamentalism flourish. She notes that "in discovering the strength of cultural identity, modern consciousness has lost the strength of its moral discernment."[38] In *L'imposture culturelle,* Beji's subtle and wide-ranging analysis demonstrates that racism and fundamentalism are two present-day manifestations of the ideology and discourse with which the concept of culture has surrounded itself.[39] For Béji, the greatest menace to the Maghreb and the West itself is the bitter truth that "the new cultural mystique has been fueled by all the political disappointments of our century."[40]

Béji's insights into the nature of the dilemmas facing the Maghreb today are innovative. She remains, to this date, an uncompromising voice on the role of the intellectual in Maghrebi society. Béji rejects all the usual platitudes about Arab identity and the need to reaffirm the role of Arabic in the context of decolonization. She writes: "If the trend today is to push a certain number of people to write in the language of 'their roots,' if this is enacted as a command, an intellectual tyranny, then I think it is an act of freedom to write in another language."[41] Béji's research, as well as her comments about the French-versus-Arabic debate, underscore the artificiality of all cultural and linguistic monoliths. For Béji, language is an element linked to the independent stance an intellectual must adopt: "If language did not exist to liberate us from all belonging [appurtenance], it could not be used to recreate belonging."[42]

Hélé Béji and the other Maghrebi francophone intellectuals discussed here all share a commitment to bear witness to the issues affecting their societies. The role of the intellectual in Maghrebi societies is no easier today than it was during the struggle for independence against the French. In his collection of essays *Penser le Maghreb,* Abdelkébir Khatibi notes that never before have the responsibilities and the burdens laid on the shoulders of Maghrebi intellectuals been greater. Regardless of the language they choose to express themselves, Khatibi points out that intellectuals in the Maghreb—a region "engaged in decisive change"—are inextricably bound to their historical moment and their land of birth, even as their work transcends national boundaries.[43] Maghrebi intellectuals who write in French focus an international spotlight on the strengths and weaknesses of their societies. Their expressed goals are to stimulate debate and dialogue with others, both at home and in international forums. The reactions their writings provoke range from total indifference to violent hostility, but most observers must respectfully acknowledge that French-language intellectuals in the Maghreb have accomplished repeatedly the task Khatibi has laid out for them: "to accompany the history of his or her epoch."[44] At the same time, the works of francophone intellectuals in the Maghreb direct our attention to the individuals and the events that shape this history itself.

Notes

Unless otherwise noted, all translations from the French are my own.

1. For the purposes of this essay, the term "francophone intellectuals" simply refers to individuals who have published either works of fiction or books of a scholarly nature in the French language, either in the Maghreb or—as is more often the case—in France. I do not include in this group the government techno-crats in Algeria, Morocco, or Tunisia who use French as a "working language." My interest in this analysis is to focus on individuals who have, through their publications, achieved a recognized status as intellectuals, both in their countries of birth and in Europe and North America.

2. Khan, "Algerian Intellectuals," 295.

3. Ben Jelloun, "Le français tel qu'on le rêve," 60.

4. Khatibi, *Penser le Maghreb,* 3–4.

5. Schemeil, "Préface: Passeurs entre deux rives," 13.

6. Addi's essay, "Les intellectuels qu'on assassine," makes several interesting points. However, his entire analysis is grounded on the simplistic assumption that francophone intellectuals work to support the state, which is seen as a modernizing force, while Arabic-language writers defend the traditional structures of their society (131). Unfortunately, when presented in this manner, the multitude of differences among Algerian intellectuals, between their ideas and writings—whether francophone or arabophone—are reduced to deceptively simple proportions. Where, then, would the French writings of Islamic scholars like Malek Bennabi or Mohammed Arkoun fit in? Furthermore, when the novelist Rachid Boudjedra writes fiction in Arabic, he is unsparing in his critique of traditional and patriarchal values.

7. The language issue in Algeria is more complex than in any other nation of the Maghreb. The recent civil crisis has exacerbated the antagonisms between linguistic groups, and the Algerian government continues to manipulate ethnic and social divisions that are drawn along linguistic lines. In December 1996, the Algerian National Transition Council (CNT) passed a law that would prohibit the use of any foreign language in official meetings. Designed to completely eliminate French from the seat of power, and as a peace gesture to Islamic militants, the new law still does not permit any official forum for the use of Berber languages. For further discussion of the language issue and the political heritage of French versus Arabic usage, see the works by Gilbert Grandguillaume and Djamila Saadi.

8. Sayad, "Intellectuels à titre posthume," 5.

9. Burgat, *L'islamisme en face,* 164.

10. For other analyses of the relationship between francophone and arabophone intellectuals and their perceived roles in Algerian society, see Addi, Mediene, Burgat (especially his chapter entitled "Algérie: L'Islamisme contre les intellectuels"), Tengour, and Benrabah. Perhaps the most insightful of these analyses is that of Yves Lacoste. In "Les causes spécifiques du drame algérien," he advances the hypothesis that the political, social, and educational consequences of the language issue have a profound (and often overlooked) importance in determining the causes of the Algerian crisis.

11. Sayad, "Intellectuels à titre posthume," 5.

12. Addi, "Les intellectuels qu'on assassine," 130.

13. Lacoste, "Les causes spécifiques du drame algérien," 12–13.

14. Benmouhoub, "Une interview de Tahar Djaout á la revue *Tin Hinan,*" 211–12.

15. "Hommage à Tahar Djaout," 17.

16. Burgat, *L'islamisme en face,* 155.

17. Boudjedra's status as a francophone intellectual is somewhat problematic. Although he began as a French-language novelist with *La répudiation,* he subsequently turned to publishing fiction in Arabic after 1981. Boudjedra has explained his decision to write in Arabic by his desire to "modernize" the Arabic novel. However, even though Boudjedra began to write in Arabic, he closely collaborates with his Lebanese translator, Antoine Moussali, for the French version of his novels that appear almost immediately after their publication in Arabic. For further information regarding Boudjedra's significant contributions to Algerian literature, see Gafaïti.

18. Gafaïti, "Rachid Boudjedra: The Bard of Modernity," 90.

19. Boudjedra, *FIS de la haine,* 12.

20. Ibid., 16.

21. Ibid., 35.

22. Ibid., 9–10, 20–22.

23. Ibid., 26–28.

24. Ibid., 69.

25. Ibid., 134.

26. At present, there has been no independent confirmation of the rumors that Mimouni's grave was defiled.

27. Mimouni, *De la barbarie en général et de l'intégrisme en particulier,* 87–92.

28. Mimouni's fictional works have also suffered from the vicissitudes of a regime that rarely has been able to accept criticism. For an interesting account of how French literary circles influenced the Algerian regime to finally accept a limited distribution of Mimouni's works in Algeria after 1985, see Gafaïti, "Rachid Mimouni entre la critique algérienne et la critique française."

29. Mimouni, *De la barbarie en général et de l'intégrisme en particulier,* 95–98.

30. Spear, "Politics and Literature," 39.
31. Kaye and Zoubir, *Ambiguous Compromise,* 42.
32. Ibid., 43.
33. Ben Jelloun, *L'homme rompu,* 33.
34. Ibid., 223.
35. Bekri, "On French-Language Tunisian Literature," 179.
36. Béji, *Le désenchantement national,* 14.
37. Béji, "Hélé Béji par elle-même, 33.
38. Béji, *L'imposture culturelle,* 117.
39. Ibid., 54.
40. Ibid., 152.
41. Béji, "Hélé Béji par elle-même," 33.
42. Béji, "La langue est ma maison," 22.
43. Khatibi, *Penser le Maghreb,* 4.
44. Ibid., 5.

10.

THE MAGHREBI ECONOMIES AS EMERGING MARKETS?

Nora Ann Colton

The Maghrebi states have witnessed drastic change and faced many difficulties since securing independence from France. In the past, political instability, coupled with too much government control and regulation, has caused much of the international financial and business community to shun the Maghreb and to focus instead on emerging superstars in Southeast Asia. The 1990s, however, have been a period of transformation in the Maghreb region. Countries now hungry for riches from abroad are rapidly opening up their economies, hoping to attract much-needed foreign investments. In an era when foreign aid has dried up, the race for private investors comes with costs as well as benefits, however. Countries eager to become market superstars easily ignore some of the more pressing issues of their societies in an effort to attract investors.

The three Maghrebi states' lack of attractiveness to investors has resulted partly from their having pursued some form of state capitalism after their independence. In an attempt to spread the fruits of independence as well as to make up for the lack of an indigenous entrepreneur class, the governments of those states used foreign aid and revenues from natural resources to build an inefficient and stagnant bureaucratic machine. By the 1980s, they were burdened by state enterprises and were hence compelled to restructure their economies through privatization and liberalization. They hoped that reforms would help bring in foreign direct investments.

The push to become emerging markets has revitalized the Maghrebi economies and stock markets. According to Andrew Hovaguimian, the

International Finance Corporation (IFC) director for Central Asia, the Middle East, and North Africa, "the sleeping beauties have awakened."[1] Morocco, Tunisia, and Algeria have been attempting to sell off many state-owned enterprises to foreign and domestic entrepreneurs. They also have been opening their economies to foreign investments, particularly by lifting controls and regulations which discourage international investors. As a result, Morocco and Tunisia most likely will be added soon to the IFC's index of emerging-market stocks available to foreign investors.[2] All three countries have concluded that the foreign aid that was available during the Cold War has ended, so only private investment remains for development. International statistics bear out the conclusion: in 1996, investment of private capital in emerging markets rose to $239 billion, more than four times the amount of international aid to the same countries.[3]

This chapter focuses on the factors that have led the Maghrebi states, since the early 1980s, to pursue privatization and liberalization, and on the prospects for their success.

The changes in the global economy have caused much debate in the Maghrebi states, but the intermittent political instability in the region has weighed heavily on those states' attempts to become emerging superstars. Today, the prevalent belief in the region is that privatization is not a mere choice but the key to survival in an era of globalization. That belief has spurred those states, which had been cautiously pursuing privatization and liberalization, to pursue them aggressively.

Inside the Maghrebi states, however, the rhetoric of democracy has given way to economic needs. As in the Near East, the Maghrebi states have slowed the process of democratization, fearing loss of control and replacement by opposition parties that have stronger grassroots support. The governments justify much of their retrenchment on the basis that Islamic fundamentalism lurks within their societies and needs to be stamped out.

In some circles in the Middle East today, the Maghreb is commonly referred to as the "next Southeast Asia." Jonathen Chew of GT Management, for instance, believes that the first criterion for identifying a market that is poised for fast growth is a government willing to change financial and economic policies in favor of a place in the international market.[4] The opening of stock markets in the region, coupled with the rapid pace at which legislation for privatization and liberalization is being passed in Morocco, Tunisia, and Algeria, conforms to that first criterion.

The governments of Morocco, Tunisia, and Algeria for some time now have been selling off assets to private interests, such as individuals or corporations. Liberalization also has been introduced to expand the economic freedom of the private sector and to encourage foreign investment, with a particular interest in portfolio investors. The IMF and the World Bank are playing a prominent role in assisting the three states in meeting their goals.

The second criterion for assessing whether a region or country is about to "take off" is to determine whether the obstacles that caused the country to be noncompetitive in the past have been removed.[5] Among the factors that once made Maghrebi countries unattractive were state capitalism and instability, coupled with little or no regional cooperation. The Maghrebi states have abandoned their former economic structures, which the ruling regimes dominated, in favor of a more market-oriented system. While some degree of political liberalization has taken place, the regimes have kept a firm hold on their societies.

Morocco

Morocco has been hailed as a foreign direct investment success story. Foreign direct investment in Morocco increased from $122 million a year in 1985–89 to $407 million a year in 1990–93, reaching an all-time high in 1997 of $1.2 billion.[6] Morocco now boasts thirteen stockbrokers, a revitalized stock exchange, and investment bankers eager to surpass Morocco's current fifteenth-place ranking in stock-market performance.[7]

In the early 1980s, Morocco was economically troubled. It turned to the IMF and World Bank for capital, and, as usual, the IMF and World Bank required economic reforms for their help.[8] Implementing the reforms produced destabilization. In January 1984, Moroccan students began protesting the increase in university fees, which led to a general demonstration against the hardship suffered under the IMF and World Bank program; however, King Hassan II quickly ended the demonstration with the brutal assistance of the army.

The government continued its economic reforms by restraining spending, revising the tax system, ameliorating the banking system, lifting import restrictions, lowering tariffs, and liberalizing the foreign-exchange regime.[9] As a result, the Moroccan economy improved somewhat. The figures for per capita income, inflation, and the deficit all show signs of improvement. In 1996, inflation reached a record low of 3.0 percent, while the budget deficit stood at about 3 percent of GDP, with GDP growth measured at 11.8 percent.[10]

The 1989 privatization law called for privatizing 112 firms by the end of 1995. It was amended in late 1994 to add 2 additional firms and to extend the deadline to the end of 1998. The privatization of more than one hundred government entities, including the important energy sector, has helped boost the economy.[11] In November 1989, parliament abrogated a 1973 law requiring majority Moroccan ownership of firms in a wide range of industries.[12] In 1993, the government repealed the 1974 decree that limited foreign ownership in petroleum refining and distribution, allowing, for example, Mobil Oil to buy back the Moroccan government's 50 percent share of Mobil's Moroccan subsidiary.[13]

The Moroccan government has changed various rules to attract foreign investment, including creating a number of investment incentives such as exemption from corporate income taxes and import duties. Foreign investment is permitted in all sectors except agricultural land and a few sectors that are deemed important to the state such as phosphate mining.[14]

The banking reforms in Morocco have been more crucial than the selling off of state enterprises. The government most likely will come to the rescue of any failing bank, because banks are still the centers of financial transactions in the country. Morocco has sixteen major banks and five government-owned specialized institutions. Approximately fifteen credit agencies and about ten leasing companies also exist. Other financial institutions remain underdeveloped, including several insurance companies, pension funds, and, of course, the Casablanca stock market.[15]

Until the early 1990s, asset markets were controlled directly by the old French-style *encadrement* system, which allocates sectoral lending among banks. Since financial liberalization, credit is supposed to be allocated freely, with the central bank using indirect methods, such as reserve requirements, as a means of controlling the interest rate and credit volume.[16] Initially, with liberalization, credit expanded rapidly.

Morocco began phasing in Basle standards in 1992;[17] furthermore, Moroccan banks are supervised as a group and must provide statements audited by certified public accountants. Moroccan banks recently have maintained a low spread of 4 percent,[18] but Morocco is being pressured to increase competition and further liberalize the banking sector.[19]

Probably the two factors that most threaten the health of the Moroccan financial sector are its macroeconomic volatility, which is clearly linked to agriculture, and the government's overinvolvement in the banking sector. Although 1996 was a great year for the Moroccan stock market, posting 30 percent returns with GDP growth of 11.8 percent and an inflation rate of 3 percent, 1995 was a period of recession and 1997 is expected to show no growth,[20] primarily because the economy relies heavily on agriculture. In fact, the 1996 GDP growth, excluding the agricultural sector, was only 3.8 percent.[21]

In spite of all the euphoria about the Moroccan economy, unemployment has remained around 16 percent for the past few years.[22] Clearly, Morocco's economy needs further reform so that the health of the financial sector will affect more clearly the overall economy.

The Moroccan government continues to exploit banks for political ends by using them to channel domestic savings to finance government debt. Banks were also required to hold a part of their assets in government bonds paying below-market interest rates.[23] One of the main criticisms of Morocco's banking system by those doing business in Morocco is that corruption and official bureaucracies remain strong. The government is attempting to change the use of commercial banks by the treasury. A decision was made to reduce the minimum securities held by commercial banks from 20 to 15 percent in a move to gradually abolish obligatory lending to the treasury. Banks no longer have to subscribe to treasury bills at below-market rates, so they should have more capital for loans.[24]

The government has liberalized the foreign exchange. The Moroccan dirham is convertible for all current transactions and for some capital transactions, notably capital repatriation by foreign investors (especially if the original investment is registered with the foreign-exchange office). The central bank sets the exchange rate for the dirham against a basket of currencies of its principal trading partners, namely the French franc and other European currencies. The rate has been stable since a 9 percent devaluation in May 1990.[25]

On the positive side, Morocco's foreign debt recently has declined steadily, although it remains a burden on the economy. Foreign debt fell from 128 percent of GDP in 1985 to 59 percent in 1996. Tourism and workers' remittances have been important foreign-currency earners. Worker remittances reached $2.27 billion in 1991, the second-highest inflows to a country in the Middle East and North African region. The budget deficit has dropped significantly because of privatization. It stood at 3.0 percent of GDP in 1996 and may remain the same in 1997 despite predicted higher inflation and an agricultural downturn resulting from the sale of state assets.[26] Nonetheless, Morocco must diversify more because it still depends on agriculture, and the government has fewer and fewer assets to sell. Much of the phenomenal increase in foreign investment in 1997 was a product of the privatization of SANM refining company at $360 million and $263 million from payments by Asia Brown Boveri (ABB) for an initial portion of an electricity production concession.[27]

Agriculture is an important sector of the Moroccan economy, but recently it has suffered a decrease. Agriculture accounts for about 15 to 20 percent of GDP and employs about 40 percent of the workforce; however, it has failed to attract much foreign interest.[28] Agriculture, in fact, has attracted less than 1 percent of foreign direct investment.[29] The recent drought in the region has caused declining yields in exports of fruits and vegetables, thus slowing Morocco's growth in 1994 and 1995. Morocco has also had to import more grain as production hit record lows in 1995. In 1994, cereal production was reported at 9.2 million metric tons, compared to just 1.6 million in 1995.[30] In 1996, cereals recovered to 10 million tons but were expected to drop to 6 million in 1997.[31]

In spite of the drought, agriculture will continue to be an important sector for export growth; in fact, the drought has emphasized the necessity for better water management. Ninety percent of Morocco's agriculture depends on rain, but the government is seeking to improve water management through well-digging and introducing irrigation technologies.

The fishing industry is another key sector of the economy. It earned $500 million from exports last year. Although that industry appears to grow steadily, it now faces the expectation of rapid growth such as it experienced in the early 1990s. The waters around Morocco are overfished, and much tension has developed with Spain over Spanish fishing in Moroccan waters.[32]

The industrial sector is flourishing as a result of the export of phosphate and its derivatives, such as phosphoric acid and fertilizers. Since its integration into the global economy and the signing of a number of free-trade agreements, the Moroccan phosphate industry represents one-third of the Moroccan manufacturing sector.[33] Morocco is also a leading producer and exporter of industrial minerals, which include copper, fluorine, lead, barite, and iron; and the country is involved in oil refining.[34]

The textile industry also has much potential but needs more regional cooperation if it is to live up to its potential goals. Although foreign direct investment in Moroccan textiles has been limited, European companies have subcontracted with Morocco for clothing production. The key to expanding the market for Moroccan textiles will be to devaluate its currency to an appropriate level and to keep wages down. Minimum wages are around $0.85 an hour.[35] So far, Morocco has expanded employment without a significant increase in wages or productivity, making its unit labor cost higher than that of its East Asian competitors and making a regional approach to the textile industry vital.

Overall, reforms have contributed to lower inflation, lower fiscal and current-account deficits, and modest growth in per capita income during the last decade. Morocco, which began its trade reforms early, has virtually eliminated quantitative trade restrictions, attracting much more foreign direct investment, which averaged $516 million between 1992 and 1995.[36] In spite of all the gains, however, unemployment remains high and investor interest in Morocco's agriculture remains limited.

Morocco has put in place a typical IMF and World Bank structural-adjustment program in hopes of stimulating exports and encouraging private investments from home and abroad. Much of what has been accomplished is helping to repay the debt, but the price has been high for many of the citizens, especially the unemployed. In spite of the recent economic success, unemployment remains at 16 percent at the end of 1997; especially high unemployment among university graduates fuels social unrest. In Southwestern Morocco, unemployed university graduates joined a sit-in outside the regional office in Sari of the opposition Socialist Union of Populist Forces to protest government policies on employment. Thousands of university graduates have held demonstrations and hunger strikes recently in hopes of a government response to unemployment. In fact, these educated youth are not alone, as miners in Eastern Morocco have begun to demonstrate against the authorities' closure of a coal mine in Jerrarda, one of the few sources of employment for that region. The government's response has proven consistent: security forces have been used to break up protests with only casual rhetoric for further job creation. Although privatization and liberalization appear to be paying off by attracting foreign direct investments, they may only be short-term speculative investments if reforms in Morocco do not increase.

Tunisia

"Taking into account the new world-trade agreements and our country's partnership accord with the European Union, we must continue our efforts for higher growth while respecting the criteria of rigorous management,"[37] according to Tunisia's central-bank governor, Mohammed Beji Hamda. His words represent a new way of thinking which has many watching Tunisia as a likely candidate for foreign direct investment.

Tunisia had little capital and a meager private sector when it gained its independence. Initially, Tunisia entered a period of state-directed economic development. President Habib Bourguiba created a number of state monopolies, along with controls on foreign trade and prices. Even the private businesses were not without linkages to the state, but as early as 1970, Tunisia attempted to restructure its economy.[38] The price of any major change appeared too high, however, so Tunisia never implemented more than superficial change. The public sector, in fact, flourished at the expense of the private sector until the mid-1980s, when Tunisia ran into a balance-of-payment problem.[39] Coming on the heels of the 1982 debt crisis in Latin America, international sources of funding for such problems had dried up except through the IMF and World Bank; therefore, Tunisia resorted to these financial institutions for assistance.

Tunisia has been a model country in implementing its structural-adjustment program. Much of the program involved trimming the state bureaucracy. At the beginning of the program, state-owned enterprises numbered around 189, but by the end of 1994, the government had cut this number to 143.[40] The Tunisians continued to sell off firms after structural adjustment. The government probably did not sell state-owned businesses any faster than it did because it wanted to avoid mass layoffs and resulting increased unemployment. The government would like to see the reforms create new private-sector jobs to replace inefficient public-sector employment.

Like Morocco, Tunisia sacrificed political freedom to ensure that the structural-adjustment program would be implemented with minimal risk to the regime. Disturbances did take place, and the government dealt with them swiftly and decisively. As in Morocco, many of the demonstrators were young, unemployed people, often with high school and university education.[41] The state at present is overseen by a group of pragmatic politicians who are firmly committed to economic liberalization while justifying intolerance toward opposition groups.

The Tunisian structural-adjustment program has run more smoothly than those of other countries because the labor movement has not played a strong opposing role. The National Labor Federation (UGTT) makes up less than one-fifth of the labor force; furthermore, the UGTT has been co-opted into the privatization program and has yet to pose any threat to the program.[42] Labor's perceived indifference to unions, in fact, has led many foreign firms to demand that employees sign agreements prohibiting union membership.[43] The government is privatizing a number of public enterprises but remains cautious about selling those that employ many, for fear of creating dissatisfaction among laborers—dissatisfaction that presently does not exist.

Tunisia has approached privatization using the British model of "cleaning up" many of the less successful ventures before offering them for sale.

Tourism, Tunisia's single most important sector for generating foreign exchange, enjoyed the fruits of such a cleanup early on. The government spent 27.5MD in 1984 to tidy up unprofitable hotels owned by the state before offering them in direct sales to second parties.[44] The government's method of selling off firms via direct sales has created many debates within government circles in Tunisia. The central bank and those more directly involved in the bourse believe that selling companies through the stock exchange enhances the development of the economy and capital markets. As the government sells off more companies, it probably will sell them through the stock market. The bourse has now introduced a system of electronic trading, and in 1996 a new share-trading system was introduced to correct overpricing.[45]

Privatization has not been without costs. Unemployment has risen to 16 percent. Wages appear to be lagging at a time when the depreciation of the local currency in Tunisia has raised the cost of imported equipment and goods, in turn fueling inflation, which has averaged between 5 and 6 percent in recent years.[46] Furthermore, the human-rights picture is dismal. In October 1992, Amnesty International stated that more than nine thousand Islamists had been detained at some point over the previous two years.[47] Furthermore, the government has kept a tight grip on civil society and opposition politics. The independent press engages in self-censhorship to keep from being closed down while the parliament remains the domain of the ruling party.[48]

Despite its problems, however, Tunisia has had one of the highest per capita GDP growth rates in the Middle East during the 1990s. It has also had one of the highest growth rates for nonoil exports, at 10.5 percent. In addition, textiles now stand as one of the largest employers of Tunisia's export-related sectors, providing great potential for additional growth.[49]

The Tunisian government has encouraged foreign direct investment. Like many emerging market "wannabes," the government has been easing many restrictions to allow foreign and domestic entrepreneurs to operate in Tunisia. The reforms actually began in the 1970s under Prime Minister Hedi Nouira. These initial reforms were an attempt to rescind much of the hold Ben Salah had on the economy prior to his ouster in 1969.[50] His government passed a series of laws aimed at opening the economy in the 1970s and early 1980s, before putting the structural-adjustment program in place.[51] Those early laws were aimed at foreign investors, giving them tax concessions and duty-free imports of equipment and raw materials as a means of fostering foreign direct investment. Later, when the IMF and World Bank structural-adjustment program was phased in, private investment in Tunisia took off. In 1970, private investment was at $16 million; by 1986 it had risen to $159 million.[52] Total foreign investment in Tunisia from 1980 to 1993 is estimated to have exceeded $2.85 billion.[53]

By 1994, however, a new unified investment code was needed to replace the early liberalization laws. The new code is intended to simplify investment further and, indirectly, to encourage private investment in industries in which the government believes Tunisia has a competitive advantage. Some of the features of the new code exempt investors from taxes on 35 percent of reinvested profits and income and allow investors to use an accelerated-depreciation schedule for long-term capital. Limited taxation on capital goods exists, with a host of incentives for export-oriented businesses.[54]

Despite having opened markets to foreign direct investment, Tunisia has been accused of moving too slowly at opening up firms to foreign ownership and capital-market reforms. Tunisia still limits foreign ownership of firms to 49 percent.[55] In the past, the government did not allow investors to invest directly in Tunisia, but this appears to be changing. In 1996, the Tunis stock exchange announced the first sale of shares in a Tunisian company to foreign investors.[56]

The most significant changes in the financial sectors relate to the role of the central bank, which is planning to increase its advisory capacity in the economy. The central bank has deregulated interest rates and allowed commercial banks to extend long-term credit while continuing to closely monitor Tunisia's level of external debt.[57]

Tunisia, unlike so many developing countries today, has never rescheduled any of its debt. External debt service has recently increased, but it increased because the Tunisian dinar was devalued in 1993. Approximately 73 percent of the country's foreign debt is in U.S. dollars or dollar-linked currencies. The central bank uses a sophisticated debt-portfolio-management system by aligning debt characterized by seasonal variation and by aligning debt-service payments with the currencies of anticipated export receipts.[58] Tunisia has never had to reschedule its debt, so investors consider the country a good credit risk. This has helped Tunisia secure the resources it needed to get its export-led growth off the ground.

Overall, Tunisia appears to be creating real growth. Aside from tourism (Tunisia's single most important generator of foreign exchange), textiles, and petroleum, agriculture has been a strong sector; however, a drought during 1993–95 severely affected agriculture. In Morocco, agriculture represents 21 percent of the GDP, but in Tunisia, agriculture represents only 15 percent.[59] Furthermore, privatization of state-owned farms and the incentives that have been offered to investors in the new investment code have spurred growth in poultry, dairy, and livestock. The government also has begun a program to improve the infrastructure, with tenders being issued in communication, roadways, and waterworks.

Tunisia has opened itself to the global economy through its membership in GATT and accords with the European Union.[60] At the end of 1996, the Tunisian GDP's average growth rate was 4.5 percent, with an average inflation rate between 5 and 6 percent. Furthermore, the government budget deficit decreased from 5.5 percent of GDP in 1986 to 2.6 in 1994, while debt service, as a percentage of exports, declined from 27.9 to 18.5 percent.[61] It is no surprise, then, that Tunisia is being hailed as an IMF and World Bank success story in spite of its slow pace of privatization and democratization.

Algeria

In spite of political instability since 1991, Algeria has been attempting to phase in an IMF and World Bank structural-adjustment plan. The absence of capital and an indigenous private sector led to a socialist experiment of heavy state intervention, especially in the hydrocarbon sector of the economy. The government succeeded in developing hydrocarbons into a revenue generator; however, after years of state intervention under the authoritarian regime of Houari Boumediene, Algeria proved unable to create a diversified economy which would sustain development for the people. The country depended on the hydrocarbon industry and became the victim of fluctuating oil prices.[62]

Like Tunisia, Algeria began the slow process of reforming its economy before it was compelled to do so by international organizations. Algeria, having implemented its own version of socialism rather than state capitalism, was much more sensitive to its inability to produce results; consequently, it abandoned the socialist experience to enter into an economic strategy with more market orientation. The reformation was to be known as the *infitah* (opening) of the Algerian economy under the leadership of President Chadli Bendjedid, but the inability and unwillingness of the regime to implement timely reform proved catastrophic. Much of the foot-dragging by the regime was an attempt to create support for economic austerity measures by casting them in the nationalist roots of the 1954–62 revolution. However, in a country with a rapidly growing young generation who did not identify with this rallying cry, the government's rhetoric fell on ears that were not only deaf but even hostile.[63]

Privatization of state-owned enterprises was not pursued at all; meanwhile, the manner in which liberalization was ushered in appears to have fueled political upheaval, as the government had overestimated its ability to win the people's support by using nationalism as the main playing card. The citizens, after two decades of socialism, were not committed to the changes that were taking place; nor were they prepared economically to endure them. The restructuring of the economy and the concomitant ending of the welfare state were imposed on citizens who were apprehensive about the ability of reforms to succeed and the burden they were being asked to bear by a regime perceived to be corrupt and inept at managing the state's affairs.[64]

The riots of October 1988 were the turning point for Algerian reforms. In their aftermath, the regime accelerated political liberalization and economic reform. A group of pragmatic technocrats was brought to the forefront to carry out the reforms; thus, since 1989 and despite moments of hesitation, the Algerian government has acted much more decisively in implementing reforms.

One of the major difficulties Algeria faced before the IMF intervention was its balance of payments. With mounting imports, it no longer could pay the installments on its foreign debt and simultaneously finance its growth investment. In 1994, Algerian authorities concluded an IMF agreement and a subsequent Paris Club debt rescheduling of $5.3 billion, which allowed the central bank of Algeria to rebuild its holdings of hard currency. In May 1995, the bank concluded a $3.2 billion rescheduling of its commercially held foreign debt. The IMF also extended credits totaling $1.8 billion for the reform program.[65]

The bloody fight between the Islamic movement's extremist wing and the state security services has hurt Algeria's economy and reform by deterring foreign investment. Although it has been reluctant to privatize public firms, Algeria attempted a pilot project in 1995 by putting five public hotels up for sale, but because of the unstable political situation, it has had few offers.[66] The dilemma for Algeria is that, in order for the structural-adjustment program to succeed, the country needs to have the type of economic and political stability that will promote private-sector activities. Unemployment (estimated at 25 percent) and inflation (16 percent), in fact, have helped to fuel the violence.[67] As World Bank president James Wolfenshohn stated during a visit to Algeria, "The world must feel that there is a change in Algeria. The Algerian problem is often discussed abroad, and it is necessary to show to the world that Algeria is getting out of the violence cycle."[68] President Liamine Zeroual's administration has worked hard to end that cycle. In November 1995, presidential elections were held in the hope of bringing about national reconciliation. Legislative elections were held in June 1997 as part of an institutionalization process, which were concluded in late 1997 when municipal and departmental elections were held. Yet the bloodletting in Algeria reached its all-time high in 1997, and the international support that the regime had enjoyed began to dissolve with its inability and unwillingness to bring about a political solution. In fact, in a policy reversal, France criticized the Algerian authorities' handling of domestic affairs. The French Foreign Ministry spokesman Yves Doutriaux was quoted as saying, "It is every government's duty to enable its citizens to live in peace and safety by putting an end to violence."[69]

The market-oriented reform measures implemented in Algeria in the last two years are impressive by any standard. The socialist state has definitely become a thing of the past. Foreign trade has undergone a process of liberalization. In the last year, the government has abolished lists of restricted import goods. The state also has made foreign exchange more readily available to importers in both the private and public sectors by allowing commercial banks to buy foreign exchange from the Algerian central bank (BCA). The dinar has been devalued, in the hope that one day it will be fully convertible. The government is attempting to control inflation by following a policy of strict austerity, in which spending in many categories (such as on infrastructure and wages for public-sector workers) fell after adjustment for inflation. The government is also tightening monetary policy. Interest rates are averaging 24 percent and, with inflation still high, there is little indication that those rates will change soon.[70]

State enterprises, which make up most of the industrial sector, are being reformed without, however, showing much sign of improvement. Most of the problems those firms face are endemic to socialist enterprises: poor management and low use of capacity. The government continues to restructure many of those firms and to close others. The IMF and the World Bank are now calling on Algeria to privatize them, but the current political situation makes prospects for buyers slim.

Capital markets and portfolio investments are not on the government's agenda. Authorities instead seek more foreign investment and have introduced an attractive investment code, modeled on those of Tunisia and Morocco. The code, which took effect in 1993, offers many incentives for foreign investments. However, without political stability, much of the economic reform appears to be in vain. Algeria, meanwhile, has no choice but to continue its structural-adjustment program, because it can ill afford to lose its backers, who insist upon a formula of privatization and liberalization.

The hydrocarbon sector has not been affected significantly by the political violence. A 1986 law governs exploration, exploitation, and pipeline transportation of hydrocarbons and allows foreign companies to enter into joint ventures with the state hydrocarbon giant, Sonatrach. In 1991, an amendment to the original law allowed foreign companies to own up to 49 percent of the production of existing oil fields. It also provided for foreign participation in natural-gas exploration.[71] Since 1991, a number of American companies signed exploration and production contracts. Sonatrach, the state-owned firm, plans to invest about $14 billion over the next four years to raise its export earnings from $8.6 billion in 1994 to $12.2 billion by 1999.[72]

Another important sector in the Algerian economy is agriculture. Although it suffered droughts in 1993–94 and again in 1997, agriculture is expected to grow over the next few years. Farmers have delayed investing until state-owned lands are transferred to private ownership. The agricultural sector makes up 12 percent of GDP. All controls have been lifted from produce prices, and subsidies for agricultural production and guaranteed minimum wages for farm workers have been abolished. Agriculture employs nearly one-fourth of the labor force. The key crops include cereals, dairy products, and fruits and vegetables.[73]

Because of the violence, Algeria remains inhospitable to emerging-market capital. However, the atmosphere may change if political reforms accompany the economic restructuring.

Conclusion

When most of us think of emerging markets, the countries of Southeast Asia come to mind. These countries have consumed 70 percent of the foreign direct investment into developing countries.[74] Furthermore, these economies have created much debate and even challenges to the discourse of development. Most of Southeast Asia has earned the status of newly industrialized without the perceived pitfalls of foreign aid that have plagued Latin American, Africa, and the Middle East. Yet their success has not mollified certain individuals who see human rights and freedom to be variables as important as economic growth and prosperity. What makes the Southeast Asian model interesting is the delinking of economic development from political liberalization.

Experts have long agreed that economic development has a political component. The debate appears to be whether effective governance/development and democracy can be separated. If effective governance is essential for development and capital generation, are freedom and democracy?

Few observers associate Southeast Asia with democracy, but they definitely associate it with economic growth. In fact, much of the political stability that investors historically have found attractive in the region is due to the brutality and "no-nonsense approach" of the regimes. However, some academics and professionals have been persuaded by the Southeast Asian model. For them, the absence of political freedom is not an issue, for these observers believe that once economic development is achieved, political freedom will follow. Little empirical evidence supports this theory.

If we think about development without real democracy in North Africa, we should not be naive about its pitfalls. Foreign direct investment is, by its very nature, volatile; consequently, a political undercurrent left to fester could have major implications. These implications would be compounded by external funding to support the economy. In 1995 and 1997, Southeast Asian countries experienced alarming shocks in their economies, illustrating the unreliable nature of foreign investment.[75]

In 1995, equity and bond markets in Hong Kong, Thailand, Indonesia, Singapore, and much of the rest of Asia slid sharply, forcing governments to intervene to support their currencies. Although some analysts blamed an earthquake in Japan and others blamed the Mexican debt crisis, others blamed something much less specific: the emerging-market mutual funds, which for many countries are becoming the faceless foreign aid of the 1990s. According to Lipper Analytical, a research firm, in 1990 there were nine such American funds, with total assets of $775 million, investing in equities in the Pacific region; by 1994 there were forty-four, with assets of $12 billion.[76] Bond funds dedicated to Asian emerging markets have grown rapidly, too.

These firms began selling their assets in January 1995 for a number of reasons. First, many fund managers were unnerved by the Mexican crisis and wanted to bring down their overall risk exposure as quickly as possible. Second, others wanted to move cash from Asia to Latin America, where prices were lower.

In 1997, Southeast Asia had been hailed as anything but a success story. Southeast Asian currencies, led by Indonesia, fell in the second half of the year at record levels. In fact, a number of these countries have been forced to seek IMF bailouts along with measures to restructure their economies.

However, inside Indonesia and other Southeast Asian countries is a belief that noneconomic factors and political maneuvering undermined their countries' currencies. In fact, Indonesian officials have been so bold as to accuse investors and business persons of spreading negative rumors to sabotage the economy and then profit off the situation.[77]

There are many lessons to be learned from this Asian experience. First, North African states need to appreciate that direct investment, and not flightier portfolio investments, may reduce a country's risk to volatile finances. Consequently, Tunisia's slow approach to opening its capital markets may prove to be its saving grace, for no matter how strong the economic factors of a country are, they can be brought down when financing is risk averse.

Second, predictability of central-bank action is crucial to effective competition for an often volatile pool of international capital.[78] Banking crises and financial liberalization appear to be walking hand in hand; consequently, a cautious approach to liberalization, with rules and regulation that avoid the pitfalls of other countries, is all the more important for North Africa.

Finally, issues of political freedom and human rights often come up in the context of Southeast Asia; however, they appear at present to take second place to economic growth. Morocco, Tunisia, and Algeria have all suppressed political opposition in their pursuit of economic success. As the case of Algeria has echoed through the region, suppression of opposition groups often can have a high price down the road. This "new foreign aid," in the form of foreign investments, will move to another region or country. It is also insufficient to herald Southeast Asia as an example in an era when popular wisdom rejects a narrow definition of development. In much of the development literature today, sustainable development is an important topic of discussion. It takes into account structural transformation of an economy, along with preservation of the environment and a political system that provides for human rights and freedom—effective governance. Although the North African states, including Algeria, have made many cosmetic changes to their political systems, none have gone far enough to sustain them in the future.

The past few years have witnessed much positive economic change in a number of North African countries, along with a much more pragmatic approach to dealing with other regional actors. However, we must not let the economic successes overshadow the need for more prudent reforms.

Notes

This paper is part of a larger study on emerging markets in North Africa.

1. Dourian, "Banker Says North African Markets Stir."
2. "Looking to Join the Caravan," 75.
3. "Banking in Emerging Markets Survey," 6.
4. Taylor, "Fringe Benefits," 62.
5. Ibid.
6. "Foreign Investment in Morocco Triples in 1997."
7. "Looking to Join the Caravan," 75.
8. U.S. Department of State, *Economic Policy and Trade Practices: Morocco.*
9. Ibid.
10. International Market Insight, *Economic Trends: Morocco.*
11. U.S. International Trade Administration, *Morocco: Executive Summary.*
12. U.S. International Trade Administration, *Morocco: Investment Climate.*
13. U.S. Department of State, *Economic Policy and Trade Practices: Morocco.*
14. U.S. International Trade Administration, *Morocco: Investment Climate.*
15. Country Commercial Guides, *Morocco: Trade and Project Financing.*
16. Ibid.
17. U.S. International Trade Administration, *Morocco: Investment Climate.* The Basle Accord of 1988 requires commercial banks in signatory countries to have capital equal to at least 8 percent of their risk-adjusted assets.
18. World Bank, *Claiming the Future,* 27.
19. At a conference sponsored by *Euromoney Magazine,* there were calls for further liberalization of the banking system (International Market Insight, *Economic Trends: Morocco*).
20. "Morocco's Economy Seen at Zero Growth in 1997."
21. Ibid.
22. U.S. Department of State, *Economic Policy and Trade Practices: Morocco.*
23. Country Commercial Guides, *Morocco: Trade and Project Financing.*
24. Dourian, "Moroccan Banks Gear Up for Competition."
25. U.S. Department of State, *Background Notes: Morocco.*
26. "Morocco's Economy Seen at Zero Growth in 1997."
27. "Foreign Investment in Morocco Triples in 1997."
28. U.S. Department of State, *Background Notes: Morocco.*
29. From 1992 to 1995, agriculture received substantially lower foreign investment inflows than other sectors in the economy (Louraoui and Hammoud, *Industry Sector Analysis, Morocco: Franchising*).
30. U.S. International Trade Administration, *Morocco: Economic Trends and Outlook.*
31. "Morocco's Economy Seen at Zero Growth in 1997."
32. U.S. International Trade Administration, *Morocco: Economic Trends and Outlook.*

33. U.S. Department of State, *Background Notes: Morocco.*

34. Ibid.

35. U.S. International Trade Administration, *Morocco: Investment Climate.*

36. Louraoui and Hammoud, *Industry Sector Analysis, Morocco: Franchising.*

37. Barrouhi, "Tunisia's Central Bank Calls for Higher Growth."

38. Harik, "Privatization and Development in Tunisia," 212.

39. U.S. Department of State, *Economic Policy and Trade Practices: Tunisia.*

40. U.S. International Trade Administration, *Tunisia: Economic Trends and Outlook.*

41. Seddon, "Riot and Rebellion in North Africa," 119.

42. There are many reports that the UGTT receives substantial subsidies from the government in addition to their officially mandated monthly contributions. See U.S. Department of State, *Economic Policy and Trade Practices: Tunisia.*

43. U.S. International Trade Administration, *Tunisia: Investment Climate.*

44. For a more detailed account on how this sector has been privatized, see Harik, "Privatization and Development in Tunisia," 216–18.

45. "Looking to Join the Caravan," 75.

46. U.S. Department of State, *Economic Policy and Trade Practices: Tunisia, Key Economic Indicators.*

47. *Human Rights Watch World Report, 1993,* 344.

48. Ibid.

49. Ibid.

50. Harik, "Privatization and Development in Tunisia," 211.

51. Ibid., 222.

52. Ibid.

53. U.S. International Trade Administration, *Tunisia: Investment Climate.*

54. U.S. Department of State, *Economic Policy and Trade Practices: Tunisia.*

55. "Looking to Join the Caravan," 75.

56. Barrouhi, "Tunisia Makes First Share Offering to Foreigners."

57. U.S. International Trade Administration, *Tunisia: Economic Trends and Outlook.*

58. U.S. Department of State, *Economic Policy and Trade Practices: Tunisia.*

59. World Bank, *Claiming the Future,* 116.

60. U.S. Department of State, *Economic Policy and Trade Practices: Tunisia.*

61. U.S. International Trade Administration, *Tunisia: Domestic Economy.*

62. For a discussion of Algeria's political economy prior to implementing reforms, see Vandewalle, "Breaking with Socialism."

63. Ibid., 190.

64. Colton and Woodworth, "North African Miracle."

65. U.S. International Trade Administration, *Algeria: Economic Trends and Outlook.*

66. Ibid.

67. U.S. International Trade Administration, *Algeria: Domestic Economy.*

68. "World Bank Chief Ends Algeria Visit on High Note."

69. "France Presses Algeria on Reforms After Massacres."

70. U.S. International Trade Administration, *Algeria: Economic Trends and Outlook.*

71. U.S. Department of Energy, *Algeria: Country Analysis Brief.*

72. U.S. International Trade Administration, *Algeria: Economic Trends and Outlook.*

73. Ibid.

74. "Race for Competitiveness and High Growth," 1.

75. "World's Emerging Markets All at Sea," 67.

76. Ibid.

77. "Minister Says Non-economic Factors behind Free-fall of Rupiah."

78. These lessons are discussed in the broader context of emerging markets in "World's Emerging Markets All at Sea," 68.

11.

THE ARAB MAGHREB UNION: MYTH AND REALITY

Robert A. Mortimer

The Union du Maghreb Arabe (UMA, Arab Maghreb Union), founded with euphoria in 1989, has fallen far short of the hopes that were vested in it at its creation. In signing the Treaty of Marrakech, the heads of state of Algeria, Libya, Mauritania, Morocco, and Tunisia pledged to meet every six months in order to build a North African common market that would transform the region's economic capabilities. Instead, they met irregularly only six times before Morocco called for a suspension of the organization's activities in December 1995. Although the president of Tunisia sent a letter to his peers on the occasion of the eighth anniversary of the UMA in February 1997, calling upon them to overcome what he called "conjunctural difficulties" and resuscitate the organization, the fact was that major unresolved political differences had brought the UMA to a state of, at best, prolonged hibernation.[1]

Foremost among these differences was the dispute over Western Sahara which has deeply divided Algeria and Morocco since the mid-1970s. Indeed, much of the political momentum that produced the ardors of Marrakech sprang from a 1988 diplomatic rapprochement between these two states, which led in turn to the acceptance by Morocco and the POLISARIO Front in August 1988 of a United Nations–brokered plan to conduct a referendum in the contested territory. This matter, still unresolved in 1997, was sorely compounded by Algeria's domestic strife, the international sanctions leveled against Libya, and the generally turbulent situation in the Arab world—all of which distracted the presumed partners from their ambitious project of building an economic union.

Certainly the obstacles facing the UMA are economic as well as political. In *Le Grand Maghreb et l' Europe,* Bishara Khader cautioned against undue optimism regarding the union's prospects. He pointed out that in 1989 inter-Maghreb trade was only 3 percent of the member states' total trade (as compared with 40 percent for the six original partners of the EEC in 1957). Moreover, what was somewhat precipitously agreed upon at Marrakech in February 1989, Khader argued, could "just as quickly be undone."[2] The economic underpinnings being so fragile, the UMA depends even more than other regional economic schemes on the political will of the partners to place a very high priority upon regional cooperation. In the turmoil of the 1990s, this precondition has not been met.

Algeria is the geopolitical core of any Maghrebi construction, and it has been wracked by political instability virtually from the day the UMA was born. Less than a week after the signature of the Treaty of Marrakech, Algerians by referendum approved a new constitution that ended the country's single-party system. A few months later, the Front Islamique du Salut (Islamic Salvation Front, FIS) was certified as a legitimate political party, unleashing a torrent of popular opposition to the regime of Chadli Bendjedid. The challenge of the Islamists—first as an electoral rival and then as an armed insurrectionary movement—has consumed the attention of Algeria's rulers, leaving relatively little place for matters of regional integration. Moreover, the return of the military to the forefront of Algerian politics stiffened the government's posture on the Western Sahara issue. Indeed, for Algeria, the very idea of a "Greater Maghreb" was as much a geopolitical strategy for resolving this conflict as it was a project for economic union. Tensions in Algerian-Moroccan relations, especially after the unseating of Bendjedid in January 1992, have brought the UMA to a virtual standstill.

A brief review of the six UMA summits highlights how Sahrawis, Islamists, and a host of political crises affecting the region stunted the growth of the organization. The summits are extremely important because the treaty instituting the UMA designates the presidential council, comprising heads of state of the five member countries, as the supreme organ of the union. Article 5 of the treaty states that "the Presidential Council of the Union holds ordinary sessions once every six months," and Article 6 stipulates that "the Presidential Council is alone authorized to make decisions. Decisions are taken by the unanimous consent of its members." The process therefore relies upon the ability of the heads of state to meet regularly in order to build the architecture of a regional organization.

In fact, the first of the presumably semiannual summit meetings did not occur until January 1990. Both Libya and Tunisia proposed to hold a meeting in the summer of 1989 (six months after the founding date of February 17, 1989); for President Qadaffi, this could have been a splendid way to celebrate the twentieth anniversary of his takeover of power on September 1, 1989. As the UMA had little to show for its first six months of activity, however, the other members expressed reluctance to convene at that moment. Thus was established a pattern of delay that became the norm. Tunisia, which had played an active role in the drafting of the Treaty of Marrakech, was determined to host the first meeting of the presidential council, and eventually President Ben Ali convinced his colleagues to convene in Carthage in January 1990.

Tunisia, which wanted the UMA secretariat lodged in Tunis (from which the Arab League was about to depart), emerged as the organization's strongest booster at a moment when Algerian-Moroccan relations had already begun to sour over the very slow implementation of the UN peace plan for Western Sahara. At the Carthage summit, Ben Ali called upon his partners to prepare for the challenge posed by the European Community's Single European Act, which was rapidly moving Western Europe to a much more comprehensive common market. He won agreement on the principle of establishing a permanent secretariat for the organization, although no decision was taken on where to locate it. Ben Ali also brokered numerous bilateral meetings—notably between King Hassan and Bendjedid, in recognition of the renewal of political tensions between them. The Tunisians saw clearly that their hopes for a dynamic regional organization were largely hostage to the quality of Algerian-Moroccan relations. As a small state bordered by two large states, Tunisia saw the overarching framework of the UMA as a sort of potential protective shield; projecting a reputation for regional leadership also served the Tunisian national interest.

The heads of state met again in Algiers on July 22–23, 1990, a rare instance of the six-month timetable being respected. They declared their intention to implement a customs union by 1995, but this goal was not met. Otherwise, the leaders marked time with no decision on a headquarters or a secretary-general for the organization. One might well have expected Bendjedid to propose more ambitious objectives for the UMA, if only as a tactic to counter the FIS, which had just swept to victory in June 1990 local elections. Algeria had often practiced international leadership as one means to legitimize its domestic regime. Aggressive promotion of the popular ideal of Maghrebi unity might have refurbished the reputation of a president under political attack. Instead, the rise of the FIS had the effect of turning Bendjedid's attention inward.

The Persian Gulf crisis, erupting immediately after the Algiers summit, revealed a total lack of unity among the five member states of the UMA. When the Arab League convened in the aftermath of the Iraqi invasion of Kuwait to vote on a resolution sponsored by Saudi Arabia, each of the five governments managed to take a different stance. Morocco voted for it and eventually sent troops to join the American-led coalition. Libya voted against the resolution, while Algeria abstained and Tunisia absented itself altogether from the meeting in Cairo. Mauritania attended the meeting and expressed reservations about the resolution, neither voting nor officially abstaining. Although public opinion throughout the Maghreb was widely pro-Iraqi (or perhaps more specifically against the deployment of Western military forces in the Arab world) the member governments of the UMA did little to coordinate their diverse policy responses to the eventual war in the Gulf.

Likewise, the events of Desert Storm contributed to the delay that attended the third summit, formally scheduled for January 1991 but actually held two months later in Ras Lanouf in Libya. On this occasion, however, King Hassan was absent, and the meeting served little purpose. Indeed, the main decision reached was to reconvene once again in Libya in "extraordinary session" shortly thereafter, ostensibly to assess the consequences and fallout of the just-completed Gulf War. Yet after members fixed a date first of April 25 and then of June 8, this plan was ultimately abandoned as a new phase of Algeria's political crisis broke out in May–June 1991.

Instead, the diplomatic calendar shifted to the fourth summit, which by diplomatic rotation ought to have been held in Mauritania. Morocco, however, was eager to reassert its role in Maghrebi affairs as the Sahrawi question was moving back into the diplomatic spotlight with the deployment of the first contingent of the United Nations Mission for the Referendum in Western Sahara (MINURSO) in early September 1991. The king thus twisted the arm of President Ould Taya, who had his hands full with the impending Mauritanian elections. Ould Taya deferred to Hassan, and the summit took place in Casablanca on September 15–16 (minus Colonel Qadaffi, who thus returned the king's snub of the Ras Lanouf summit and began to distance Libya from the organization).

In hosting summit number four, Morocco was seeking several objectives. One was to secure Rabat as the headquarters for the UMA rather than to allow the organization born in Marrakech to slip away to Tunis. In this the king was successful, while Tunisia settled for the consolation prize: the post of secretary-general, which was bestowed upon the Tunisian Mohammed Amamou a month later. The latter, a career diplomat and former ambassador to Rabat, had been serving as Ben Ali's special diplomatic advisor and secretary of state for Maghrebi affairs prior to his nomination as "Mr. Maghreb."[3] If King Hassan was rewarded with the headquarters, he was less fortunate in achieving his other goals. He hoped, somewhat unrealistically, to place the Western Sahara issue on the agenda so that his partners might express their backing for the Moroccan approach to the UN referendum. The local press called upon Morocco's UMA partners "to distance themselves once and for all from the secessionist misdirection" which had "hobbled the unionist process."[4] Algeria, however, persuaded the others to leave this matter to the United Nations; neither did the organization vest King Hassan with any particular mandate for his upcoming trip to Washington or adopt any common stance on the Madrid Middle East Peace Conference, scheduled for the following month.

Rather, the fourth summit served essentially to parcel out the future institutions of the UMA. The parliament, or consultative council (*majliss choura*), composed of twenty representatives per member state, was to hold its session in Algiers. The judicial organ, entrusted with interpretation of the Treaty of Marrakech and UMA conventions, was to sit in Nouakchott. An investment and foreign-trade bank was to be located in Tunis, while Libya was assigned the responsibility of setting up a Maghrebi university and academy of sciences. Thus, some two-and-a-half years after its founding, the UMA established a more permanent organizational framework, especially insofar as the secretariat was concerned. With the exception of the latter, however, none of these institutions ever really functioned: the consultative council, after an inaugural session, has been in adjournment since 1992; the three-story building provided to house the court in Nouakchott is practically empty; the academy and university have become "exclusively Libyan institutions"; and the bank, once projected to open in 1996, is still officially in the planning stage.[5] Moreover, more than a year passed before the next "semiannual" summit meeting could be convened.

The ideal time for Mauritania's turn to host the summit appeared to be February 17, 1992, the third anniversary of the founding of the regional organization. The coup in Algeria (where the army had just deposed Bendjedid), Libya's tribulations with France, Britain, and the United

States (which were demanding the extradition of Libyan nationals suspected of terrorism), and Mauritania's own electoral timetable all got in the way, however; therefore, the summit was postponed to May, then to June, then to September. Clearly the Nouakchott summit was not a high priority for the embattled regimes of North Africa as the months slipped away throughout 1992. Finally a date was set for November, but at the last moment, both Qadaffi and King Hassan announced that they would not be present.

Instead, this became the occasion for the Algerians to return in force as the new president of the High State Committee (HCE), Ali Kafi, arrived with a large and diverse delegation on what was his first trip abroad since assuming that post in July after the assassination of Mohammed Boudiaf. Although Morocco was represented by its prime minister and Libya by its ambassador to Morocco, the presence of the Algerian, Tunisian, and Mauritanian heads of state seemed almost a throwback to December 1983, when Mauritania joined Algeria and Tunisia in the Treaty of Fraternity and Concord, viewed by many observers as the point of departure for the notion of a "Greater Maghreb."[6] Once again, the Tunis-Algiers-Nouakchott axis appeared to be the backbone of a region to which Libya's attachment was ephemeral and Morocco's circumstantial. By the same token, the decision to rotate the chairmanship back to Ben Ali in January 1993 highlighted Tunisia's role as the most committed of the member states to the organization. Ben Ali is the only chief of state to have been present at every summit, and Tunisia was the only member to have ratified all UMA conventions as of November 1992. It was agreed that Ben Ali would hold the chairmanship for twelve months, the members having acknowledged at Nouakchott that the notion of semiannual summits was overambitious.

The fifth "summit" (absent two heads of state) also finally provided an annual operating budget of $1.75 million (or $350,000 per member state) to the secretariat, for which Amamou had assembled a modest staff of fifteen civil servants recruited from the member countries. Urged along by President Ben Ali, the secretariat during 1993 generated a number of joint projects and draft agreements on relatively noncontroversial topics, like building a trans-Maghreb highway or constructing other regionwide facilities. These functional projects did not immediately spill over into a heightened spirit of cooperation, however. Even the new timetable of annual summits proved beyond the reach of the organization, as the political uncertainty in Algeria took priority over region building. Only after Liamine Zeroual was installed as Algeria's new executive, at the end of January 1994, did Ben Ali undertake to organize another UMA summit.

This sixth (and to date, last) summit took place in Tunis in April 1994. As he had four years earlier, Ben Ali tried to rally the troops around the theme of regional integration. But once again, not all the commanders were present, Hassan II and Qadaffi absenting themselves yet another time. Both leaders felt that the organization had failed them: in the king's case, it had not cleared the way to a definitive Moroccan takeover of Western Sahara; in the colonel's case, it had done little to persuade the great powers to lift the sanctions that the Security Council had placed on Libya. Almost all that the Tunis summit achieved was to pass the torch of the UMA chairmanship from Ben Ali to Zeroual.

The latter, however, lacked the Tunisian's dogged commitment to the regional idea; moreover, he had his hands full with the emergence of the Armed Islamic Group (GIA), whose terrorist exactions were even more disruptive than the political challenge of the FIS. Zeroual invested little political energy in the UMA, organizing a meeting of member-state finance ministers in January 1995, for example, to discuss such burning issues as tax harmonization policy or planning for the (today still unimplemented) investment and trade bank. After a year of desultory attention, Zeroual was preparing to hand the chairmanship on to Qadaffi when Libya announced that it would not accept that honor, on the grounds that the UMA "had not succeeded in meeting the aspirations of the Maghrebin people for unity, economic integration, and freedom of movement."[7] It remained only for Morocco's December call for a freeze to cast a deep chill over the organization.

The founders of the UMA (of whom all but Bendjedid remain at the head of their respective states) were right to call for frequent and regular summitry. The fact that only six summits have been held during a period for which sixteen were originally projected (through February 1997) attests not to an error on their part but rather to an insight into the necessity of top-level political cooperation as an absolute requirement of regional integration in the Maghreb. The review of the breakdown of summitry underscores the fact that the concept of a Grand Maghreb was, and remains, much more a diplomatic than an economic artifact. The political will of the heads of state is the motor that drives or stalls the regional construct. Lengthy delays attended the first, third, and fifth summits, because one or another head of state had a political reason to put off the conference; even the sixth failed to take place within the new annual schedule because of national political concerns. The logic of national interest has consistently overridden the logic of functional cooperation or economic integration.

The reasons for the breakdown of the UMA process are the mirror image of the determinants of its initial creation. The impetus that produced the UMA in 1989 had much more to do with diplomacy than economic cooperation. Both Algeria and Morocco conceived of the organization as a regional framework within which a solution to the long disagreement over the status of Western Sahara could be finessed.[8] Just a month before the treaty signature, King Hassan had held unprecedented talks with representatives of the POLISARIO Front, and there was widespread optimism that the United Nations soon would supervise a referendum on the destiny of the former Spanish colony. The problem was that Algeria and Morocco were each assuming that the other would back off from its previous stance in the dispute for the sake of advancing cooperation in the new regional organization. It appeared that the question of whether Western Sahara became the sixth entity within the AMU, as an independent state or as a southern province of Morocco, might lose enough salience for both sides to risk their chances in a referendum.

In retrospect, it is clear that each side misread the other's intentions. They exaggerated the long-term impact of the rapprochement of 1988. King Hassan read Bendjedid as a pragmatic reformer and did not anticipate the political challenge that led to Bendjedid's removal. Bendjedid gambled on a mellowing of the Moroccan stance, which never occurred. Despite the deployment of a United Nations force whose mission was to organize such a referendum, neither side—the Algerian-backed POLISARIO Front nor Morocco—has backed down on the crucial procedural question of voter eligibility (Morocco essentially seeking to pack the voting lists with individuals not on the 1974 census rolls).[9] Morocco's obstructionist posture has left Algeria ill disposed to forge ahead with regional integration.

Certainly the unresolved Western Sahara issue is not the only matter to undermine the Algerian-Moroccan rapprochement of the late 1980s. Tension attendant upon the Islamists' destabilization of Algeria has further harmed their relationship. There have been Algerian complaints about Moroccan laxity in preventing guerrillas or weapons from crossing the border. A severe flare-up occurred in August 1994, when a bizarre attack occurred at the Atlas-Asni hotel in Marrakech. Two Spanish tourists were murdered by individuals of French nationality of North African background. Although these French nationals had entered Morocco traveling from France, the Moroccan authorities suspected some kind of Algerian secret-service operation against the monarchy and responded by adopting a new visa requirement for Algerian citizens and persons of other nationalities of Algerian background. In turn, Algeria instituted a visa for

Moroccans and provisionally closed the border between the two presumed economic partners. This odd episode exposed the layers of mistrust that lie just below the surface of Algerian-Moroccan relations. A good deal of confidence-building will be necessary to bury this diffidence. King Hassan's 1993 remark that an FIS takeover would have been an "interesting experiment" for the other countries of the Maghreb to observe hardly helped to build such confidence.[10] At the root of these mutual suspicions, however, lay the festering Western Sahara question. Not long after the fifth UMA summit, Algeria's foreign minister observed that the union was "in serious trouble" for two reasons: "The Western Sahara, which needs to be settled before the construction of the Maghrebin Union, and the differences in economic orientations of the member countries at present."[11] While the latter must be addressed (and were momentarily exacerbated by the return of Belaid Abdesselam, Algeria's socialist economic czar of the 1970s, as prime minister), the grain of sand that is the Western Saharan problem is the most severe irritant between the two states whose collaboration is the sine qua non of Maghrebi integration. This is a matter of high politics for Morocco and the POLISARIO Front; it is a matter of prestige and geopolitical interest for Algeria. While it has appeared for some time that Algeria is prepared to let the issue be settled by referendum, it is not prepared to abandon POLISARIO in the negotiations over the criteria for eligibility to participate in the vote. So long as this matter remains contentious, the incentives for strengthening the union are weak.

In the absence of compelling political incentives, the temptation to focus instead on collaboration with Europe is strong. All the member states of the UMA trade far more with the European Union than with one another, and there has been little evolution in this situation over the past three decades. In 1970, for example, 78 percent of Algeria's trade was with Europe; in 1992, the figure was 71 percent. For Morocco, the comparable figures were 66.5 percent in 1970 and 64 percent in 1992. For Tunisia, the figure grew from 64 percent to 75.6 percent.[12] For the group as a whole, about 70 percent of their trade is with the economies of the EU. This heavy dependence upon Europe as a trading partner manifested itself particularly in Moroccan policy. In an interview in 1993, Foreign Minister Abdellatif Filali argued that Morocco was entitled to a special relationship with the EU "because it is the country closest to Europe in the orientation of its economy, its diplomacy, and its internal policies."[13] Indeed for years, as Gregory White explains, "Morocco had projected itself to the EU as a 'Mediterranean dragon,' the 'Mexico of Europe,' and a key player in economic diplomatic endeavors."[14] White sees Morocco turning away from the "moribund" UMA already in 1992 as it redefined its priorities, opting for an essentially bilateral strategy vis-à-vis Europe. This Moroccan defection was especially significant insofar as a large part of the rationale for creating the UMA was to allow the Maghreb to bargain collectively with Europe.

In the year or two following the treaty of Marrakech, the European Community and certain of its subgroups expressed an interest in dealing with the Maghreb as a unit. A string of conferences took place between the five and various combinations of European states. In March 1990, for example, the foreign ministers of Italy, France, and Spain met in Rome with their UMA counterparts and issued a communiqué declaring the "primordial importance that they attach to the Mediterranean Basin and their . . . complete agreement on the necessity to deepen and develop their collaboration."[15] A few months later, the Franco-Arab Chamber of Commerce organized a colloquium in Marseilles attended by some 270 Maghrebins on "The Future of Cooperation between the UMA and France." In October 1990, the UMA states met with the EC's western Mediterranean subgroup (Spain, Portugal, France, and Italy) in Rome, and a follow-up meeting of the five and the four took place in Algiers a year later. These conferences discussed a variety of issues: the status of North African workers in Europe, the debt problem, and matters concerning investment, notably the Maghreb's anxiety about European capital flowing increasingly toward Eastern Europe rather than across the Mediterranean. Likewise, parliamentary delegations from the EU and the UMA met in March 1993 to pledge cooperation between the two economic groupings.

The European Commission in Brussels produced a document in April 1992 on "The Future of Relations between the European Community and the Maghreb" and has repeatedly urged the member states of the UMA to strengthen the organization as an incentive to European firms to carry out investment. Yet despite these meetings and what Dirk Vandewalle has called "pious declarations," Europe as a whole has remained skeptical about Maghrebi cooperation—and with good reason.[16] The UMA has been unable to convert itself into a convincing multilateral partner.

Tunisian president Ben Ali's attempt to reinvigorate the faltering union early in 1993 ran into a Moroccan roadblock. Abdellatif Filali emerged from a February meeting of UMA foreign ministers to declare that "everyone is in agreement that it is necessary to stop in order to see clearly what we have done and what we now have to do . . . because that will allow us to relaunch the UMA on a new solid basis."[17] In fact, as already noted, Morocco was more devoted to pursuing the vision of a special relationship with the EU than to relaunching the UMA. Thus King Hassan skipped the April 1994 summit and took no interest in promoting a further one. Twenty months later, Filali—by then Morocco's prime minister—officially called for a suspension of the activity of the (already dormant) organization.

Consistent with the UMA track record, the reasons were political and diplomatic, not economic. Algeria had, in November, raised the stalled Western Saharan issue before the UN Security Council. In arguing for direct negotiations between POLISARIO and Morocco over the ever-contentious voting lists for the long-deferred referendum, Algeria ruffled Moroccan sensibilities; POLISARIO threats to end its respect for the cease-fire only inflamed matters. As customary, when tensions flare, the two countries' press entered into a war of words as well.

Disregarding Morocco's call for a freeze, the Algerian foreign minister, Ahmed Attaf, instead convened a regular session of the UMA's ministerial council in Algiers on February 2, 1996. Not surprisingly, Morocco ignored the meeting, as did Libya for its own reasons. Once again the "five" had divided into three and two, with an Algerian-centered core and a disaffected periphery. As a quick glance at the map reveals, the core potentially encompasses Western Sahara as well. Attaf's initiative served essentially to accentuate the negative.

Throughout 1996, very little occurred to break the dual stalemate deadlocking the Western Saharan situation and its political hostage, the UMA. Zeroual sent one of his most astute negotiators, education minister Slimane Cheikh, to Morocco in July to discuss ways out of the impasse. Yet at the same time, Morocco was reinforcing its military capabilities along the wall in Western Sahara, where the first military skirmishes in five years occurred that same month. Holding the upper hand militarily, the king was in no hurry to make diplomatic concessions on the referendum. This left the burden of compromise on the Algerian side, but Algeria also was loath to let its twenty-year investment in POLISARIO slide. Zeroual traveled to Mauritania to shore up that side of his alliances before proceeding to the Organization of African Unity summit in Cameroon, where he weighed in on behalf of the Sahrawi cause there. In these circumstances, little could come of Slimane Cheikh's mission to the royal palace.

On the contrary, much as had occurred upon the first emergence of the "mini-Maghreb" of Algeria-Mauritania-Tunisia in 1983, Libya and Morocco saw reasons to improve their relations. Libya sent its secretary for Maghrebi affairs to Rabat in July 1996. The two governments agreed to rehabilitate their joint economic commission. Yet this time there was no real prospect of a remake of the Libyan-Moroccan "union" of 1984–86 (the Treaty of Oujda), and Libya recognized that the Algerian-Moroccan antagonism was the major obstacle to a viable UMA. Qadaffi, whose grievances with the organization stemmed primarily from its failure to do more to challenge the U.S.-sponsored UN embargo against his country, decided to align his policy more closely with that of Ben Ali, perennial booster of the UMA. He carried out a five-day state visit to Tunisia from October 28 to November 1, 1996, and demonstrated a fresh attitude toward the dormant organization. "The Maghrebin process," he declared, "must continue independently of prevailing circumstances," alluding to the paralysis provoked by the tensions in Algerian-Moroccan relations.[18] The very Qadaffi who had declined the chairmanship of the UMA in 1995 now sought to stir new life into the "Maghrebin process."

Qadaffi's new stance nonetheless was primarily grounded in Libyan national interest. He desperately needed allies to break out of the diplomatic isolation into which his country had been cast (because of charges of involvement in the sabotage of two civilian airliners). Cooperation with Tunisia on bilateral as well as regional matters was as promising a strategy as any to assist Libya diplomatically. Tunisians regularly have crossed the border to find employment in Libya, even though these exchanges have been interrupted periodically by political tensions (notably the Gafsa raid in 1980) and arbitrary expulsions of workers; and Libyans have found consumer goods in Tunisian markets that are unavailable in Tripoli.[19] Thus, the Tunisian-Libyan rapprochement of 1996 was as much a bilateral move as one to resuscitate the regional process. At the same time, it accorded Tunisia greater diplomatic flexibility than a hardening of the Tunis-Algiers-Nouakchott axis would permit, a freedom of maneuver that was in Tunisia's interest. In other ways as well Tunisia sought to compensate for the disappointing performance of the UMA. As Moncef Mahroug has put it, "Although they continue officially to proclaim their faith in Maghrebi integration, [the Tunisian leaders] are convinced that this endeavor has once again been put on hold for the foreseeable future. And henceforth they are acting accordingly."[20] Mahroug reports that Tunisia has carried out a trade-expansion campaign with a wide range of partners in the Arab world and beyond. While not neglecting the Maghreb, the Tunisians sent trade or diplomatic missions to sixteen Arab countries in 1996, giving particular attention to Kuwait, Egypt, and the Palestinian Authority. Meanwhile, despite a visit to Tunis by Algerian prime minister Ahmed Ouyahia in December 1996, they found their commerce with that country undermined by its preference for barter arrangements and other barriers. Thus, despite Ben Ali's continuing role as the conscience of Maghreb unity, Tunisia has looked out for its immediate national interest as much as the other member states.

In his eighth anniversary message to his fellow heads of state, the Tunisian president reiterated his "firm intention to pursue our collective action" in order to build upon the UMA's early achievements. Only King Hassan, it was reported, replied to Ben Ali's plea, citing his own willingness to "overcome all the handicaps" that have hamstrung the organization.[21] Nevertheless, Morocco has set its own conditions for ending the freeze on organizational activities. When Algeria (which has formally held onto the chairmanship of the group in the absence of a further summit) proposed to convene the seventh summit in November 1996, Morocco objected to the idea on the grounds that it was incumbent upon the two states to normalize their relations first. So far, they have disagreed over the proper procedure by which to do this. Algeria has proposed that experts and government ministers confer to seek solutions to the problems that divide the two countries in order to lay the groundwork for a meeting of the two heads of state. Morocco, to the contrary, has called for a summit between King Hassan and President Zeroual as the key to unlocking the stalemate.

It would appear that the king recalls his 1987 summit with Chadli Bendjedid, which ushered in the earlier rapprochement. This was followed by a five-party summit at Bendjedid's residence in Zeralda in 1988, which in turn paved the road to the triumphal Marrakech summit of February 1989. The king has not forgotten that the founding treaty of the UMA relied heavily upon the mechanism of regular summit meetings to carry forward their ambitious vision of Maghrebi unity. He believed then that summitry would nurture a spirit of cooperation in which such matters as Sahrawi self-determination would fade into insignificance alongside the dynamism of regional economic growth. For his part, President Bendjedid appears to have shared this optimism—except that he expected it to lead to Moroccan cooperation in a referendum based on the 1974 census. In this he was deceived.

The Algerian scholar Ahmed Mahiou has observed that "one of the errors at attempts at union in the Arab world is to have a strictly political view of the problem, neglecting the economic, technical, social and human dimensions."[22] Certainly Mahiou is correct to point to the "nitty-gritty" of functional cooperation, yet this is not where the insurmountable difficulties have arisen. On the contrary, under Secretary-General

Amamou, the various technical sub-bodies of the UMA have gone about their business. Transport specialists, for example, met in Fez in November 1992 to plan the TransMaghreb Highway (a $15 billion project, of which some one hundred kilometers had been completed by 1995); energy ministers met in Mauritania that same year to order feasibility studies for a regionwide industrial oil factory; the Maghrebin Union of Farmers was organized under UMA auspices and met in Tunisia in 1993; and just before the 1995 freeze, the infrastructure committee met in Rabat to discuss such matters as fiber-optic cable installation and water-resource planning.

These functional activities have not sufficed to move the UMA to higher ground. They are necessary but not sufficient components of a process of regional integration. Political incentives were crucial at the founding of the UMA, and resolving the region's single most important international dispute remains a prerequisite to relaunching the process. Maghreb unity requires a serious commitment to cooperation between the two most important states in the region. The border war of 1963, the rivalry between the patrimonial monarchy and the socialist republic of the late 1960s, and then the clash of interests over the destiny of Spain's Saharan enclave have rendered the Moroccan-Algerian relationship more fratricidal than fraternal. The perennial rhetoric of fraternity has yet to overcome the enduring issues of geopolitics.

In his February 1997 letter to President Ben Ali, the king of Morocco expressed his desire to see the UMA realize its full potential. In proposing to organize the long-delayed seventh summit, Algeria likewise demonstrated a wish to move ahead. Both states understand perfectly well that compromise of some kind on the Saharan question is the missing link. So long as they construe their national interests in such a way as to foreclose such a compromise, the UMA will slumber fitfully on and Maghrebi unity will remain a dream.

Notes

Portions of this chapter are adapted from my earlier article "Regionalism and Geopolitics in the Maghreb."

1. Mahroug, "A quand la relance?" 27.
2. Khader, *Le Grand Maghreb et l' Europe*, 64.
3. So dubbed in a profile in *Jeune Afrique* 1663 (November 19–25, 1992): 8.
4. *Le Monde*, September 19, 1991.
5. Mahroug, "A quand la relance?" 26.
6. On the origins of the UMA, see Mortimer, "Maghreb Matters," 160–75;

and Mary-Jane Deeb, "The Arab Maghrebi Union and the Prospects for North African Unity," 189–203.

7. *Africa Research Bulletin* 32, no. 1 (January 16–February 15, 1995).

8. For an elaboration of this argument, see Mortimer, "The Greater Maghreb and the Western Sahara," 169–86.

9. Zoubir and Pazzanita, "The United Nations' Failure in Resolving the Western Sahara Conflict." For an account of the early tribulations of the United Nations Mission for a Referendum in Western Sahara (MINURSO), see Durch, "Building on Sand: UN Peacekeeping in the Western Sahara."

10. As reported in *Jeune Afrique* 1673 (January 28–February 3, 1993): 6. The king later withdrew his provocative observation.

11. *Africa Research Bulletin* 30, no. 1 (January 1993): 10843.

12. Rouadjia, "L'UMA mise à mal," 853.

13. *Africa Research Bulletin* 30, no. 2 (February 1993): 10879.

14. White, "The Mexico of Europe? Morocco's Partnership with the European Union," 112.

15. *Le Monde,* March 24, 1990, as cited by Rouadjia, "L'UMA mise à mal," 854.

16. Vandewalle, "Uneasy and Unequal Partners: A European Perspective on Change and Development in North Africa," 96.

17. *Africa Research Bulletin* 30, no. 2 (February 1993): 10879.

18. *Africa Research Bulletin* 33, no. 10 (October 16–November 15, 1996): 12772.

19. On Tunisian-Libyan relations, see Grimaud, *La Tunisie à la recherche de sa sécurité;* and Mary-Jane Deeb, *Libya's Foreign Policy in North Africa.*

20. Mahroug, "Par-delá l'UMA," 20.

21. Mahroug, "A quand la relance?" 27.

22. Rouadjia, "L'UMA mise à mal," 853.

Part III

The Maghreb in World Affairs

12.

THE GEOPOLITICS OF THE WESTERN SAHARA CONFLICT

Yahia H. Zoubir

At the close of the 1980s, the Maghreb emerged from a long period of tension and distrust into what seemed a process of integration, cooperation, and conflict resolution. That process was institutionalized following a series of political developments, which included the reestablishment of diplomatic relations between Algeria and Morocco in May 1988 and King Hassan's meeting with POLISARIO leaders in January 1989. The crowning achievement of those political developments was the formation of the Arab Maghreb Union (UMA) in February 1989. Despite progress toward entente, the Western Sahara dispute between the Algerian-backed POLISARIO and the Kingdom of Morocco remained one of the major obstacles in intra-Maghrebi relations, for neither country has altered its respective position in any fundamental way.[1]

Much has been written about the Western Sahara conflict,[2] but some geopolitical aspects of the twenty-three-year-old dispute deserve further treatment, especially in this post–Cold War era. This chapter will focus on Morocco's stakes in Western Sahara and on the influence that the conflict exerts on Algerian-Moroccan relations, and, by extension, on the UMA. The underlying thesis in this chapter is that Morocco will have much to lose from a defeat in the referendum and that Moroccans intend to stay in the disputed territory regardless of the illegality of their occupation. Furthermore, this chapter will show that, notwithstanding Morocco's virtual annexation of Western Sahara, Algeria's geopolitical interests remain as strong as ever. The chapter will also deal with the roles of the United States, Spain, and France in the conflict.

A Brief Historical Background of the Western Sahara Conflict

A territory claimed by Morocco, Western Sahara is a former Spanish colony (1884–1976) located along the Atlantic Ocean in Northwest Africa. The Western Sahara covers 260,000 square kilometers (100,000 square miles). Approximately seventy-four thousand Sahrawis (Arab-Berber speaking) were reportedly living in Western Sahara in 1974. Now, in the late 1990s, the total Sahrawi population is believed to have reached close to three hundred thousand.

The United Nations, since the early 1960s, has called for a referendum on self-determination for the Sahrawi people. Spain ceded her former colony to Morocco and Mauritania in November 1975 before officially withdrawing from the land in February 1976. The POLISARIO Front, formed in May 1973 to liberate the colony, proclaimed on February 27, 1976, the creation of a new state, the Sahrawi Arab Democratic Republic (SADR), which became a full member of the Organization of African Unity (OAU) in 1984 and was recognized by seventy-six countries. Moroccan and Mauritanian troops have, however, dominated the territory despite SADR claims to be an independent republic. Mauritanian troops occupied the area until 1979. Morocco, after annexing the abandoned Mauritanian sector and adding it to its own occupation zone, has since maintained and strengthened its military and administrative control and holds about two-thirds of the "useful" (that is, richest) part of the land.

Even though the international community has never sanctioned Morocco's claims of sovereignty over the territory, Moroccans still maintain that Western Sahara is an integral part of the Kingdom of Morocco. Since 1976, Morocco has strengthened its hold on the territory it occupied by stationing several thousands troops inside electronically protected earthen walls. Moroccan authorities have strongly encouraged the establishment of Moroccan settlements. The occupation of Western Sahara led to tension with Algeria, which has sheltered tens of thousands of Sahrawi refugees in the Tindouf area and provides, to this day, military, diplomatic, and logistical support to POLISARIO and to the SADR's government in exile.

In May 1988, Algeria and Morocco reestablished diplomatic ties, which Morocco had broken in March 1976 in retaliation for Algeria's recognition of the SADR. In August 1988, Morocco and POLISARIO accepted a UN peace plan, which included holding a "referendum on self-determination for the Sahrawi people." The referendum scheduled for 1992 never took place, resulting in a stalemate because of Morocco's demand to include tens of thousands of additional voters and POLISARIO's refusal to acquiesce to the demand. In summer 1997, the prospects for a referendum remained remote, especially because the United Nations withdrew part of the Mission for the Referendum in Western Sahara (MINURSO). The mandate, due to expire in September 1997, was renewed in order to give yet another chance for the peace process. A new date for holding the referendum was set for December 7, 1998. In May 1998, it became evident that the referendum was unlikely ever to occur because the Moroccans simply would not risk the verdict at the polls, thus creating the worst setback for the monarchy in its thirty-seven-year rule. Algeria's refusal to allow Morocco to appropriate Western Sahara and Morocco's determination to make further claims on the territory will continue the impasse, hence hindering progress toward regional integration.

Western Sahara: A Barren Land?

The considerable wealth of Western Sahara is often overlooked but the huge deposits of phosphates led the Spaniards to invest heavily in them. The reserves, estimated at more than 10 billion tons, could make Western Sahara one of the biggest exporters of phosphates in the world.[3] Other valuable minerals, such as iron ore, titanium oxide, vanadium, iron, and possibly oil abound throughout the territory,[4] so Morocco today (like Spain until 1975) is reluctant to relinquish the region.

Fishing also figures importantly into the economy of Western Sahara because its four-hundred-mile-long coast borders on one of the richest fishing zones in the world. About 2 million tons of fish could be caught off the coast in any year.[5]

Moroccan Expansion in the Occupied Territory

The incessant POLISARIO attacks on Moroccan positions in Western Sahara compelled Morocco to invest on three levels. First, they built sixteen hundred miles of defensive sand walls, completed in 1987, around the "useful triangle." Second, they maintained an armed force of 120,000 to protect the occupied sectors. Third, they encouraged settlements of Moroccans and initiated economic development in the centers of Layoune, the capital, Smara, Boujdour, and Dakhla.

The building of the defensive walls was effective but expensive. Most observers consider that, until the completion of the walls in 1987, the kingdom was spending more than $1 billion annually.[6] The expense was somewhat relieved by the rescheduling of Morocco's debt and by assistance from France and Saudi Arabia. But the war still resulted in a considerable increase in Morocco's foreign debt and in periodic food riots and social unrest in the kingdom.[7]

Since its beginning, the conflict in Western Sahara has provided King Hassan an opportunity to increase social control in Morocco. He skillfully made Western Sahara an issue of national resolve. Today, the general population, as well as the opposition parties, supports the policy on Western Sahara as strongly as does the monarchy. Such unified support explains how Morocco has succeeded in preventing the United Nations from holding a "fair and regular" referendum in Western Sahara.[8]

Although the Western Sahara conflict causes international concern, its regional effects are even more crucial. Despite intermittent periods of peaceful coexistence, from May 1988 until the assassination of Algerian President Mohammed Boudiaf in June 1992, Algerian-Moroccan relations worsened, and, by March 1996, had eroded to a dangerous level. In fact, on February 27, 1996 (the twentieth anniversary of the SADR), Moroccan troops were reported to be deploying along the Algerian border.[9] Renewed hostilities between the POLISARIO and Morocco leading to a confrontation between the two Maghrebi states seemed imminent.

Algeria, Morocco, and the Western Sahara Dispute

The reestablishment of diplomatic relations between Rabat and Algiers in May 1988 produced a new political climate in the region. The new relations held out the promise, albeit temporarily, of a resolution of the dispute. Renewed ties between the two competing regional powers also held out the possibility of a new era in intra-Maghrebi relations.

Algeria wanted to settle the conflict over Western Sahara through the Maghrebi Union, but the Union lost its usefulness once President Chadli Bendjedid's rapprochement with Morocco developed. As soon as the Moroccan government believed that its relations with Algeria were more important than dealing with POLISARIO and believed that Algeria was more interested in forging stronger ties with King Hassan than with supporting the Sahrawis, the Moroccan government decided to resolve the dispute on its own terms, circumventing the Maghrebi Union.

Morocco and POLISARIO had agreed to the UN peace plan, which included such provisions as a cease-fire and a referendum on self-determination; therefore, Algerian policymakers believed that King Hassan favored a political solution. They also believed that such a solution would satisfy all sides and thus promote Maghrebi integration. The Moroccans

presumed that two factions had formed within the Algerian political system regarding Western Sahara and that Chadli Bendjedid was one of the
moderates or "liberals" sympathetic to the king's position. The Moroccan government felt confident that if Bendjedid were offered a face-sav-
ing solution, he would accept it and distance himself from POLISARIO.

The reality at the end of the 1980s was that Algeria and Morocco were
both interested in improving their bilateral relations, so both sides seemed
inclined to concentrate on domestic problems and trade issues. In Algeria, clearly, the UN peace plan and its acceptance by Morocco and
POLISARIO motivated those in the government who favored a rapprochement with Morocco (albeit at the expense of the Sahrawis) to strengthen
relations with Morocco and to create a Maghrebi union that would ex-
clude the SADR. Some analysts exaggerated the importance of the disagreements among the Algerian leaders on Western Sahara.[10] In reality,
those who supported POLISARIO never allowed Morocco's supporters
to gain the upper hand. The Algerian military and the diplomatic corps,
including the newer generations, maintained a consistent position.

Moroccan officials hoped that improved relations with Algiers, the turmoil in Algeria, the existence of divergent views within the Algerian leadership on the conflict, and the pragmatism shown by Bendjedid would all
work to their benefit. A chill in relations in late 1988, however, did compel King Hassan to agree to meet POLISARIO leaders just six weeks before the Maghrebi summit scheduled for mid-February 1989. Many factors, however, gradually bolstered King Hassan's position: his assured
refusal to hold further meetings with POLISARIO leaders; the creation of
the UMA without the participation of the SADR; Algeria's increasing preoccupation with internal problems; the strong influence exerted by some
of Bendjedid's close associates less favorable to the SADR; and the defec-
tions of a few important POLISARIO officials to Morocco. The king believed at the time, as did many observers, that Algeria's domestic problems would compel it to soften its stance on Western Sahara. However,
Algeria, though confronted with an incipient civil war since 1992, did
not allow Morocco to have its way in Western Sahara. The late 1980s
thus ended with neither Algeria nor Morocco having fundamentally altered its respective position on Western Sahara.

Morocco, Algeria, and the Western Sahara in the 1990s

By 1990, improvement in Algerian-Moroccan relations, on one hand, and
overall amelioration of Maghrebi ties, on the other, did not signify an

end to the regional conflict. Neither the government nor the legal opposition in Morocco indicated that it would relinquish Western Sahara, so each continued to oppose withdrawing Moroccan military forces and administrative personnel. In October and November 1989, the POLISARIO had demonstrated that the conflict was far from resolved by launching fierce attacks against Moroccan military positions in Western Sahara. Just before the UMA meeting scheduled in Algiers on July 22, 1990, Algeria's foreign minister, Sid Ahmed Ghozali, made a statement that defined the core of the conflict in Algerian-Moroccan relations: "The potential for economic and political cooperation in the Greater Maghreb is extraordinary; however, there still remains one major problem: the conflict in the Western Sahara."[11] A review of the two neighbors' policies to defend their respective positions demonstrates the continued importance of the issue.

Algeria

Notwithstanding the many crises that have shaken Algeria, POLISARIO's chief ally, Western Sahara, remains a major preoccupation in spite of the UN peace plan. Even if the plan has relieved Algerian policymakers who argue that the UN will bear the main responsibility in case of failure, they strongly believe that the illegal annexation of the territory to Morocco will have dangerous ramifications. While aid to the Sahrawis fell off in the early 1990s, it has, in fact, increased since 1994.[12] The severe domestic problems in Algeria took precedence over Western Sahara. Since late 1992, however, Algeria has reaffirmed its stance on the issue. High-ranking Algerian officials avow that Morocco has been the prime beneficiary of the reestablishment of diplomatic relations between the two countries. In 1997, Algeria's attitude reverted to the one Algerian officials adopted in the late 1970s and early 1980s—that is, supporting the Sahrawis while encouraging them to negotiate a settlement. Algerians have expressed disappointment about the delay of the referendum.[13] They felt outmaneuvered by the Moroccans when, on December 19, 1991, less than two weeks before his term in office ended, UN secretary-general Javier Perez de Cuellar, in his final report to the UN Security Council, capitulated to Morocco's persistent demands for changes in the criteria of voting eligibility. President Mohammed Boudiaf (January–June 1992), more sympathetic to the Moroccan position on Western Sahara, issued a statement reiterating Algeria's firm commitment to an honest referendum, after encouragement from the military to do so.[14] Although the former defense minister, Khaled Nezzar, assured the Sahrawis that the annexation of the Western Sahara to Morocco was absolutely unacceptable for Algeria, he reportedly frankly admitted to them that total independence was unattainable and that they should seek an alternative between independence and annexation by Morocco.[15] Certainly, economic difficulties, as well as perhaps pressure from France, strongly influenced Algeria's position. Simply put, in view of its own socioeconomic and political concerns, Algeria could no longer afford to provide the same support to the Sahrawis as it had done previously, but it still entirely opposed the handing over of the disputed land to Morocco.

In 1993, Algerian policymakers admitted candidly that they had neglected the question of Western Sahara and that they should reexamine their policy.[16] The Algerian military communicated to King Hassan that Algeria would not tolerate Moroccan annexation of Western Sahara.[17] In fact, in that same year, relations between Algeria and Morocco had reached such a low ebb that the king publicly admitted the tension with Morocco's eastern neighbor.[18]

The UMA began stagnating, in large part because of the Western Sahara issue. The stagnation resulted from the alleged support that the Moroccans (and the Libyans) were providing to the opponents of the Algerian state, as well as from the alleged involvement of some Moroccan officers in arms movement at the Algerian border.[19] In a letter to the Algerian newspaper, El-Watan, published on February 2, 1998, Khaled Nezzar, former defense minister, revealed that in 1993–1994, Morocco had sought to blackmail Algeria. According to Nezzar, the Moroccans asked the Algerian authorities to end their support for the Sahrawis in exchange for Morocco's extradition of Abdelhak Layada, head of the Armed Islamic Group (GIA). The closing of the borders between the two countries in August 1994, following a terrorist attack in Marrakech, highlighted the growing tension in the region.

Recently, Algeria's leaders have tried to prevent their foreign policy from merely reflecting internal problems. They aspire to regain the respectable diplomatic and political role that they played on the world stage until the mid-1980s, and they have tried to refute doubts about their position on Western Sahara—a position for which Algeria used its best diplomats and to which it devoted considerable resources. Officials at the highest levels, including President Liamine Zeroual,[20] have reiterated Algeria's commitment to the Sahrawi cause.

From December 1995, the prospect for holding a fair referendum greatly diminished. Algeria accused UN secretary-general Boutros Boutros-Ghali of blatantly favoring Morocco.[21] Morocco, in turn, accused Algeria of meddling in the process and sought a freeze in UMA activities, a request that Algeria disregarded without, however, succeeding in giving the UMA new life.[22]

The Algerian regime has been empowered by its quest to revive Algerian nationalism. The relative strength that the regime has gained since the presidential elections of November 16, 1995, and the recent lucrative contracts that the regime has signed with foreign oil companies, coupled with the relative weakening of the Islamist insurrection, have bolstered Zeroual's government. The inability of the Islamist insurrection to topple the regime and the new strength the authorities have acquired impelled Algeria to reassert its influence in the region. The country's renewed confidence and good economic prospects (the continued insecurity throughout the country notwithstanding) have provided Algerian leaders with more leverage to conduct foreign policy relatively independent of outside political and economic pressures. Algerian policymakers do not feel that economic cooperation with Morocco could offset Algeria's support for POLISARIO, because Western Sahara is both a political and a psychological issue. Although Algeria wishes to establish a certain level of supremacy in the region, Algerians are motivated primarily by genuine geopolitical concerns. Fears of Morocco's irredentist claims over Algerian territory are still real in the minds of the Algerian political-military establishment.

Morocco

Morocco has maintained an unwavering position on Western Sahara. The chief objective remains the integration of the territory into the Kingdom of Morocco, preferably with UN approval. Moroccans have argued steadfastly that Western Sahara is theirs and have accepted only reluctantly the idea of holding a referendum, although they have made it plain that such a referendum can only affirm their annexation of the territory. King Hassan has mobilized the entire country in order to promote his version of the referendum. In the meantime, the authorities have encouraged Moroccans to settle en masse in the territory, where an infrastructure has been put in place to allow them to live in more favorable conditions.[23] Despite its illicit character, the settlement has continued and has been publicly criticized by members of MINURSO.[24] Evidence indicates that Morocco's delaying tactics are aimed at having the vote go in its favor,[25] which explains the Moroccan demand that the UN include thousands of additional, allegedly Sahrawi, voters residing in Morocco.

In October 1994, Moroccans flooded the United Nations Identification Commission with more than 120,000 new applications, thus buying more time by forcing Boutros-Ghali to drop his February 1995 deadline and to propose another date for the referendum. King Hassan anticipated that the delay would not alienate his Western allies, because the latter, concerned about the deterioration of the situation in Algeria, have been more preoccupied with maintaining stability in the kingdom than with insuring that the peace process be implemented.

Morocco's policy has been to regain its diplomatic losses of the 1970s and 1980s and to capitalize on the Algerian crisis to strengthen its own position in the region. Unlike Algeria, which has looked to Africa for backing on Western Sahara, Morocco continues to seek international support from the West and from the Gulf monarchies. The image of Morocco that the authorities seek to project is one of stability in the region, a bulwark against radical Islamism. In many ways, this Moroccan tactic has succeeded because France granted King Hassan overwhelming support on Western Sahara, presumably to avoid destabilization of the kingdom. The issue of identification of voters, the delay in the referendum, the existence of a cease-fire since September 1991, and the turmoil in Algeria all have allowed Morocco to strengthen its de facto annexation of Western Sahara.

The United States

Despite its proclaimed neutrality in the conflict, the United States, until recently, has provided considerable political and material support to Morocco, a longtime ally.[26] Under President George Bush, however, U.S. policy toward the conflict was much more evenhanded than under the previous administrations, for a number of reasons: (1) the considerable improvement of American-Algerian relations greatly diminished the perception of Algeria as a radical state opposed to U.S. interests; (2) the growing attention of the U.S. Congress to the conflict has also played a role in the change of attitude among Republicans and Democrats alike;[27] and (3) the U.S. has supported the UN peace plan since its elaboration in 1988.

In October 1991, the United States Congress passed a resolution calling for a "free and fair referendum." The resolution urged President Bush to "take appropriate steps to ensure that the [UN] Security Council takes firm action in the event of any failure to comply with, or attempt, to delay the peace plan which has been adopted."[28] Congress conducted its own inquiry into Western Sahara. It dispatched a congressional team to the region in January 1992. George A. Pickart submitted a report, in which his congressional team charged Morocco with obstructing the work of MINURSO.[29] During testimony before the Congress, administration officials conceded that Morocco's demand for additional voters in the upcoming referendum was indeed contradictory to the initial UN peace proposal.[30]

U.S. policy suffers from inconsistency. For example, the vote in the UN Security Council on March 2, 1993, effectively saved the peace plan. However, despite Morocco's human-rights violations (which the U.S. government itself has reported)[31] and despite the hurdles the Moroccan authorities have created for MINURSO's operations, the United States continues to provide Morocco with economic and military aid. Furthermore, although they have expressed their willingness to talk to all sides involved in regional conflicts throughout the world, American policymakers have declined to meet officially with POLISARIO representatives.[32] U.S. decisionmakers have yet to more forcefully encourage Morocco to comply with UN resolutions.

The United States still values its relationship with Morocco, a traditional ally, upon whom "we have long relied . . . as a stable and constructive force in the region."[33] The United States appreciates Morocco's position on Middle East issues and its "moderation in North Africa." Americans continuously applaud Hassan's willingness to continue providing transit rights for U.S. military forces en route to the Middle East,[34] so U.S. security and economic assistance to Morocco has been steady. Furthermore, "Morocco's continued eligibility for excess defense articles under the Southern Region Amendment will allow us to continue our military cooperation that has yielded concrete benefits in the Gulf War."[35]

The primary concern of the United States in the Maghreb since 1992 has been the situation in Algeria. The uncertainty in Algeria has been the prime reason why merely maintaining the status quo in the Western Sahara conflict became acceptable. The rise of radical Islamism in Algeria and the chaos that analysts anticipated as a result of an Islamist victory at the polls strengthened Morocco's importance in the eyes of several European countries, particularly France. The fear of Islamism also accounts for France's full endorsement of Perez de Cuellar's proposal for additional voters. From the perspective of some American policymakers, then, a referendum—especially one favorable to the Sahrawis—might destabilize Morocco. If both Morocco and Algeria were destabilized, the consequences for Europe would be dire: destabilized Morocco could facilitate the rise of radical Islamism in that country, especially when the U.S. seeks "to encourage Morocco's role as a stable anchor in the region."[36] At the same time, however, the United States could not allow Morocco to assume power in Western Sahara or to hold a seemingly less-than-fair referendum. Allowing Morocco to usurp power in Western Sahara or to influence the referendum would not only discredit the United States and the United Nations, but might also lead to a much-feared confrontation between Algeria and Morocco. Wanting to prevent such a confrontation may explain why the United States has tolerated the long postponement of the referendum.

The Clinton administration, until late 1996, had favored Morocco and its wishes about Western Sahara. Officials in the Department of State and the Department of Defense admitted that integrating Western Sahara into Morocco might prove the best solution, although they maintained that a UN settlement agreed to by the warring parties might be less costly politically.[37] The unwillingness of the U.S. Congress to continue funding UN operations also accounted for the administration's lack of resolve to bring an end to the stalemate.

In March 1997, former secretary of state James A. Baker accepted the appointment of special UN representative for Western Sahara. The new UN secretary-general, Kofi Annan, understood early on that U.S. leadership would be critical to an effective referendum. The appointment also reveals that Baker, who elicited strong U.S. support, believes the issue important enough to warrant a genuine attempt at achieving a peaceful resolution. The appointment, in December 1997, of yet another American diplomat, Charles F. Dunbar, to serve as UN special envoy for Western Sahara indicated increased U.S. interest in bringing an end to the conflict. An attempt to do so would be particularly significant because Algeria may be on the verge of overcoming its domestic crisis and Morocco is nearing a delicate succession phase.

A United Nations success would definitely alleviate Congressional criticism against the world body. For the administration, resolving the Western Sahara dispute, which has adversely affected Moroccan-Algerian relations, would remove a major obstacle for the United States to pursue a more potent regional policy and, perhaps, to diminish French influence in the Maghreb—traditionally the France's *chasse gardée*. But it remains to be seen how vigorously the French will oppose the U.S. drive to establish American influence over the African continent.

Spain

One cannot study Western Sahara without considering Spain's part in the conflict.[38] As the colonial power since 1884, Spain concluded in 1974 that independence of the territory was inevitable. The Spaniards hoped that the Sahrawis would maintain close ties with Spain after independence, but the Spanish government, for various reasons, failed to keep its commitment to organize a referendum on self-determination. Spain, in compliance with the Madrid Tripartite Accords of November 1975, transferred the administration of the territory to Morocco and Mauritania effective February 26, 1976. The transfer (or "de-administration") allowed Spain more flexibility as it pursued a complex policy, the aim of which was to balance its relationship with the Maghrebi protagonists.

Despite its incongruity, Spanish policy is marked by a profound sense of culpability. This is the underlying reason why Spanish policymakers still insist that their country transferred the administration of, not the sovereignty over, the territory to Morocco and Mauritania. It also explains their steadfast recognition of "the right of the Sahrawi people to self-determination." Spain, in fact, recognized POLISARIO in 1978 as the "sole and legitimate representative of the Sahrawi people in struggle."[39]

The undignified manner with which Spain left its former colony accounts for the country's constant willingness to ensure that the conflict is fairly resolved. Spain has therefore supported unequivocally the UN peace plan and the referendum. In October 1988, for instance, Spain voted in favor of UN Resolution 43/23, which advocated negotiations between POLISARIO and Morocco. Spanish policymakers also believe that a credible UN initiative and a negotiated settlement before the referendum are the best ways of resolving the conflict.[40]

Spain has sought to play a decisive role in the peace process in Western Sahara; for example, it sent representatives to identify those Sahrawis who would be eligible to vote. Spain also contributed 10 percent ($3 million) of the budget of the UN census commission and provided the UN secretary-general with its list of voters. Morocco has succeeded in blocking some of Spain's goodwill initiatives, such as keeping Spanish peacekeeping troops out of the MINURSO. Spain's dilemma undoubtedly stems from the nature and importance of its interests in Morocco, so its support for the Sahrawis is inevitably limited and always remains guarded. The preeminence of relations with Morocco, coupled with the changing situation in Algeria, has compelled the Spaniards—in spite of their sizable interests in Algeria—to avoid acting in any way that would result in destabilizing Morocco. For the Spaniards, such destabilization could easily result in a mass exodus of Moroccans to Europe or to a repetition of the Moroccan Green March, but this time King Hassan could order the march into the Spanish enclaves of Ceuta and Melilla.

Spain's policy has consisted of humanitarian aid: food (about $2.5 million a year); scholarships to Sahrawis to study in Spain; medical assistance to and treatment of Sahrawis; and the proliferation of "sister cities." Such aid to the Sahrawis is meant to proclaim, in a peculiar way, the rejection of the occupation of Western Sahara by Morocco.[41] Spain's greatest wish is, obviously, that the conflict will end and that a free and fair referendum will be held. The heavy historical burden would then be lifted from Spain's conscience.

France

France has opposed staunchly and consistently an independent Sahrawi state.[42] French officials contend that another "micro state," under the influence of Algeria, would not bode well for the Maghreb. The reality, of course, is that France has an important presence in Morocco and, despite the historical volatility of its relations with its former protectorate, its interests in the kingdom at all levels are considerable.

So far in the 1990s, Algeria's problems have completely preoccupied France. Fearing a spillover of the Algerian crisis into Morocco, France has decided to help the monarchy remain strong. The French believe that a destabilized kingdom would be fraught with dangerous ramifications. A close analysis reveals that whenever the situation in Algeria worsens, France endeavors to delay the referendum in Western Sahara by strengthening Morocco's position with the UN Security Council.

France has provided the Moroccan monarchy with considerable economic, political, and military support, while trying not to alienate Algeria—a country in which France has immense commercial and other interests. Concern with the succession in Morocco and with the prevailing socioeconomic conditions was instrumental in the French government's recent decision to reduce the Moroccan debt and to sign important economic agreements with the kingdom.[43]

France's policy toward the two Maghrebi states has not always been consistent, creating the appearance that there existed not one but several French foreign policies. France (like the United States) perceives Morocco as a bulwark against the spread of radical Islamism in the region, so POLISARIO and the Sahrawis elicit little sympathy in France—not even among the socialists, who traditionally favor self-determination of peoples and national liberation movements. The conservative government of French president Jacques Chirac has extended greater and more-open support to Morocco. According to well-informed sources who wished to remain anonymous, France pressured some African countries to withdraw recognition of the SADR, and successfully, for in Spring 1997, Benin, Burkina Faso, Chad, Congo-Brazzaville, and Togo gave in to the pressure. This policy has been so successful that only a minority of the African countries in the OAU recognize the SADR.

France has, however, not succeeded in persuading Algeria to stop supporting POLISARIO in exchange for French and European economic and financial aid. In the 1980s, French authorities believed that if Chadli Bendjedid stayed in power, the Western Sahara conflict would be settled in Morocco's favor.[44] The interesting question now is whether a recovery from its domestic crisis will allow Algeria to take a strong position on Western Sahara despite France's opposition and maneuvering. The staunchly nationalistic factions in the Algerian military are willing to continue supporting POLISARIO. So far, they have refrained from providing sufficient military supplies to allow Sahrawi forces to resume hostilities against Morocco, for fear of involving Algeria in a direct confrontation with Morocco. The Algerian military clearly has avoided simultaneously facing the Islamist insurgency domestically and its Moroccan adversary externally. But if the UN peace plan fails (quite a plausible development) and if the Algerian domestic crisis ends, Algeria probably will allow POLISARIO to resume hostilities against the Moroccan occupying troops in Western Sahara.[45]

Conclusion

The problem of Western Sahara continues to be a major thorn in the side of intra-Maghrebi relations and is likely to remain so until the problem is completely resolved. The question is important to both Algeria and Morocco. For Morocco, the conflict, since its inception in 1975, has served as a catalyst for national unity. It also has helped King Hassan to justify the economic hardship suffered by many Moroccans. The investments in Western Sahara, coupled with the military costs, impeded the Moroccans from risking a referendum. Although the economic cost for the Algerians has been less than that for the Moroccans, the political and psychological investment is just as great. For Algerians, the Western Sahara situation is less a question of prestige than an issue of geopolitics and a struggle for power with its neighbor. The conflict over Western Sahara has prevented both countries from entering a period of lasting cooperation and trust, thus preventing Maghrebi integration. There is no reason for optimism: without the use of outside force (an unlikely scenario), Morocco will never leave Western Sahara.

As has been seen in this chapter, the conflict in Western Sahara is also important to outside powers. What seems to become increasingly obvious, however, is that U.S. leadership in resolving regional conflicts and/or imposing solutions to such conflicts (through the UN or alone) may well extend to the Maghreb—traditionally a French sphere of influence. The question, of course, is whether the United States is willing to assume that role.

Notes

I would like to thank Robert A. Mortimer for his comments on an earlier draft of this chapter.

1. Zoubir, "The Western Sahara Conflict," 225–43.

2. de Froberville, *Sahara Occidental;* Zoubir and Volman, *International Dimensions;* Hodges, *Western Sahara;* and Zartman, *Ripe for Resolution,* chap. 2.

3. Balta, *Le Grand Maghreb,* 168.

4. Hodges and Ball, "Is There Oil in the Western Sahara?" 14; Balta, *Le Grand Maghreb,* 168.

5. Decraene, "La question du Sahara Occidental reste un important facteur d'unité nationale," 41.

6. Damis, "Morocco and the Western Sahara," 166. The figures vary from one author to the other. On the military expenditures proper, see Volman, "The Role of Military Assistance in the Western Sahara War," 151–68; see also chapter 13 in this volume.

7. Seddon, "Morocco at War," 122 ff.

8. Zoubir and Pazzanita, "The United Nations' Failure in Resolving the Western Sahara Conflict," 614–28.

9. *L'Authentique* [Algiers], February 27, 1996.

10. Grimaud, "La diplomatie sous Chadli ou la politique du possible," gives an exaggerated importance to this split; for a different view, cf. Zoubir, "The Western Sahara Conflict."

11. *Al Sharq al Awsat* (in Arabic), July 10, 1990.

12. Most Sahrawi leaders interviewed on this issue have confirmed this point. But, unquestionably, there was some noticeable change in the attitude of some Algerian officials vis-à-vis the Sahrawis in the late 1980s. The situation had changed dramatically by the end of 1992. Interviews with officials in the Algerian ministry of foreign affairs and the ministry of defense show that even the new generation of officials and officers support the Sahrawi cause and reject an illegal annexation of the territory by Morocco.

13. See, for instance, interview of Mohammed Salah Dembri, former minister of foreign affairs, in *El Moudjahid* [Algiers], February 9, 1994.

14. See the good analysis Jacques Barrin provided in *Le Monde,* March 13, 1992.

15. Grimaud, "La diplomatie sous Chadli," 434.

16. Interviews by the author with Algeria's foreign minister and other foreign ministry officials, both in Algeria and abroad.

17. Interview by the author with high-ranking military officers, Ministry of National Defense, Algiers, March 1993.

18. King Hassan's interview on French TV, channel TF 1's *7 sur 7,* May 16, 1993; see also Soudan, "Algérie-Maroc: Faut-il craindre le pire."

19. *E1-Watan* (Algiers), May 23, 1993.

20. See excerpt from Liamine Zeroual's message to Robert Mugabe, president of Zimbabwe and president of the OAU's Liberation Committee, published in *El-Watan* (Algiers), August 18, 1994.

21. de Froberville, *Sahara Occidental.*

22. Ouazani, "UMA: 3 + 2." See *Reuter,* February 1, 1996. In May 1997, Algeria blamed Morocco for the continued impasse. See *AFP* (Algiers), May 3, 1997.

23. For the more recent wave of settlements, see *West Africa,* July 18–24, 1994, 1277.

24. Author's interview with a medical doctor, member of MINURSO, April 20, 1994, Madrid. Other former members of MINURSO confirmed this. An interview of a medical doctor from the MINURSO was published in *Témoignage Chrétien* (Paris), reprinted in *El-Watan* (Algiers), May 6–7, 1994. Several nongovernmental organizations have reported the many complications Sahrawis and MINURSO personnel have faced in the occupied Western Sahara. See, in particular, the reports submitted to the UN Economic and Social Council, Human Rights Commission, *E/CN. 4/Sub. 2/1994/NGO32,* August 17, 1994, and *E/CN.4/Sub.2/ 1994/ NGO/20,* August 8, 1994. De Froberville, "Sahara Occidental: Échec du plan de paix," and Tami Hultman, "UN Peace Effort Is Seen at Risk in W. Sahara," *Washington Post,* March 14, 1992, A15–16, had already reported the obstacles the Moroccan authorities posed to MINURSO.

25. *New York Times,* March 5, 1995. See also U.S. Department of State, *Western Sahara Country Report on Human Rights Practices for 1996,* January 30, 1997: "The Moroccan Government has undertaken a sizable economic development program in the Western Sahara as part of its long-term efforts to strengthen Moroccan claims to the territory," 1.

26. For a detailed study of U.S. policy toward the Western Sahara dispute, see Zoubir and Volman, "The United States and Conflict in the Maghreb," 10–24; and Zunes, "The United States and the Western Sahara Peace Process," 131–46. The military aid diminished due to budgetary constraints in the United States.

27. Zoubir and Volman, "The New World Order and the Case of the Western Sahara," 108–20.

28. House of Representatives, *House Concurrent Resolution 214,* 102nd Congress, 1st session, 1991.

29. United States Senate, Committee on Foreign Relations, *The Western Sahara,* 12. In the late 1990s, the U.S. Congress was strongly supportive of a just solution to the conflict (see United States House of Representatives, 105th Con-

gress, 1st Session, H. RES. 245, expressing the sense of the House of Representatives in support of a free and fair referendum on self-determination for the people of Western Sahara September 25, 1997).

30. *Statement by Assistant Secretary of State John R. Bolton Before the Subcommittee on Africa Regarding the UN Referendum in the Western Sahara,* February 26, 1992, 6.

31. U.S. Department of State, *Country Reports on Human Rights Practices for 1994,* February 1995. See also, U.S. Department of State, *Morocco Country Report on Human Rights Practices for 1996,* January 30, 1997.

32. For a similar remark, see the commentary in *The Washington Post,* June 13, 1993.

33. *Statement of Assistant Secretary of State for Near Eastern Affairs Robert Pelletreau Before the House Foreign Affairs Committee Subcommittee on North Africa, September 28, 1994* (Washington, D.C.: Government Printing Office, 1995), 51.

34. U.S. Department of State and U.S. Defense Security Assistance Agency, *Congressional Presentation for Security Assistance Programs: Fiscal Year 1993,* 245–46.

35. Pelletreau, *Statement of Assistant Secretary of State for Near Eastern Affairs Robert Pelletreau Before the House Foreign Affairs Committee Subcommittee on North Africa,* 52.

36. Ibid., 53.

37. Interviews by author with U.S. officials, Washington, D.C., May 1996 and January 1997.

38. The best study of Spanish colonization of Western Sahara is that of Aguirre, *Historia del Sahara Español—La Verdad de una Traición.* For a study of Spanish foreign policy, see Berramdane, *Le Sahara Occidental,* 127–38, 217–31; Naylor, "Spain, France, and the Western Sahara, 17–51."

39. Berramdane, *Le Sahara Occidental,* 129.

40. Interview by the author with Spanish official, London, May 24, 1995.

41. Interviews by the author with POLISARIO and Spanish officials in Madrid, April 21–23, 1994.

42. Grimaud, "Algeria and Socialist France," 262.

43. *Le Monde,* January 16, 1996.

44. Attali, *Verbatim—Chronique des années 1981–1986,* 466.

45. Interview by the author with Algerian military officers in charge of national security.

13.

FOREIGN ARMS SALES AND THE MILITARY BALANCE IN THE MAGHREB

Daniel Volman

This chapter will examine and analyze the arms trade in the Maghreb and its impact on the regional military balance. Although foreign arms sales to Libya and Tunisia will be briefly summarized, this chapter will be focused on the Algerian-Moroccan military balance because of its direct connection to the war in Western Sahara (the only major military conflict that has occurred in the region over the past two decades), its impact on the ongoing efforts of the United Nations to resolve the conflict in Western Sahara, and its implications for regional stability.

Foreign Military Assistance to Morocco and Algeria during the Saharan War

During the Saharan war, Morocco purchased nearly $4 billion worth of arms and other types of military equipment from France, its former colonial protector (see Table 13.1). This accounted for roughly 50 percent of the total military hardware acquired by the Royal Moroccan Armed Forces during this period.[1] The most expensive types of weaponry that Morocco bought from France consisted of sophisticated jet combat aircraft. Designed for operations against ground forces and equipped with radar warning receivers and electronic countermeasures to defend against SA-6 and SA-7 surface-to-air missiles, these aircraft were used to mount effective attacks against POLISARIO Front troops in Western Sahara.[2] According to Lieutenant Colonel David Dean of the U.S. Air Force, the author of a unique study of the military aspects of the Saharan conflict, Gazelle helicopter gunships equipped with antitank missiles and other ground-attack weaponry were used to do "credible work in the war zone flying flank reconnaissance for moving ground forces," deployed by the Royal Moroccan Army.[3]

The Royal Moroccan Army also purchased substantial quantities of military hardware from France. In combination with military training provided by French military instructors, both in Morocco (roughly 250 French military instructors were stationed in the country throughout this period)[4] and in France, these sales had a major impact on the strength of

Table 13.1. Major arms sales to Morocco, 1975–1988

Supplier	Number	Type of equipment
Austria	121	Kuerassier light tanks
France	24	F-1CH Mirage fighter aircraft
	15	F-1EH Mirage fighter aircraft
	24	SA-341 Gazelle helicopter gunships
	24	AlphaJet counterinsurgency aircraft
	30	AMX-13 light tanks
	360	VAB armored personnel carriers
	100+	AMX-F-3 155mm self-propelled howitzers
Germany	70	UR-416 armored personnel carriers
	10	Do-28 transport aircraft
Italy	28	SF-260 trainer aircraft
South Africa	c. 100	Eland and Ratel armored cars
Switzerland	10	AS-202 trainer aircraft
United States	100	M-48 tanks
	420	M-113 armored personnel carriers
	60	Vulcan 20mm self-propelled air-defense gun systems
	37	M-48 Chaparral surface-to-air missile batteries
	55	155mm towed and self-propelled howitzers
	6	F-5A fighter aircraft
	14	F-5E fighter aircraft
	6	OV-10 counterinsurgency aircraft
	15	C-130 transport aircraft
	2	KC-130 tanker aircraft

Sources: IISS, *Military Balance, 1979–1980,* 96; IISS, *Military Balance, 1987–1988,* 107–9; IISS, *Military Balance, 1989–1990,* 108–10; Dean, *Air Force Role,* 16, 42, 44–47, 59, 61–62, 67–69.

the Royal Moroccan Armed Forces and on the course of the Saharan war. In particular, the French-produced Mirage aircraft and Gazelle attack helicopters gave Morocco an essential ability to find and attack the highly mobile ground forces of the POLISARIO Front, while French-produced armored vehicles and self-propelled artillery provided some of the vital mobility and firepower that Morocco needed to launch attacks on POLISARIO forces outside of the earthen walls that were constructed to protect Moroccan troops garrisoned in Western Sahara.

During the same period, Morocco bought more than $750 million worth of military equipment from the United States through the U.S. Foreign Military Sales program and an additional $150 million worth through the Commercial Sales program.[5] This constituted about one-fourth of the total foreign military assistance obtained by Morocco during the Saharan war. The most costly type of weaponry that Morocco acquired from the United States, as in the case of military assistance from France, was jet combat aircraft. These were designed primarily to intercept enemy aircraft, not to attack ground troops, and were intended to strengthen Morocco's ability to defend itself against Algeria's substantial fleet of fighters and bombers. Moreover, they were designed for use against troops who did not possess air-defense missiles such as the Soviet-produced SA-6 surface-to-air missile, which was first deployed by POLISARIO troops in 1981. These planes, therefore, were not useful for attacks on POLISARIO ground forces and proved highly vulnerable to POLISARIO missile defenses, which brought down about a dozen of these aircraft over the course of the war.[6]

While the OV-10 propeller-driven counterinsurgency aircraft (unlike the F-5s) were low-technology planes designed for ground attack, they were intended for use only against lightly armed guerrilla forces. These aircraft, Lieutenant Colonel Dean reported, were "too slow and too vulnerable to SA-7 attacks to use in the war zone" and "have never been used for combat missions" in Western Sahara.[7]

The U.S.-supplied aircraft that played the most important role in the Saharan war were actually C-130 transport planes and KC-130 aerial tanker planes. During the early years of the war, before Morocco built the series of defensive earthen walls in the territory, it was very difficult (if not impossible) for Morocco to move troops and supplies by road without falling victim to attacks by POLISARIO forces. But the "Royal Moroccan Air Force accomplished this important, and often overlooked, mission of supplying Moroccan ground forces in the cities and remote garrisons with its fleet of C-130 cargo planes."[8] In 1980, Morocco also began using one of its fleet of C-130 transport aircraft as an airborne reconnaissance and command center. This plane is equipped with side-looking radar for surveillance and defense against missile attacks. When refueled in the air by the KC-130 tanker aircraft, which Morocco bought from the United States, it can remain airborne for long periods of time, detecting POLISARIO forces on the ground and directing attacks mounted by Moroccan combat aircraft.[9]

Morocco also obtained a sophisticated American-produced ground-surveillance and air-defense radar system manufactured by the Westinghouse Corporation. This deal included the construction of the Royal Moroccan Air Force's command center at Salé, which is linked to radar stations throughout Morocco and Western Sahara, and the installation of a network of radar stations and ground sensors along the defensive earthen wall built by Morocco in Western Sahara, which was used to detect POLISARIO troop movements and to direct artillery fire against POLISARIO units.[10]

The Royal Moroccan Army also purchased substantial quantities of U.S. weaponry. Along with French-produced equipment, this provided Moroccan ground troops with the mobility and firepower that they needed to attack POLISARIO forces outside of the defensive earthen walls.

In addition to weaponry and other military hardware, the Pentagon provided military training to Moroccan troops, both in-country and in the United States. For example, in 1982, a three-man U.S. training team was dispatched to the Moroccan F-5 base at Meknes for two months to provide training and to evaluate the performance of U.S.-supplied F-5s in the war. A team of twenty U.S. Army counterinsurgency experts were also sent to Morocco to train a special battalion of Royal Moroccan Army troops for commando-style operations against POLISARIO Front SA-6 units.[11] During the course of the war, the Pentagon provided training at installations in the United States to more than fifteen hundred Moroccan troops through the U.S. International Military Education and Training Program. This included training in combat flying and the use of other U.S.-supplied equipment, counterinsurgency tactics, and military command and control.[12]

The remainder of the weaponry and other military equipment that was acquired by Morocco during the course of the war (some $1 billion worth) was acquired by Morocco from a variety of other European arms-producing countries, China, and South Africa.[13]

Between 1975 and 1988, Algeria bought almost $9 billion worth of weaponry and other military equipment; nearly all of this came from the

Soviet Union (see Table 13.2).[14] In addition, the Soviet Union dispatched one thousand military personnel to Algeria to train Algerian troops and maintain Soviet-produced military equipment.[15]

Limited amounts of military hardware were *independently* transferred by Algeria to the forces of the POLISARIO Front over the course of the Saharan war. Although it is impossible to quantify these transfers, they included such potent weapons as SA-6 and SA-7 surface-to-air missile systems (which were used with considerable success against Moroccan aircraft), ZSU-23 self-propelled 23mm anti-aircraft guns, anti-tank weapon systems, artillery, BMP-1 armored cars, and a small number of T-54 and -55 tanks obtained by Algeria from the Soviet Union prior to the outbreak of the war.[16]

The acquisition of this weaponry by the POLISARIO Front enabled Sahrawi soldiers to defend themselves, to a certain extent, against Moroccan aerial attacks and to counter the firepower possessed by Moroccan troops garrisoned at strong points along the defensive earthen walls they constructed in Western Sahara. Without these capabilities, it would have been far more difficult for POLISARIO forces to move about in Western Sahara or to mount effective assaults against Moroccan strong points.

Table 13.2. Major arms sales to Algeria, 1975–1988

Supplier	Number	Type of equipment
Soviet Union	400	T-62 and T-72 tanks
	320	BTR-50, BTR-60, and BTR-152 armored personnel carriers
	920	BTR-2, BMP-1, and BMP-2 armored cars
	65	SA-6 surface-to-air missile systems
	N/A	SA-7, SA-8, and SA-9 surface-to-air missile systems
	18	Su-7 ground-attack aircraft
	20	MiG-23 ground-attack aircraft
	15	MiG-23 fighter aircraft
	35	MiG-21 fighter aircraft
	48	Mi-24 helicopter gunships
United States	17	C-130 transport aircraft

Sources: IISS, *Military Balance, 1987–1988*, 94–95; and IISS, *Military Balance, 1989–1990*, 95–96.

As can be seen from the above description of Moroccan and Algerian arms acquisitions, Algeria was able to increase its position of military superiority—in terms of weaponry—relative to Morocco. In part, this was due to the fact that Moroccan arms acquisitions were oriented toward weaponry better suited for use in the counterinsurgency campaign in Western Sahara than in a conventional war with Algeria. Furthermore, the Algerian government enjoyed a substantial financial advantage because it could use the revenue from oil and gas sales to buy far more arms than Morocco could afford to purchase.

The principal strategic consequence of Algeria's continued and expanding military superiority was that it was impossible for the Moroccan government ever to consider seriously the launching of attacks on POLISARIO Front political bases and Saharan refugee camps located near Tindouf in southwestern Algeria, despite King Hassan's repeated threat to conduct such cross-border operations. It thus enabled the Algerian government to continue providing military assistance and other support to the POLISARIO Front with virtually no risk that this would result in a conventional war with Morocco.

The economic consequences of Moroccan and Algerian arms acquisitions were also significant. Virtually all of Morocco's purchases of American-produced weaponry were financed with money provided by the United States through the Foreign Military Sales Financing program ($475 million in low-interest credits and $200 million in grants between 1975 and 1990).[17] The credits, however, had to be repaid with interest, thus forcing spending cuts for economic development and social services and increasing the burden of Morocco's external debt. Other weapons purchases were funded either by Morocco itself (adding further to the country's economic problems) or by the government of Saudi Arabia, which gave up to $1 billion to the Moroccan government annually in grants until 1988, when Saudi Arabia ended its financial aid program.[18]

For its part, Algeria had to use a substantial proportion of its oil and gas revenues to finance its arms acquisitions, which reduced the ability of the government to promote economic development in that country, particularly when oil and gas prices began to decline in the mid-1980s. Thus, while the Saharan war's direct economic impact on Algeria was small, the indirect cost of maintaining a position of military superiority (at least to the extent that this was necessary to deter a conventional war with Morocco as a result of Algeria's relationship with the POLISARIO Front) was quite large and contributed significantly to the country's economic problems and the resulting political unrest.

Foreign Military Assistance to Morocco and Algeria since the End of the Cold War

Since the end of the Cold War, there have been a number of major developments in the military and political situation in the Maghreb. These include the agreement by the government of Morocco and the POLISARIO Front to the UN peace plan for Western Sahara in 1988, the agreement by the two combatants to a cease-fire and the arrival of a UN peacekeeping force (MINURSO) in the territory in 1991, the continued failure of the United Nations to conduct a free and fair referendum on the future status of the territory up to the present time, and the democratization process in Algeria. As a result of these developments—and domestic economic problems in both countries—average annual spending on arms acquisitions by Morocco and Algeria has declined by roughly 50 percent since 1988.

Between 1989 and 1994 (the most recent year for which data is available), Morocco has obtained some $690 million worth of arms and other military equipment (see Table 13.3). French sales declined sharply and now account for only about 10 percent of the total military hardware acquired by Morocco; the United States has become the largest single source of supply, accounting for about 30 percent of the total; and the remainder has come chiefly from Spain and Italy.[19]

Table 13.3. Major arms sales to Morocco, 1989–1994

Supplier	Number	Type of equipment
France	15	VAB-VCI armored cars
	10	AMX-10 armored cars
	35	FH-70 155mm towed artillery
Italy	2	Assad-class missile corvettes
Spain	7	CN-235 transport aircraft
	4	Lazaga missile frigates
United States	1	C-130 electronic warfare aircraft
	2	UH-60 liason helicopters
	300	M-60 tanks (NATO surplus)
	20	M-113 armored reconnaissance vehicles
	20	M-44 155mm self-propelled artillery
	26	M-198 155mm towed artillery

Sources: IISS, *Military Balance, 1987–1988,* 108; IISS, *Military Balance, 1989–1990,* 109–10; IISS *Military Balance, 1995–1996,* 142–43; and IISS, *Military Balance, 1996–1997,* 125, 128–29.

During this same period, Algeria obtained some $1.4 billion worth of weaponry and other military equipment, primarily from the Russian Federation and former Warsaw Pact countries in Eastern Europe (see Table 13.4).[20]

The dissolution of the Soviet Union led to a dramatic decline in Algerian purchases of weaponry produced in Russia and other former Soviet republics, weapons that Algeria preferred because they were compatible with the training and maintenance capabilities of their armed forces (see Table 13.5). By 1994, however, arms purchases from former Soviet re-

Table 13.4. Major arms sales to Algeria, 1989–1994

Supplier	Number	Type of equipment
Egypt	200	Fahd armored personnel carriers (for Gendamerie)
Russia et. al.	30	T-62 tanks
	200	T-72 tanks
	150	OT-64 armored personnel carriers
	48	BVP-2 armored personnel carriers
	135	BMP-2 armored cars
	20	D-74 155mm towed artillery
	20	D-30 155mm towed artillery
	35	ZS3 155mm self-propelled artillery
	150	ZS1 122mm self-propelled artillery
	48	BM–14–16 140mm multiple rocket launchers
	150	M-37 82mm mortars
	120	B-10 82mm recoilless launchers
	12	T-12 100mm antitank guns
	80	D-44 85mm antitank guns
	35	ZU-23 23mm air-defense gun systems
	15	ZPU-2 and -4 14.5mm air-defense gun systems
	10	Su-24 ground attack aircraft
	20	MiG-23 fighter aircraft
	5	Il-76 transport aircraft
United States	3	C–130–30 transport aircraft

Sources: IISS, Military Balance, 1987–1988, 94–95; IISS, Military Balance, 1989–1990, 96; IISS, Military Balance, 1995–1996, 142–43; and IISS, Military Balance, 1996–1997, 125, 128–29.

publics, and from former members of the Warsaw Pact that produced the
same equipment, rose again, although not to previous levels. In September 1994, for instance, Algeria began taking delivery of forty-seven Russian Mi-8 helicopter gunships equipped for counterinsurgency operations.[21] Furthermore, in November 1994, French newspapers revealed that French defense firms—with the approval of the government—were selling night-vision systems for helicopter gunships, communications equipment, and light infantry weapons to Algeria to equip its counterinsurgency forces.[22] That same month, the Algerian interior ministry bought nine secondhand AS-350B Ecureuil helicopters from Eurocopter, a Franco-German consortium, and additional deliveries were made in February 1995.[23] In July 1995, *Jane's Defence Weekly* reported that Algeria was

Table 13.5. Annual value of arms imports, 1977–1994 (in millions of current U.S. dollars)

Year	Algeria	Libya	Morocco	Tunisia
1977	600	1,400	300	50
1978	800	2,300	440	10
1979	550	2,900	470	90
1980	725	2,600	350	140
1981	1,200	3,200	340	60
1982	1,200	3,100	270	60
1983	675	2,200	320	40
1984	750	2,100	210	130
1985	500	1,600	110	340
1986	625	1,200	100	30
1987	700	625	410	50
1988	825	950	220	30
1989	625	1,100	110	30
1990	310	370	230	40
1991	130	410	60	30
1992	5	80	90	20
1993	20	0	70	20
1994	140	0	130	50
Total	10,380	26,135	4,230	1,220

Sources: U.S. Arms Control and Disarmament Agency (U.S. ACDA), *World Military Expenditures and Arms Transfers (WMEAT), 1988,* 74, 93, 96, 106; U.S. ACDA, *WMEAT, 1995,* 111, 133, 136, 147.

planning on buying, for around $200 million, seven hundred Akrep Scorpion armored vehicles built by Otokar, a Turkish defense firm; these were intended to improve the mobility of troops engaged in operations against armed Islamic groups.[24] And in January 1998, the South African arms manufacturer Denel signed a $20 million contract with Algeria for the sale of a Seeker remote-piloted reconnaissance aircraft. The plane, with sophisticated surveillance equipment, is to be delivered within two years.[25]

The Algerian military also experienced difficulty, for a time, in obtaining the spare parts, other components, and specialized technical assistance it required to maintain and deploy its existing stockpile of military equipment. But Algeria was soon able to find new sources for these goods and services from a wide variety of countries and, consequently, has not had much trouble keeping its arsenal operational.[26]

The Current Algerian-Moroccan Military Balance and the Peace Process in Western Sahara

As of early 1997, Algeria's military strength—in terms of weaponry—remains significantly superior to that of the armed forces of Morocco. Algeria's military advantage has diminished to a certain extent, but continued arms acquisitions by both countries have largely served to maintain the overall military balance. At the same time, however, the Algerian military has committed a substantial portion of its military personnel and equipment to the ongoing internal conflict with the armed groups associated with the Islamic Salvation Front (FIS) and other Islamic extremist groups. In 1995, for example, the Algerian defense budget rose to 58.8 billion dinars ($1.3 billion), which accounted for 21 percent of Algeria's total budget (compared to 18 percent in the previous year, when 39.8 billion dinars were devoted to the defense budget).[27] As long as this internal conflict continues, the requirements of this counterinsurgency campaign will reduce the capability of the Algerian military to engage in a possible conventional war with Morocco or any other country.

Due to these factors, there has been a small shift in the balance of military capabilities in favor of Morocco. But because Algeria previously enjoyed a significant advantage relative to Morocco, this shift is of little practical importance with regard to the outcome of a military confrontation between the two countries. There is little doubt that if a war broke out in the immediate future (which is not likely), Algeria would be able to successfully defend its territory and would prevail over Morocco in a fairly short time. Of more potential consequence for the future military balance in the region, and for relations between Algeria and its neighbors more generally, is the possibility that the ongoing conflict within Algeria might eventually undermine the loyalty of the conscripts who serve in the Algerian military or might even lead to the emergence of an Islamic extremist government in Algeria. However, neither of these prospects appears at all likely.

The prospects that the United Nations' efforts to achieve a peaceful resolution of the conflict in Western Sahara will collapse, thus leading to a resumption of fighting between the armed forces of Morocco and of the POLISARIO Front, will essentially be determined by political calculations rather than by military factors. Both Morocco and the POLISARIO Front have retained their military capabilities vis-à-vis each other. Morocco's current military power has already been described. As to the current strength of the POLISARIO Front, the International Institute for Strategic Studies reports that the POLISARIO arsenal now contains one hundred T-55 and T-62 tanks; more than fifty BMP-1 armored cars; twenty to thirty Brazilian-produced EE-9 Cascavel military vehicles; twenty-five D-30/M-30 122mm howitzers; fifteen BM-21 122mm multiple rocket launchers; fifty ZSU-23 self-propelled 23mm antiaircraft guns; AT-3 Sagger antitank guided missile systems; SA-6, -7, -8, and -9 surface-to-air missile systems; and a variety of captured Moroccan military hardware, including light tanks, armored personnel carriers, and armored cars (although it is not known how much of this captured equipment is in operating condition).[28] Thus, POLISARIO forces are clearly in a position to resume military operations in Western Sahara if the POLISARIO Front should decide to take this step. Indeed, according to Commander Douglas Kring Dryden, an American naval officer who served as a MINURSO military observer and who, in his own words, enjoyed "unhindered access to the Sahrawi refugee camps in Algeria and was the first military observer to travel throughout the entire POLISARIO area of operations," POLISARIO "has a clear capability, if planned and executed correctly, to seriously effect a military decision."[29]

Foreign Military Assistance to Libya and Tunisia

Between 1977 and 1994, Libya used the massive revenues from its oil sales to buy more than $26 billion worth of weaponry and other military hardware (see Table 13.6). About three-fourths of this came from the Soviet Union, Czechoslovakia, Poland, and other members of the Warsaw Pact Organization. The remainder came from France, Italy, West Ger-

Table 13.6. Major arms sales to Libya, 1975–1994

Supplier	Number	Type of equipment
Brazil	100	EE-11 Uturu armored personnel carriers
	400	EE-9 Cascavel armored cars
Czechoslovakia	18	L-410 transport aircraft
France	1	RASIT artillery and vehicle-mounted radar system
	10	Combattante II missile boats
	11	SA-316 light helicopters
Italy	20	G-222 transport aircraft
	1	Assad-class missile corvette
Russia	250	T-72 tanks
	350	BTR-40, BTR-50, and BTR-60 armored personnel carriers
	250	BRDM-2 armored cars
	800	BMP-1 armored cars
	450	multiple rocket launchers
	48	Frog-7 surface-to-surface missiles
	55	Scud-B surface-to-surface missiles
	2	Koni missile frigates
	3	Nanuchka II missile corvettes
	6	Osa II missile boats
	3	Foxtrot submarines
	55	MiG-25 fighter aircraft
	80	MiG-23 fighter aircraft
	6	Su-24 fighter-bomber aircraft
	60	Su-20 and-22 fighter-bomber aircraft
	16	An-26 transport aircraft
	20	Il-76 transport aircraft
	12	Mi-35 helicopter gunships
	40	Mi-25 helicopter gunships
	32	Mi-8 and Mi-17 transport helicopters
	30	Mi-2 transport helicopters
United States	5	L-100 transport aircraft
Yugoslavia	80	G-2 Galeb trainer aircraft

Sources: IISS, *Military Balance, 1979–1980*, 96; IISS, *Military Balance, 1981–1982*, 86; and IISS, *Military Balance, 1996–1997*, 139–40.

many, other Western European producers, Yugoslavia, China, and other suppliers.[30]

Between 1977 and 1994, Tunisia purchased more than $1.2 billion worth of arms and other military equipment; about half of this came from the United States, a sixth from France, and the remainder from Austria, Italy, and Brazil (see Table 13.7).[31]

Conclusion

This chapter shows that the military rivalry between Morocco and Algeria led them to acquire large quantities of major conventional weapons systems and that this military buildup had a significant impact on the course of the conflict in Western Sahara up to the time of the acceptance of the UN peace plan by Morocco and the POLISARIO Front in 1988. It also demonstrates that their continued rivalry has led both countries to acquire substantial amounts of additional weaponry since the end of the

Table 13.7. Major arms sales to Tunisia, 1975–1994

Supplier	Number	Type of equipment
Brazil	18	EE-11 Uturu armored personnel carriers
France	500	Milan antitank missile systems
	1	RASIT artillery and vehicle-mounted radar system
	3	Combattante III missile boats
	3	P-48 missile boats
	5	SA-341 Gazelle helicopter gunships
Italy	110	F-6614 armored personnel carriers
United States	30	M-60A1 tanks
	54	M-60A3 tanks
	140	M-113 armored personnel carriers
	65	TOW antitank missile systems
	25	M-48 Chaparral surface-to-air missile batteries
	15	F-5E fighter and F-5F trainer aircraft
	4	C-130B and C-130H transport aircraft
	2	HH-3 antisubmarine-warfare helicopters

Sources: IISS, *Military Balance, 1979–1980*, 98; IISS, *Military Balance, 1981–1982*, 88; and IISS, *Military Balance, 1996–1997*, 148.

Cold War and the conclusion of a cease-fire in Western Sahara. And it makes clear that both Morocco and the POLISARIO Front are capable of returning to the battlefield if the United Nations fails to resolve the conflict in Western Sahara through a free and fair referendum.

Notes

1. U.S. Arms Control and Disarmament Agency (U.S. ACDA), *World Military Expenditures and Arms Transfers* [hereafter *WMEAT*], *1970–1979*, 127; *1972–1982*, 95; and *1988*, 96, 111.

2. Dean, *Air Force Role*, 44, 46, 62, 67–69.

3. Ibid., 61.

4. David Coetzee, "France Bids to Turn the Colonial Clock Back," 26; and Tony Hodges, "François Mitterand, Master Strategist in the Maghreb," 20.

5. U.S. Defense Security Assistance Agency (U.S. DSAA), *Foreign Military Sales Facts* [hereafter *FMS Facts*], *as of September 30, 1985*, 38–39; U.S. DSAA, *FMS Facts, as of September 30, 1989*, 46–47; and U.S. DSAA and U.S. Department of State (DOS), *Congressional Presentation for Security Assistance Programs, Fiscal Year 1991*, 48.

6. Dean, *Air Force Role*, 62.

7. Ibid., 16.

8. Ibid., 42.

9. Ibid., 45–47, 59.

10. Ibid., 46, 57–58.

11. Ibid., 68–69.

12. U.S. DSAA, *FMS Facts, as of September 30, 1989*, 86–87, 94–95; and U.S. DSAA and U.S. DOS, *Congressional Presentation for Security Assistance Programs, Fiscal Year 1991*, 19.

13. International Institute for Strategic Studies (IISS), *Military Balance, 1979–1980*, 96; *1981–1982*, 96; *1982–1983*, 114; *1985–1986*, 81–82; and *1987–1988*, 107–9.

14. U.S. ACDA, *WMEAT, 1970–1979*, 127; *1972–1982*, 95; and *1988*, 96.

15. IISS, *Military Balance, 1982–1983*, 70; and *1989–1990*, 45.

16. IISS, *Military Balance, 1987–1988*, 109; and *1989–1990*, 95–96.

17. U.S. DSAA, *FMS Facts, as of September 30, 1985*, 24–25, 47; U.S. DSAA, *FMS Facts, as of September 30, 1989*, 32–33, 57; and U.S. DSAA and U.S. DOS, *Congressional Presentation for Security Assistance Programs, Fiscal Year 1991*, 11.

18. Dean, *Air Force Role*, 40.

19. U.S. ACDA, *WMEAT, 1995*, 136.

20. Ibid., 111.

21. "Moscow to Supply Algeria with 47 Helicopter Gunships," *Interfax*, 1310 GMT, September 24, 1994.

22. "Ministry Unwilling to Comment on Algerian Arms Sale," *Le Monde,* November 10, 1994, 24; and "Comments on Arms Delivery to Algeria," *Foreign Broadcast Information Service—94-242,* December 16, 1994, 19.

23. Centre de Documentation et de Recherche sur la Paix et les Conflits (CDRPC), *Observatoire des transferts d'armements: Rapport 1995,* 131.

24. "More Resources Given to Defence."

25. Newton Kanhema, "Algeria Buys Arms from South Africa," Panafrican News Service, October 12, 1997; "South Africa Sells Reconnaissance Plane to Algeria," Reuters News Service, January 27, 1998; and "Algeria to Get Spy Plane," *West Africa,* February 9–15, 1998, 178.

26. Interview by the author with senior Algerian military officer, May 31, 1996.

27. "More Resources Given to Defence."

28. IISS, *Military Balance, 1995–1996,* 143.

29. Dryden, "Western Sahara."

30. U.S. ACDA, *WMEAT, 1970–1979,* 127; *1972–1982,* 95; *1988,* 112; and *1995,* 133.

31. U.S. ACDA, *WMEAT, 1970–1979,* 127; *1972–1982,* 95; *1988,* 111; and *1995,* 147.

14.

UNITED STATES POLICY IN THE MAGHREB

Yahia H. Zoubir and Stephen Zunes

U.S. officials do not perceive the Maghreb as an entity but instead perceive it as individual countries. In spite of its remarkable geopolitical location, the United States has never ascribed as much importance to the Maghreb as it has to the Near East. American policymakers have been interested in the Maghreb insofar as it may affect the stability of Europe, especially southern Europe. During the Cold War, the United States sought to prevent communist influence in the Maghreb and to promote Western security and economic interests. Despite its close security and political ties with Morocco and Tunisia, however, the United States relinquished its role as a key player to France, the major former colonial power in the region. Only recently has it become possible to speak of a reasonably defined U.S. policy in the Maghreb. Officials previously formulated policies toward particular nations, which varied according to specific circumstances. Since the end of the Cold War, though, modest elements of a regional policy seem to be emerging. As part of its larger global strategy, the United States is now emphasizing economic liberalization.

This chapter reviews U.S. policy toward each Maghrebi country (excluding Mauritania), including Western Sahara.

Algeria

In spite of its relative regional and international influence, Algeria never constituted a priority for the United States. Although periods of cordiality and good economic ties have existed from time to time between the two countries, Algerian-U.S. relations have been marked by misunderstandings, suspicion, and, at times, great antagonism, because U.S. and Algerian foreign policies clashed over such issues as the Arab-Israeli conflict, Vietnam, Western Sahara, Nicaragua, Cuba, and Grenada. After independence, Algeria forged a radical foreign policy and assumed leadership in the Non-Aligned Movement, the Organization of African Unity, and other international organizations which often opposed U.S. objectives and interests. Worse yet, Algeria's privileged relations with the Soviet Union, America's archenemy, placed the two countries on a collision course.[1]

Notwithstanding the ideological and political differences between the two countries, U.S. policymakers pursued a pragmatic policy which did not allow foreign-policy disagreements to undermine advantageous economic relations. Substantial commercial interests, mainly in the hydrocarbons sector, induced the pragmatism. That pragmatism also occasionally stemmed from a willingness of both countries to find common ground on a number of political issues, especially as they pertained to the Maghreb and the Near East.

In the late 1980s, both the Reagan and Bush administrations sought better relations with Algeria. In view of Algeria's increasing pragmatism in foreign policy in the same period, the main U.S. objective was to encourage Algeria's liberalizing its economy, though the United States did little to strengthen democratization, which developed in 1989–91. The United States relied on Europe to provide foreign assistance and guidance to the Maghrebi countries, because events in Eastern Europe and in the Middle East were much more important to the United States.

The lack of political, military, or ideological ties prevented the United States from exerting much influence in Algeria, and despite the substantial commercial interests, the United States has provided insignificant bilateral foreign-assistance programs to the country. Unlike Morocco or Tunisia, Algeria has therefore never been a close friend of the United States. Obviously, the traditional instruments of influence necessary for that to happen were simply missing.

The fact that Algeria has never been vital to U.S. strategic, economic, or political interests and that the United States has traditionally exerted little influence over the country partially explains why the United States has pursued a seemingly ambivalent policy during the civil conflict that has destabilized the country since January 1992. Although Algeria previously had not been vital to U.S. economic interests (Algerian Islamists showed no particular hostility toward U.S. holdings in the country), it became so in 1992 because the crisis in the country posed a threat to

Morocco and Tunisia, close friends of the United States. Algeria's increased significance stemmed from the rise of political Islam in the Arab world, a phenomenon that Washington perceives as a threat to U.S. interests.

The crisis in Algeria has highlighted the various divisions within the U.S. government over the Islamist issue. "Confrontationalists" have opposed strongly the growing power of the Islamists because they perceive it as a destabilizing force and a threat to U.S. political and economic interests.[2] "Accommodationists" have taken a much less alarmist attitude. They believe that Islamic revivalism is a natural progression in Islamic societies and does not necessarily represent a threat to the West or to democracy. They do not perceive Islamism as a monolithic movement; in fact, some view the nonviolent Islamists as a diverse social force that will compel authoritarian regimes to democratize.

U.S. policy toward Algeria following the cancellation of the electoral process in January 1992 has undergone three phases. The first phase can be characterized as one of ambivalence. The initial U.S. reaction to the cancellation of the second round of the legislative elections, in which the Islamic Salvation Front (FIS) was poised to win an absolute majority in parliament, was one of "concern," without condemning the cancellation as such. The United States felt that the cancellation conformed to the constitution.[3] The United States altered its statement on Algeria almost immediately afterward in order to establish its neutrality in the conflict between the Islamists and the regime.[4] During that first phase, the United States pursued a wait-and-see approach, which avoided any implicit or explicit support for either side, but the United States did indicate that it did not oppose the coming to power of "moderate" Islamists who accepted the democratic game and who did not challenge U.S. interests (the security of Israel, the Middle East peace process, and economic liberalization) in the Maghreb and in the Middle East.[5]

The second phase, which began with the Clinton administration, coincided with the worsening crisis in Algeria (bombings; the slaying of journalists, intellectuals, and foreigners; followed by government repression). That phase lasted from mid-1993 until the second half of 1995, during which most American officials were convinced that it was only a matter of time before the Algerian government collapsed. Fearful of a repeat of the revolution in Iran in 1979, some policymakers felt that the U.S. government should reach out to the Islamists and "check what they are up to." During the second phase, the views of the "accommodationists" prevailed. U.S. policy was driven by opportunism: the coming of the Islamists to power was seen as a real possibility. U.S. officials routinely com-

municated with the Islamists, and a representative of the FIS acted relatively freely in the United States. In fact, one may speculate that the United
States was considering using Algeria as a laboratory for an Islamist regime. As a former CIA analyst put it:

> If the Algerian regime is doomed, then the logic of encouraging co-
> operation with moderate Muslims . . . seems compelling. If U.S.
> officials can talk to the FIS, perhaps they can improve America's
> reputation among fundamentalists, diminishing the chances of the
> United States being portrayed again as the implacable enemy of Is-
> lam . . . Indeed, according to some observers, the United States in
> Algeria could experiment with dealing with fundamentalism, thereby
> fine-tuning a long-term approach and revamping our image in the
> militant Islamic world without jeopardizing much—and certainly
> not a strategic partner, as was the risk in pre-Revolutionary Iran.[6]

Whatever the motivations of U.S. policymakers, they favored a compromise in Algeria between moderate Islamists and the regime. U.S. officials unceasingly tried to persuade the Algerian government to reach a
compromise between the moderate forces on each side. Having made plain
its opposition to extremists in the Islamist movement and to the so-called
eradicationists in the government, the United States hoped that such a
settlement in Algeria would isolate the extremists, thus bringing an end
to the bloodshed. The United States found itself at loggerheads with France
until at least mid-1995. U.S. officials felt that the January 1995 Sant'Edigio
Platform, which brought together seven opposition organizations, including the FIS, but was rejected by the Algerian authorities, the smaller secular parties, and the major moderate Islamist party HAMAS (today, Movement for a Peaceful Society), could provide the basis for national
reconciliation. While pushing for compromise, the United States severely
criticized the Algerian regime for its failure to carry out market reforms,
to respect human rights, or to establish a more democratic system. Though
suspicious of the Islamist movement, U.S. policymakers downplayed the
possibility of the movement creating a "domino effect" in the region.
However, many in the United States, the governments of Tunisia, Morocco, and Egypt, and the NATO allies considered Islamists an immi-
nently possible threat.

The third phase coincided with a more perceptible shift, albeit incremental, in U.S. policy toward Algeria. The shift was determined by several factors: increased concern among America's NATO allies, especially

the Europeans, about terrorism in Algeria and its export to France; the disintegration of the Islamist movement and the emergence of armed, extremely violent Islamist groups who obeyed no logic but their own; the regime's relative success in the antiterrorist struggle; and, perhaps most important, the presidential election of November 1995, which provided the regime with a modicum of legitimacy that it hitherto had lacked. Since then, the United States, though still critical of the regime, has adopted a policy of "positive conditionality."[7] That policy consists of supporting the regime as long as it broadens and accelerates reconciliation and economic reforms, holds elections, and enters into discussions with the opposition, including the moderate Islamists. The positive way in which the United States expressed its support for the June 1997 legislative elections is an example of its new policy.[8] Indeed, unlike France, the United States felt that, despite some irregularities during the elections, the elections were a step in the right direction of political evolution in Algeria.

The United States undoubtedly will continue supporting the Algerian regime as long as it pursues a course of action that satisfies Washington. Algeria has become an increasingly attractive market to U.S. business, especially Algerian oil projects, which are worth billions of dollars and may increase once stability is reestablished in the country. Those projects partly explain why the United States has backed IMF and World Bank agreements and Paris Club debt rescheduling for Algeria. The moderation of Algerian foreign policy has helped improve the country's image in Washington. With a few exceptions, U.S. policymakers believe that Algeria supports the Arab-Israeli peace process; they have appreciated especially Algeria's participation, in March 1996, in the "Summit of the Peacemakers" at Sharm al-Sheikh, Egypt, and its international cooperation against terrorism.[9] In spite of a vacillating policy in early 1998 due to the horrible massacres committed against civilians in Algeria, the United States proclaimed publicly on January 12, 1998, that those massacres were the work of the brutal Armed Islamic Group. Clearly, the United States continued to support the Algerian regime but continued to demand that the Algerian government take steps to guarantee human rights and to prevent the defense groups, armed by the government to defend themselves against the GIA, from committing atrocities. U.S. insistence on an international investigation of the massacres stemmed from the perceived necessity to be in line with the European Union rather than from any conviction that the government in Algiers was involved in any of those massacres.

Libya

The United States has had a series of major disputes with Libya since Muammar Qadaffi assumed power in 1969. The primary cause of recent U.S.-Libyan confrontation has been Libya's alleged role in international terrorism. That confrontation has resulted in a series of severe reactions by the United States, including the bombings of two Libyan cities in 1986. More recently, in 1992 and 1993, the United States succeeded in influencing the UN Security Council to impose a series of sanctions against the government of Libya. The sanctions resulted from Libya's failure to extradite two of its citizens to Great Britain or to the United States, where they were to face criminal charges in the bombing of Pan Am Flight 103 over Scotland in 1988.[10] The sanctions, combined with low oil prices, certainly have affected the Libyan economy adversely, substantially reducing investments in the oil industry. They also have harmed Libya's impressive advances in health care, education, and welfare,[11] but according to the former assistant secretary of state Robert Pelletreau, "there are significant differences between the U.S. position on enhanced sanctions and that of our allies."[12] The failure of the United States to persuade its allies and others to extend the embargo to include the purchase of Libyan oil has prevented the sanctions from being more effective in toppling the regime. U.S. hostility has also placed Qadaffi in his favorite position—that of a "beleaguered revolutionary, standing firm against the forces of imperialism and neo-colonialism."[13]

The Libyans appear reluctant to comply with the extradition demands because they believe that the United States would block the lifting of sanctions even if they did comply. They seem convinced that the Clinton administration's target is not the indicted men but the regime itself.[14] The Libyans find no incentive in U.S. policy to improve their behavior, and they believe the United States has pushed for those sanctions knowing that, in view of Libyan and Arab public opinion, Qadaffi can ill afford to turn over the suspects.

In August 1996, responding to the failure of other countries to back the hard-line, anti-Libyan position of the United States, President Bill Clinton signed a law introduced by Senator Alfonse D'Amato. The law imposes a secondary boycott on foreign countries and companies breaking the UN embargo against Libya by selling such prohibited items as weapons, airplanes, or airplane parts.[15] The motivations for the D'Amato Act may extend beyond its announced goal of curbing terrorism; it may exert U.S. pressure on weaker countries because of other issues, as well.

According to that law, the president can "determine" that a person, company, or government is violating the act, and the aggrieved party has no recourse to challenge the president's determination in court or anywhere else.[16] With so much freedom of interpretation, a president can thus impose sanctions or other punitive measures based more on political considerations than on any objective criteria. The law obviously strengthens the tools by which the United States can force Middle Eastern and North African countries to cooperate with its strategic and economic agenda, including pro-Israeli interpretations of the Middle East peace process. The bill provides for an array of sanctions, including banning the sale in the United States of products of culpable firms. The United States, paradoxically, has opposed vehemently the same type of secondary boycotts when Arab states applied them to companies doing business in Israel. As with similar extraterritorial laws against Cuba and Iran, even America's strongest allies have raised fierce objections to the D'Amato law.[17] As U.S. officials openly admitted, "Our major trading partners, chiefly Canada, Europe, and Japan, are strongly opposed to this sanctions legislation because they consider it to be an attempt to force U.S. policy on their citizens. . . . These governments are also reluctant to adopt measures that will mean a loss in business for their companies. Some doubt whether economic pressure will succeed in altering the behavior of Iran and Libya."[18]

U.S. threats against Libya reached new heights in 1996 when some American officials implied that the United States would launch a first-strike nuclear attack against an alleged underground chemical weapons factory near Tarhuna, in the Libyan desert. Secretary of Defense William Perry declared that destroying Libyan chemical weapons capability "could require, could include the use of nuclear weapons."[19] The threat was credible because the United States is believed to be developing a new atomic bomb, known as the B61–11, designed to penetrate underground to destroy just such installations.[20]

The United States feels little incentive to moderate its position toward Libya. For instance, when President Clinton threatened military action against Libya's alleged chemical-weapons facilities, Republicans attacked him for not adopting an even tougher stance. Few in the United States seem willing to defend Qadaffi's regime, given its often-brutal repression of domestic and exiled critics and its ties to international terrorism.

U.S. policy toward Libya is part of the "rogue-state" doctrine. U.S. national security officials have defined rogue states as those that possess substantial military capability, seek to acquire weapons of mass destruction, and violate "international norms." According to former national security advisor Anthony Lake, "our policy must face the reality of recalcitrant and outlaw states that not only choose to remain outside the family [of nations] but also assault its basic values . . . [and] exhibit a chronic inability to engage constructively with the outside world."[21] Lake further argued that, just as the United States took the lead in "containing" the Soviet Union, so it must now also bear the "special responsibility" to "neutralize" and "contain" those "outlaw states."[22]

The threat that Libya and similar "rogues" pose to the United States or its allies seems highly overstated.[23] The rogue-states doctrine is directed against the Libyan regime, among others, but the doctrine affects ordinary Libyans, already suffering from despotic rule, more than it affects the regime. In fact, instead of weakening the regime, the doctrine tends to feed popular anti-Americanism in the region.[24] More important, U.S. policymakers have failed to convince Libyans that they are truly concerned about the well-being of the population in the region. Libyans, instead, suspect that the regime is the target because of its refusal to bow to U.S. hegemony. The irony is that the rogue-states doctrine, along with the sanctions imposed upon Libya, have given Qadaffi the credibility and legitimacy he otherwise would not receive from the Libyan population, a fact readily accepted privately by some U.S. officials.

Morocco

The United States and Morocco have a long-standing special relationship. They have had a treaty of friendship since 1787, the longest unbroken peace agreement that the United States has maintained with any country in the world. Morocco is rich in mineral resources, which may become more important to the United States, and it is strategically located in the northwest corner of Africa, bordering both the Atlantic and Mediterranean coasts, including the Straits of Gibraltar. Morocco has, since its independence in 1956, received more U.S. aid than any other Arab country except Egypt. Indeed, since the beginning of the war over Western Sahara in 1975, Morocco has obtained more than one-fifth of all U.S. aid to Africa, totaling more than $1 billion in military assistance alone. The United States played a major role in reversing the war over Western Sahara to Morocco's favor through large-scale economic and military aid, military advisors, and logistical assistance.[25]

The end of the Cold War made Morocco's strategic location less significant, thus weakening the standard U.S. rationale for its pro-Moroccan bias. Algeria's moderate policy and moves toward democracy, coupled with the belated acknowledgment by U.S. analysts that the Sahrawi nationalist movement, the POLISARIO Front, could not be completely defeated militarily by the Moroccan Armed Forces, also caused the United States to reassess its relations with Morocco. The United States began quietly urging Morocco to seek a compromise on Western Sahara and to institute needed economic and political reforms. George Bush, both as vice president and president, asked the U.S. State Department and European leaders to encourage the king to accelerate the process for holding the referendum in Western Sahara.[26] The dramatic decline of Marxism-Leninism in Africa lessened the need for Morocco as a surrogate state.[27]

U.S. military and economic assistance remains at a relatively low level, but Morocco has since rebounded as an important ally. The first reason for this rebound was Morocco's support for the Gulf War, including sending Moroccan forces to Saudi Arabia. Morocco supported the allies despite previous collaboration with the Iraqi government, widespread sympathy for Iraq among the Moroccan population, and the striking parallels between Iraq's occupation of Kuwait and Morocco's occupation of Western Sahara. The second reason was the instability in Algeria. The Algerian regime was fighting for its very survival; its capacity to counter Moroccan ambitions was thus limited. The specter of a radical Islamist revolution in North Africa placed Morocco once again in the role of bulwark against extremist, anti-Western forces. King Hassan's success in curbing radical Islamist movements in his own country made him a particularly useful buffer against such forces. The third reason was the relative weakness of the POLISARIO against Morocco because of the cease-fire and the stalemate in the peace process, which clearly worked to the POLISARIO's disadvantage. The shift in the balance of forces lessened the urgency to pressure Morocco to reach a compromise with its weakened opponent. Assistant Secretary of State for International Organization Affairs John R. Bolton acknowledged that Morocco had been "unhelpful" in the peace process. However, he candidly conceded that Morocco's role in supporting U.S. foreign policy had to be taken into account in determining the U.S. response.[28] The predominant view in diplomatic circles in Rabat was that King Hassan would lose his throne if he lost the referendum.[29] The fourth reason Morocco regained its importance as a U.S. ally relates to Morocco's role in U.S.-led peace initiatives, hence clearly showing that King Hassan could still play an important part in supporting U.S. strategic interests. Morocco has supported the Middle East peace process and has contributed armed forces to UN peacekeeping missions in Bosnia, Somalia, and elsewhere. A fifth reason can be linked to the increase in free-market economic reforms, which include large-scale privatization that coincides with American ideological goals. Those reforms have also made Morocco more attractive for U.S.-based multinational corporations.[30]

Morocco, however, remains less pivotal to the United States than it was during the height of the Cold War in the mid-1980s, and the United States has become less critical to Morocco. The Europeans—especially the French, who have made the development of northern Morocco a "duty" and "an absolute priority" (in part to stop the important production of cannabis in that region)—have supported Morocco more than they used to, thereby lessening Morocco's dependence on the United States and diminishing the influence Americans once had in Morocco. "U.S. policy in Morocco [still however] seeks to preserve the long friendship and cooperation we enjoy on a variety of issues and to encourage Morocco's role as a stable anchor in the region."[31]

Western Sahara

In the 1990s, U.S. policy toward the conflict in Western Sahara has been less noticeably pro-Moroccan. The end of the Cold War, the moderation of the foreign policy toward Algeria (POLISARIO's main ally), and the existence of a UN peace plan approved by Moroccans and Sahrawis, coupled with the perspective of a UN-OAU-sponsored free referendum, were instrumental in changing U.S. policy. The United States made it clear that it supported the peace process and that a freely held referendum would be the deciding factor about the future of the territory. The United States was initially strongly committed to the peace process. However, the Gulf War, the Algerian crisis, and the factors mentioned above resulted in a policy shift back toward a more pro-Moroccan stance. Like the French, Americans were concerned that the Algerian crisis would spill over into Morocco; therefore, maintaining the kingdom's stability became a necessity. Some U.S. officials were privately more inclined to see the conflict resolved to Morocco's advantage. However, the United States seemed more officially committed to a genuinely free referendum in order to determine the final status of the disputed territory. Former assistant secretary of state Robert Pelletreau stated unequivocally that "we consider it important that any referendum organized by the UN be perceived as free and fair so that the results will be respected and enduring and contribute to the stability of the region."[32] Even though the United States supported the peace process, it put little pressure on Morocco to enter negotiations with Sahrawi leaders, as it had done under the Bush administration.

The United States, however, has maintained communications with the POLISARIO, both through the embassies in Algiers and Rabat,[33] and through high-ranking officials as well—a change since the Reagan era, when such communications were forbidden. High-level meetings began in 1990, when Secretary of State James A. Baker met quietly with the Sahrawi Arab Democratic Republic's president Mohammed Abdelaziz in Windhoek, Namibia.

The threat by the U.S. Congress to cut off aid to UN peacekeeping forces would have affected the United Nations Mission for the Referendum in Western Sahara (MINURSO). But that threat should be interpreted as a reaction to the UN's incompetence and failure to resolve conflicts rather than as any bias against the peace process in Western Sahara. Many congressional leaders, in fact, show more sympathy for the Sahrawis than do members of the executive branch. The U.S. administration has blamed both Morocco and the Sahrawis for the stalemate, which has persisted since 1992. Yet despite the United States' proclaimed neutrality in the conflict, the seemingly impartial and hands-off U.S. approach has inevitably favored the status quo, particularly given the great inequality in relationship between the Sahrawis and the Moroccan occupying forces. The United States has never hinted that it would block any movement toward an independent Sahrawi state, but it has never indicated that it favors such an outcome, either.

As with Indonesia's occupation of East Timor, Turkey's occupation of northern Cyprus, and Israel's occupation of neighboring Arab lands, the United States seems reluctant to pressure its allies to withdraw from territories they seized through military force, UN Security Council resolutions and international law notwithstanding. Even state department officials, privately critical of Morocco's occupation, acknowledge that while Western Sahara is just one of several concerns in U.S. policy toward Morocco and the region, it is by far Morocco's highest foreign-policy priority.[34] As a result, Morocco's inclination to resist compromise is much stronger than the United States' inclination to push for a just settlement.

Tunisia

The main characteristic of U.S.-Tunisian relations is constancy. The serenity of the U.S.-Tunisian partnership, which has existed since the 1950s, has been threatened only by the October 1985 Israeli bombing of the

PLO headquarters in Tunis, which caused scores of civilian casualties (the United States had foreknowledge of the bombing but refused to prevent it). Mutual admiration best characterizes the relationship between the American superpower and the small, pro-Western Maghrebi state.

In the 1990s, U.S. policymakers have depicted Tunisia as a success story. A review of testimonies and public statements by U.S. officials reveals the admiration that successive administrations have had for Tunisia. They have been mostly impressed with Tunisia's free-market reforms, for which the U S. provided an inexpensive foreign-assistance program (now terminated) through the U.S. Agency for International Development. The United States had also helped Tunisia through the GATT's General System of Preferences. The predominant view is that Tunisia has made such strides in the realm of socioeconomic development that it "has in a sense graduated from U.S. assistance and is now in the enviable position of being able to offer assistance and training to lesser developed countries."[35]

U.S. appreciation for Tunisia extends beyond the usual praise for moderation and pro-Western stances in international relations. Officials in both the executive and congressional branches view favorably what they perceive as a secular society. Moreover, "Tunisia has been a regional leader in its progressive approach toward women. The high literacy rate of Tunisian women and a correspondingly low birth rate have helped save Tunisia from the severe overpopulation and unemployment problems which today confront many developing countries."[36] The U.S. state department provides an ostensibly sociological analysis of Tunisia in order to distinguish it from the other Maghrebi states: "Tunisia has a much smaller and more homogeneous society than Algeria. . . . Its own Islamist movement . . . was far less vigorous than the FIS."[37]

Of more importance, U.S. policymakers value Tunisia for security reasons. The two countries hold eleven joint military exercises every year (sixteen were scheduled for 1997)—a considerable number, especially when one realizes that it is greater than the number the United States holds with any other Mediterranean country. Those exercises "employ naval, air, special warfare, and amphibious forces from both countries."[38] The Algerian crisis led the United States to pay particular attention to Tunisia. American officials, especially at the Department of Defense (DOD), feared that the Algerian crisis might spill over into Tunisia. From a U.S. perspective, therefore, "Algeria's neighbors will be the focus of DOD efforts in the near term. These efforts are critical to the maintenance of stability in the Mediterranean and North Africa."[39] Although that statement was clearly in reaction to the possibility of terrorism expanding into Tunisia and Morocco, what was less clear was whether the United States could prevent Islamist extremists from coming to power in Algeria. However, the warning clearly applied to Libya, as well, in case the latter attempted to destabilize Tunisia. As it did during the Cold War, the United States reacted to the prospect of an unfriendly regime in Algeria by strengthening the security of its traditional allies, Morocco and Tunisia. Given that U.S. financing for the Tunisian military was terminated in 1994 and military aid to Morocco was substantially reduced (though both countries were still eligible for excess defense goods and military education programs), U.S. intent—beyond supplying anti-terrorist assistance to Tunisia—remains a mystery.

Despite its great esteem for Tunisia, the United States has been critical of its human-rights record. In 1993, for instance, Assistant Secretary of State Edward P. Djerejian stated that, "while we acknowledge Tunisia's concerns about violence, we are seriously concerned that, in the name of internal security, Tunisia dealt too harshly with some of its political opponents. Tunisia's human rights record has been marred by credible claims of torture and incommunicado detention which surfaced during last year's trials of hundreds of Islamists."[40] What is striking, however, is that, even though the state department's annual reports on human rights were not flattering to Tunisia, high-ranking officials, such as Pelletreau, avoided public criticisms of the Tunisian government's human-rights violations as harsh as those leveled against Algeria. In fact (as one observer correctly pointed out about the Maghreb), Moroccan, Tunisian, and Egyptian rulers have justified their repressive policies in the name of stability and survival. Those policies were in response to the Algerian crisis:

> Tunisia . . . has become a virtual police state. Despite the Tunisian government's success in "de-fanging" the Islamist threat and the economic boom that followed economic reforms, repression in Tunisia has worsened, rather than improved, over the past few years. Now, even secular, left-leaning opposition parties, previously considered the "loyal opposition," have been targeted by the government crackdowns. . . . Privately, Tunisian officials boast that their policies will save Tunisia from the tragedy that befell Algeria. Tunisia's tame secular elite echoes these sentiments.[41]

Tunisia's perceived moderation in the Middle East peace process, its attempts to promote better ties with Israel, and its strong security-relations with the United States will undoubtedly dissuade U.S. officials from exerting too much pressure, at least not publicly, on Tunisia to improve its human-rights record.

Conclusion

With the important exception of Libya, which has become an important focus of the rogue-state doctrine, U.S. policy toward the Maghreb appears to be based primarily on pragmatic calculations of state department professionals familiar with the region. The end of the Cold War has resulted in a shift to a more flexible policy in some areas. U.S. support for stability and reconciliation in Algeria has won particularly high marks from diplomatic observers. But the apparent return to a de facto, pro-Moroccan bias in the Western Sahara dispute and the continued fixation on Libyan leader Muammar Qadaffi could lead some in the region to question American diplomacy and could also sow the seeds of instability. The United States has been pushing Algeria, Morocco, and Tunisia toward faster and greater economic liberalization, but whether the push will lead to genuine economic prosperity capable of bringing about stability remains to be seen. Another pertinent question is whether the stability the United States has been seeking is dictated by an interest in creating the appropriate climate for access of U.S. multinational corporations to the region, thus inaugurating a policy driven largely by private economic interests. Two other questions come to mind: (1) whether such policies of economic liberalization will exacerbate social and economic disparities, thus raising the specter of renewed social disorder, and (2) what role, if any, the United States will play in solving them, especially, beyond supporting the World Bank's social safety net.

Meanwhile, the prospects for greater Maghrebi unity, though negligible at the moment (see chapter 11), could undermine U.S. efforts to isolate Libya. However, greater unity among Maghrebi nations could also reduce the perception of Libya as a major threat to American interests. American officials, however, unfortunately have discounted the possibility that Maghrebi unity would be far more likely to moderate Libyan behavior than would U.S. hostility. Instead, they have discouraged Libya's inclusion in any efforts at cooperation despite Libya's ability to interfere with those efforts.[42] National reconciliation in Algeria could pave the way for unprecedented improvement in U.S.-Algerian relations. A peaceful resolution of the Western Sahara dispute, which likely would require independence or substantial autonomy, would enable U.S. companies to

invest in the mineral-rich territory and allow for closer strategic cooperation with Morocco without the stigma of backing an occupying power.
Continued economic and political reforms in Morocco and Tunisia also
would allow for greater cooperation with those two countries and would
result in mutual benefits.

Notes

1. Zoubir, "The U.S., the Algerian Crisis, and the Question of Radical Islamism."
2. Political interests relate to the Middle East peace process and to the fall of
friendly regimes; economic interests refer to access to oil, U.S. investments, and
U.S. multinational corporations.
3. *Washington Post,* January 14, 1992.
4. *Washington Post,* January 15, 1992.
5. Djerejian, "The U.S. and the Middle East in a Changing World."
6. Shirley, "Is Iran's Present Algeria's Future?" 29.
7. Assistant Secretary of State Robert H. Pelletreau's Address on Muslim Politics, Council on Foreign Relations, New York, May 8, 1996.
8. U.S. Department of State, statement on Algeria issued by U.S. Dept. of State
spokesman Nicholas Burns, June 9, 1997, *Africa News Online.*
9. President Bill Clinton's reply to newly appointed Algerian ambassador to the
United States, July 1996. Courtesy of Algerian Embassy (Zoubir's personal ar-
chives).
10. Security Council Resolution 748 (March 31, 1992) and 883 (November
11, 1993).
11. Clark, "Sanctions and Insurrections," 11.
12. *Statement of Robert H. Pelletreau, Assistant Secretary of State for Near
Eastern Affairs before the House International Relations Committee, June 12,
1996* (Washington, D.C.: Government Printing Office, 1996).
13. Waller, "Qadhafi Ahead on Points," 20. U.S. officials concur on this point
(Zoubir phone interview with U.S. Dept. of State official, July 24, 1997).
14. Joffé, "Facing New Sanctions," 9; Joffé, "Qadhafi Ups the Ante," 9.
15. One Hundred and Fourth Congress of the United States of America, *Iran
and Libya Sanctions Act of 1996: H.R.3107.*
16. Ibid., Section 11.
17. Clark, "Sanctions and Insurrections," 11.
18. *C. David Welsh, Acting Assistant Secretary of State for Near Eastern Affairs, Statement before the House Ways and Means Committee, Subcommittee on
Trade, Washington, D.C., May 22, 1996* (U.S. Department of State home page:
http://www.state.gov/www/regions/nea/960522.html).
19. Cited by Kenneth Bacon, Assistant Secretary of Defense, U.S. DOD news
briefing, April 23, 1996.
20. Klare, "Itching for a Fight," 32.

21. Lake, "Confronting Backlash States," 45–46.

22. Ibid., 46.

23. See Klare, "Itching for a Fight," and Zunes, "Rogue States in U.S. Middle East Policy," 150–67.

24. Zunes, "Arab Nationalism and the Persian Gulf Conflict."

25. Damis, "U.S. Policy toward North Africa," 225–26. In 1997, appropriated U.S. economic assistance to Morocco was on the order of $152 million. See U.S. AID, "Congressional Presentation: Summary Tables—Fiscal Year 1998," (Washington, D.C.: Government Printing Office, 1997), 19, 25, 31.

26. Bachir Mustapha Sayed, interview by Margaret A. Novicki, *Africa Report,* May–June 1989, 60.

27. On the notion of surrogate states, see Zunes, "The United States in the Saharan War," 53–92.

28. *Statement by Assistant Secretary of State John R. Bolton before the Subcommittee on Africa Regarding the UN Referendum in the Western Sahara, February 26, 1992,* 6.

29. Kim Murphy, "Moroccan Throne Appears at Stake in a Historic Western Sahara Vote," *Los Angeles Times,* November 9, 1991.

30. "Morocco Becomes Western Outpost against Militant Islam," *Seattle Times,* February 26, 1993.

31. Pelletreau, "U.S. Policy toward North Africa," 669.

32. *Statement by Robert Pelletreau, Assistant Secretary of State for Near Eastern Affairs at Hearing before the Subcommittee on Africa of the Committee on Foreign Affairs, House of Representatives, September 28, 1994* (Washington, D.C.: Government Printing Office, 1995), 8.

33. Interview conducted by Stephen Zunes with U.S. Dept. of State official, Washington, D.C., June 5, 1997.

34. Ibid.

35. *Statement by Robert Pelletreau . . . September 28, 1994, 5.*

36. "Statement by Edward P. Djerejian, Assistant Secretary for Near East Affairs, before the Subcommittee on Africa of the House Foreign Affairs Committee, Washington, D.C., May 12, 1993," *Dispatch* 4, no. 21 (May 24, 1993): 377.

37. *Statement by Mark R. Parris, Acting Assistant Secretary of State for Near Eastern Affairs, before the House Foreign Affairs Committee, Subcommittee on Africa, March 22, 1994* (Washington, D.C.: Government Printing Office, 1995), 59.

38. *Testimony of Bruce Riedel, Deputy Assistant Secretary of Defense for Near Eastern and South Asian Affairs, before the House Committee on International Relations, the Subcommittee on Africa, October 11, 1995* (Washington, D.C.: Government Printing Office, 1996), 28.

39. Ibid.

40. "Statement by Edward P. Djerejian . . . May 12, 1993." U.S. officials have remained disappointed with Tunisia's political reforms and human rights (Zoubir phone interview with U.S. Dept. of State official, July 24, 1997).

41. Yacoubian, *Algeria's Struggle for Democracy,* 37. For a different view, cf. statement by Hon. Nick Rahal II in the House of Representatives, April 15, 1997, in *Congressional Record Online,* via GPO Access [wais.access.gpo.gov].

42. Mortimer, "Maghreb Matters," 160–75.

15.

THE EUROPEAN UNION AND THE
MAGHREB IN THE 1990S

George Joffé

It is no secret that the European Union—despite the promises of the Maastricht Treaty and the Amsterdam intergovernmental conference (both of which postulated a common EU security and foreign policy)—is still unable to articulate common political and diplomatic positions toward the world outside its frontiers, except at the level of the lowest common denominator. The reality has been that, as the EU has sought to intensify its internal cohesion, the national preoccupations of its constituent members have become ever more prominent, and this has severely hampered its abilities to formulate common positions on foreign policy and defense. The 1996–97 intergovernmental conference, which was designed, among other things, to push forward the development of such common objectives, made little significant difference to the current position of disarray (despite its proposal for an official policy coordinator), particularly over the issue of common defense policy; tensions between NATO and the WEU as options for European defense strategy remain as acute as ever. Interestingly enough, as far as foreign policy issues are concerned, apart from a general agreement over the need to expand Union membership eastward (although disagreements remain about the speed with which this should be done), the one area in which a degree of common purpose has emerged has been over the issue of the EU's policy toward the Mediterranean.

At the same time, this common policy bears all the hallmarks of the inherent problems that the formulation of EU policy always exhibits. Its political and security content is weak, for it is predominantly economic in orientation. It reflects acute European preoccupations over the evolution of the internal European scene, rather than a broader regional vision. Yet it is undeniable that there is a coherent EU policy now in place toward the Maghreb at least, and by extension to the remainder of the southern Mediterranean as well. This, in itself, is a significant achievement. The question is to what extent it can respond to the realities of the situation in the Maghreb or, indeed, to its own imperatives.

There are two major reasons for this apparent collective unity of purpose. The first reflects European concerns over migration into Europe in the context of significant levels of European unemployment in the 1990s and the consequent domestic xenophobic pressures, as well as security anxieties engendered by the situation in Algeria and the continuing problems in relations with Libya. The second concerns the need for Europe to address the geopolitical and geo-economic implications of its regional role among states along its periphery.[1] This has been translated into a differentiation between the eastern and the southern peripheries.[2] As far as the southern periphery is concerned, the anxiety of southern European states over the precedence originally given to the east after the end of the Cold War in 1991 has been coupled with a growing desire throughout the EU to see effective economic development within the region, in the hope that this may deflect migratory pressures, alongside an awareness that the piecemeal approach of the past is inadequate and that an integrated holistic relationship with peripheral states was inevitable. The anxieties of southern European states are that, since the end of the Cold War, European investment flows have been substantially directed eastward and away from the Mediterranean region. They argue that this trend will endanger issues of Mediterranean security as well as stimulate migration flows northward if economic development among south Mediterranean nonmember countries stagnates.

Given the limitations on a common security and foreign policy, the European Union's agenda toward North Africa is not, however, the only expression of European concern over the Mediterranean basin. The Barcelona process represents the limits of what currently can be achieved within the framework of the EU because of the lack of a comprehensive policymaking structure within the commission and in the council of ministers. As one commentator has remarked, admittedly in the context of the current security debate over the Mediterranean, but the comment applies in other areas equally well, "through no fault of its own, the Barcelona process is an imperfect, and even preemptive, expression of the EU's CFSP."[3] In view of the fact that individual European states have their own specific national interests connected with the Maghreb region, their individual foreign policies also need to be examined in the light of the general framework of European policy toward North Africa.

Not surprisingly, France has the most acute interest in the region, albeit for largely atavistic reasons related to its long colonial involvement in the Maghreb. At the same time, however, Italy, Spain and Portugal have long had significant commitment to good relations with Maghrebi states for reasons of security and trade—Italy, after all, depends heavily on Libyan oil as well as being the terminal for the Trans-Med gas pipeline from Algeria via Tunisia, and Spain has just begun to receive natural gas through the Trans-Maghreb pipeline from Algeria. This specificity of southern European interests in the Maghreb has been particularly marked in the context of the various collective security proposals that have emerged since the start of the 1990s, all of which have involved these four states— the Conference on Security and Cooperation in the Mediterranean (CSCM—Spain and Italy, 1990), the Five-plus-Five proposal (France, 1991), the Mediterranean Forum (Egypt, 1994), Eurofor and Euromarfor (all four states, 1996),[4] to mention only the most significant. Now, however, these concerns are also being integrated into the Barcelona process, leaving specifically national questions within the unique purview of each state.[5] And, in that context and largely prompted by the introduction of the Euro-Mediterranean Partnership Initiative, Britain and Germany have begun to consider the significance of their own relationships with the Maghreb—both within the European Union and on a bilateral basis—in ways which did not exist before.

Euro-Mediterranean Policy

The Euro-Mediterranean Partnership Initiative is the brainchild of the European commission and represents the culmination of European attempts to find a common policy toward the Mediterranean basin that reflects both a colonial legacy—particularly in North Africa—and an appropriate response to the burgeoning regionalization of the global economy. It is the latest stage in a policy that began in 1956 as an attempt to cope with the implications of the French colonial experience—primarily in North Africa, but also in the Middle East—and of the fact that Maghrebi economies were profoundly dependent on their access to the

European market as a result.[6] It was a reality that was formally recognized in the 1957 Treaty of Rome, the founding document of the European Community. Individual agreements were made with Maghrebi states to allow colonial import preferences (mainly in agricultural produce) to continue, with France as the major market. Its first formal institutionalization as a European initiative occurred in 1969, when association agreements were signed between the European Economic Community (EEC)—as the EU was then known—and Morocco and Tunisia. The existing agreements had been designed to go beyond the old system of colonial preferences by allowing virtually unrestricted access into Europe for industrial goods as well as providing special access for agricultural produce.

After 1976, the agreements were amplified by the introduction of five-year financial protocols designed to promote economic development. Although restrictions on the access to European markets of agricultural goods remained (indeed, were strengthened after Spain and Portugal joined the EEC in 1986), financial cooperation increased and each agreement was given greater specificity, taking into account the needs of individual south Mediterranean partners. In essence, however, the basic assumptions behind the agreements remained as they had in the early years, and the same fundamental relationship between the EEC and its south Mediterranean partners persisted: that of providing access in certain specific economic areas and excluding it in others, in order to protect European producers, particularly in agriculture and in the textile sector, while, at the same time, providing development aid on a bilateral basis.[7]

It is worth noting that all these arrangements were essentially devoid of political content. No interaction at a diplomatic level took place within the agreements. At the same time, however, the world outside European Community diplomacy was changing, as were the assumptions on which European–south Mediterranean links were based. With the end of the Cold War approaching and the growth in importance of human rights issues in international politics, the EEC found it increasingly difficult to maintain its resolutely economist stance, not least because of the growing importance of the European Parliament, which was fully prepared to comment on aspects of third-country behavior over which the commission preferred to draw a discreet veil. In addition, there was a crisis looming in several European states over levels of migrant labor, particularly from North Africa, at a time when European economies were increasingly subject to retrenchment in employment.[8] This, in turn, persuaded member states that the time had come to limit immigration and to persuade established migrant labor populations to return home, if possible. This process had been going on since the late 1970s, but now it acquired renewed urgency under the pressure of economic stagnation and technological change, which expressed themselves socially in increased European xenophobia.[9]

There were other problems as well. The October 1988 riots in Algeria and the subsequent rise of a mass-based Islamist movement caused considerable anxiety in European chancelleries, given the sizable migrant populations from North Africa that many of them possessed. It also reminded them that the relative stability of North Africa, compared with the Middle East, was increasingly threatened (contrary to expectations) by economic decline. This was particularly serious in view of the fact that two Maghrebi economies had been subject to major economic restructuring, Morocco since 1983 and Tunisia since 1987. Algeria, like Libya, was a major oil and gas exporter and thus had sufficient funds (or rents), in theory, to fuel development. Furthermore, all three Maghrebi economies[10] suffered from heavy burdens of foreign debt, although, in the case of Tunisia, debt levels were manageable. Algeria's foreign debt had been acquired to finance major oil and gas process plants under the Valhyd Plan, on the assumption that the consequently increased export revenues would allow the debt to be easily paid back.[11] In Morocco's case, the combination of borrowing against the expectation of increased phosphate export revenues in 1976 and the costs of the Western Sahara war had produced a similar situation a decade earlier, leading to debt rescheduling in 1983. Most of the major creditors (particularly the official creditors) were European, so the European Community as a whole felt it necessary to reconsider its policy approach to the Maghreb in particular and the south Mediterranean basin in general.[12]

By 1992 it had become evident, in the wake of the euphoria that greeted the defeat of Iraq in the Second Gulf War, that political issues could no longer be completely excluded from the European Union's agenda as far as the Middle East and North Africa were concerned. This was made abundantly and embarrassingly clear when, in 1992, the European parliament banned aid to Morocco on the grounds of its abuses of human rights, particularly in the Western Sahara conflict. Embarrassed commission officials tried to repair the damage by proposing a novel form of agreement to Morocco which would bypass the obstreperous parliament: a free-trade area agreement with the EU.

This development coincided with the growing realization that the renovated Mediterranean policy was not going to achieve its objectives, and by June 1994, at the Corfu European Union summit, European heads of state called on the commission to prepare a new policy in line with the new realities. This was embodied in a special commission document which was to form the basis of the discussions at the December 1994 Essen summit, in which the new Euro-Mediterranean Partnership Initiative was authorized.[13] At the Nice meeting of European heads of state the following June, the new policy was given the go-ahead, and during the Spanish presidency of the European Union, it was launched in November in Barcelona at a major conference of the fifteen Union members and their eleven south Mediterranean correspondents.[14] By that time, Tunisia and Morocco had already signed up to the new policy, more specific bilateral arrangements which brought them directly into the European economic area.

The Euro-Mediterranean Partnership Initiative

As was true of its precursors, the Euro-Mediterranean Partnership Initiative is essentially an economic process. It is designed, for security reasons (namely, to block economic migration into Europe) to stimulate economic development in the partnership nonmember states. It does this through the institution of bilateral free-trade agreements with each partner for industrial goods and services. Agricultural goods are excluded, for they fall under the restrictive conditions of the common agricultural policy and are subject to quota and tariff regulation to protect European producers (although the EU has promised to reconsider the situation after the year 2005). The first two agreements, with Morocco and Tunisia, provide for twelve-year transition periods before both countries are expected to remove all tariff and nontariff barriers to free trade. Similar provisions are being negotiated with Algeria. The process of transition is aided by a special five-year financial protocol, the MEDA Program, which provides Ecu 4.685 billion (down from the original Essen proposal of Ecu 5.5 billion at British insistence). MEDA funding is only available to the private sector and represents roughly 25 percent more than was available under the previous financial protocol. It will be amplified by loans of a similar size from the European Investment Bank.

There are two crucial distinctions between these new free-trade agreements and the association and cooperation agreements that preceded them. First, the financial aid prioritizes the private sector and seeks to emphasize horizontal funding. Second, for the first time, it is the recipient countries—the European Union nonmember states—that have to make the major concessions in terms of removing barriers to trade. After all, under the previous agreements, it was the European Union that offered tariff-free access to Mediterranean nonmember countries without requiring similar treatment in reverse. This has now ended, and given the volume of industrial goods that Maghrebi states import, the change will have severe implications for government revenues. Most Maghrebi states depend heavily on customs duties for revenue, and now that this has gone, they will have to find other sources of revenue. Almost certainly, this will come from indirect taxation. Tunisia, for example, has already extended the range of the value-added tax for this reason, and other states will have to do the same or introduce similar taxation systems as the problems of transition to the new bilateral free-trade areas begin to bite.

The transitions themselves are also going to be difficult for the states concerned. Tunisia has estimated that, without special conversion programs, two-thirds of its industrial sector will simply disappear under the effects of European competition. As it is, the *mise à niveau* (equalization) conversion program it has introduced is expected to save one-third of the sector, although the remaining one-third will go to the wall. The costs of the transition are estimated at $2.2 billion, of which 80 percent will have to come from foreign sources. In Morocco, the comparable costs are estimated at $5.4 billion; without such sums, 60 percent of the Moroccan industrial sector is condemned to disappear.[15]

There is a complex set of reasons for this. In part, the Barcelona process merely anticipates the requirements of the Uruguay round of the General Agreement on Tariffs and Trade (signed in Marrakech in April 1995 and now enshrined in the World Trade Organization), which requires a general reduction in external tariffs and the tariffication of nontariff barriers. This, in itself, would threaten protected domestic industries, as will indeed happen under the Barcelona process. There is, however, a more direct threat in that North African and Middle Eastern industrial sectors must now meet European production and safety standards, both to defend their domestic markets and to penetrate European markets, whether in finished products or intra-industry and intermediate goods. It is this consideration that, in the short term, has caused such anxiety in Morocco and Tunisia, where industry is primarily concerned with textiles, mechanical and electrical assembly, and agricultural processing.

As troubling are the longer-term implications of the new relationship. Given European technological superiority and the relative lack of comparative advantage offered by south Mediterranean economies, there is a considerable danger that they will become economic satellites of European manufacturers, supplying inputs but not becoming sophisticated manufacturers in their own right, along the pattern of the *maquilladora* industries along the Mexican-American border. Even worse is the danger that such suppliers, because of their export orientation, will become separated from the national economic fabric in which they are located and thus become economic enclaves in which, despite the apparent benefit they generate for national macroeconomic indicators, their internal microeconomic effects would be denied to the wider national economy. In other words, as was the experience of the multinationals in the developing world during the 1960s, "trickle-down" does not occur, and the purchasing power of the population as a whole is not increased. In such circumstances, the European-oriented sectors of the economies of south Mediterranean states will become enclaves within their own national economies. In economists' terms, they will become "leopard-spot" economies. Static and dynamic trade effects worsen these problems, such that the south Mediterranean economies' trade dependence on Europe will significantly increase to the detriment of their national economies.

The main problem with the economic basket is that, although it seeks to achieve a similar economic shock as was provided for the Spanish and Portuguese economies when these two states joined the European Community in 1986, it will not provide the convergence funding that they both enjoyed thereafter. The convergence funding, whether in terms of structural or cohesion funds, was designed to accelerate the adjustment of the Portuguese and Spanish economies (and, later, the Irish economy) to the levels of the other Community economies. So great were the sums involved that Brussels bureaucrats often joked that it was not that Spain had penetrated the European Community—it was that the European Community had penetrated Spain.

With the Barcelona process, however, no such generosity is on display: the countries concerned are not joining the Community, or the EU and the MEDA funding being provided falls into the category of official external aid. Indeed, they are not even joining the European economic area— the so-called European common economic space—and do not form part of the EU's budgetary process. By definition, therefore, convergence funding is denied them and, as eastward enlargement progresses, the likelihood of substantially increased adjustment funding will correspondingly decline. The south Mediterranean countries concerned, therefore, must pick up their essential transition funding from private foreign investment, either direct or portfolio, and this has also proved to be very difficult in the past.

If the economic outlook is so uncertain, it is reasonable to ask why south Mediterranean states have been prepared to take such a gamble. The short answer is that they have little choice, for the European Union is by far their dominant economic partner. In 1992, for example, the European Union generated 47.1 percent of the imports absorbed by the Middle East and North Africa and absorbed 38.3 percent of their exports. This dependency has increased since then and is even higher for the Maghreb.[16] In addition, there are some 2.6 million North Africans living in Europe as migrant laborers,[17] and this intensifies North African interest in closer ties with Europe, even if there is an economic cost. In any case, if sufficient private investment can be found, then the economic gamble may pay off. The hope is that the European Union ultimately will be persuaded to create an ever-closer union with the south Mediterranean world, so that free movement of goods and services eventually will be accompanied by free movement of people. In the shorter term, south Mediterranean states know that if agriculture were brought into the free-trade areas, their economic fortunes would be transformed radically. Although the EU has so far refused to consider this, it has hinted that, after 2005, the common agricultural policy may be sufficiently restrained to make such changes possible. In addition, they also know that, by 2010, the European Union intends to push for south-south economic integration, which would produce dramatic opportunities for real development in the southern region, despite the disadvantages the current agreements impose on nonmember states. Another possibility for ameliorating the process (which, however, has been completely discounted by the European Union at present) is that of debt forgiveness. Much official debt in the region is held by European states, as are significant proportions of commercial debt. Any easing of the debt-servicing burden (which reached as much as 82 percent of export earnings from goods and services in Algeria before rescheduling in 1993, for example)[18] would have dramatic effects on most North African economies. If a long-standing Tunisian proposal for the recycling of debt servicing as investment capital were adopted, it could also provide the essential investment motor for economic development.

In any case, Europe is linked to the Maghreb by its energy dependence. The Maghreb supplied 15.8 percent of European crude-oil requirements in 1995, compared with 28 percent from the Middle East. At the same time, North Africa provided 15.9 percent of European requirements in natural gas and, as in 1997, will provide 18.5 percent of this requirement.[19] Thus Europe and the south Mediterranean region have intense economic links that will make separate development of each region virtually impossible in the future. These ties, moreover, are intensified by the other two baskets of the Barcelona process. These concern political and security issues (basket 2) and social and cultural matters (basket 3). Basket 2, in essence, is concerned with introducing principles of "good governance"—democratization and respect for human rights—into the south Mediterranean region. The security issues are subsumed under the same principles as those enunciated in earlier initiatives, such as the CSCM and Five-plus-Five proposals of the early years of the decade. The political issues were introduced more as a formality into the final document than because they represented a serious European commitment to intervene in the governmental process in the Maghreb. However, for two reasons, it is becoming increasingly likely that European involvement in the process of economic development will aid in the process of political change in the region: first, because of the increase in transparency required and the consequent undermining of patterns of patronage and privilege there; and second, because of pressure from nongovernmental organizations and the European parliament.

Attitudes among National Governments

European Union policies are, however, only one part of the complex pattern of European attitudes toward the Maghreb. Since the EU is constrained to operate by consensus in foreign policy issues, national governments in Europe retain broad interests in the Maghreb region and in specific countries there in ways that outflank the concerns of the EU itself. This has long been true of France, as the former dominant colonial power there. It is also true of the other south European states—Portugal, Spain, and Italy—because of their proximity to the south Mediterranean region as well as because of their historic links with it. Interestingly enough, however, Britain and Germany—where interest in the western Mediterranean has been limited—have both begun to formulate a western Mediterranean dimension to their foreign policies now that they are involved in the Euro-Mediterranean Partnership Initiative. Their interest is increasing, perhaps, because they generate most of the MEDA funding through the size of their contributions to the overall European Union budget (17 percent of the total in the case of Britain).

South European Attitudes

There is little doubt that Spain has come to dominate southern European attitudes toward the south Mediterranean nonmember states, particularly those in the Maghreb. Not only has Spain played a major role in the formulation of the Barcelona process but it has paid particular attention to its relations with Morocco, where it has had the greatest economic interest until recently (now, perhaps, superseded by the new Trans-Maghreb pipeline, which, since November 1996, has begun to deliver gas from Algeria, via Morocco, to Spain and Portugal). Nonetheless, political relations between the two countries have been close, despite the potential problems of Morocco's claims to the two Spanish presidios of Ceuta and Melilla on Morocco's Mediterranean coastline and residual Spanish sovereign ties over the Western Sahara. The links between the two royal houses have played a significant role in this, and Moroccans look toward the Spanish experience of the transition from Franquism to the monarchy in 1975 for a guide to how their own transition from King Hassan's authoritarian rule toward the constitutionalized monarchy implied by the recent constitutional referendum may take place. The 1997 election process in Morocco, however, indicates that authoritarian attitudes die hard, and although there has been a dramatic improvement in the human-rights position there as well as in the spheres of personal freedom and freedom of the press, Morocco's progress along the path illuminated by Spain toward full democracy may be significantly slower than anticipated.

There are several reasons for Spain's leading role in the formulation of south European attitudes toward the western Mediterranean, a role that has come to the fore particularly during the 1990s. In part, this is a consequence of Spain's domestic stability and economic development as a result of its integration into the European Union. Membership in the EU, after all, ensured the survival of Spain's youthful democracy. It also reflects a growing desire by Spanish officials to play a proactive Mediterranean role—Spanish *protagonismo,* in the words of one commentator.[20] Apart from national self-interest, this attitude also reflected Spanish anxieties that the end of the Cold War would bring about a realignment of European investment patterns from the south of the continent eastward, as indeed happened. For Spain, therefore, the Barcelona process was a way of redressing the investment balance with the full authority of the EU behind it.

This emerged first in the joint Spanish-Italian proposal in 1990 for the CSCM security structure in the Mediterranean. Although this initiative proved abortive, Spain (largely at Moroccan suggestion) played a leading role in recommending the creation of a Mediterranean free-trade area and pushing the proposal through against considerable skepticism among its North European partners.[21] The interesting aspect of this situation of

Spanish activism is that it implies that, in recent years, French influence and activism over European interests in the western Mediterranean have receded.

To some extent, this impression is correct, although France, in economic terms, is still the dominant partner for Maghrebi states and the postcolonial links with the three Maghrebi states remain strong; indeed, the links have been revived by the accession of Jacques Chirac to the French presidency.[22] The major reason for this was French anxiety and ambiguity over the crisis in Algeria. President Mitterrand made little secret of his distaste for the January 1992 army-backed coup in Algiers, which interrupted the electoral process there because of fears that the Islamist movement would gain control of the political process. Yet for the French government, the specter of an Islamist takeover in Algeria was intolerable, and under the latter years of the Balladur government, French involvement in security issues—both in Algeria and in France—had become significant. This, in turn, attracted radical Islamic ire and a transfer of violence from Algeria into France itself. At the same time, relations with Tunisia declined because of French irritation with the repressiveness of the Ben Ali regime, as they did with Morocco because of a series of minor issues.

The arrival of Chirac to power was to alter profoundly the foreign relations scene.[23] The new president wasted no time in patching up relations with Morocco, making the country the target of his first foreign presidential visit. A similar visit to Tunis followed some months later, and a new sense of optimism toward France and Europe made itself felt, even in Libya, as the Qadaffi regime eagerly anticipated an end to its isolation, at least as far as France was concerned. In the event, Libyan hopes proved premature, although the French government did go out of its way to end the crisis in relations because of assumed Libyan involvement in the bombing of a UTA aircraft over Niger in September 1989. Those accused of being involved were finally indicted in absentia in early 1997, in a move that seemed designed to sweep the whole affair under the carpet. At the same time, however, France continued to support UN sanctions against Libya. Over Algeria, however, ambiguity continued, although France scaled down its military aid and supported the initiative of Algerian opposition parties for a negotiated settlement to the crisis, as proposed in the Rome Platform, suggested by them after meeting in Rome in January 1995. Shortly thereafter, however, France reaffirmed its cautious support for the Liamine Zeroual regime and for its proposed electoral process, despite misgivings in Paris that little would be achieved. It remains to be seen to what extent the arrival of a socialist government to power in France in June 1997 will affect the situation. First hints suggest that the new government will be far less indulgent toward the Zeroual regime than in the past, although the complex nature of Franco-Algerian relations may well neutralize any initiatives it may undertake.

The net result of these ambiguities has been that France was prepared to take a supporting role alongside Spain in pushing the Euro-Mediterranean Partnership Initiative ahead rather than dominating the process itself. As a result, the partnership initiative was initiated during the French presidency of the European Union in early 1995, but the detailed drafting of the final communiqué and the organization of the actual Barcelona conference were left to Spanish diplomats. Nonetheless, Spain was obliged to take heed of French concerns. France, for example, did not want a U.S. presence at the conference; Spain wanted the United States to participate as an observer. In the event, the United States did not participate at all—thus preserving the French view that the Euro-Mediterranean Partnership Initiative was a genuinely European concern in which the United States had no direct role. Of course, this stand cannot be maintained indefinitely, and issues of collective security, which will involve NATO, will also involve the United States.[24] Yet French sensitivities are still able to sway its European partners in the detailed formulation of Mediterranean policy.

The other two southern partners, Italy and Portugal, generally have played supporting roles. Indeed, Italy, after a brief period of active policy formulation over Mediterranean affairs at the start of the 1990s, under Foreign Minister Gianni de Michelis, which produced with Spain the CSCM proposal, lapsed back into its traditional subordinate role. In the past, this active formulation policy has been engendered as a result of the memory of the activism shown during the Fascist period, and, apart from concerns over access to energy (Italy is Europe's biggest importer of oil from Libya, for example, and has acute interests in Algerian natural gas because of the Trans-Med Pipeline), it has typified Italy's postwar Mediterranean policy, at least as far as North Africa is concerned.

Portugal, on the other hand, is anxious to emphasize its significance within southern European policies toward the Mediterranean, despite the fact that it does not have a Mediterranean coastline. (Rabat is the closest capital to Lisbon, and Morocco is therefore a near neighbor.) Portugal is also aware, as is Spain, that the end of the Cold War has meant the reorientation of investment flows eastward, away from the Mediterranean region. It, therefore, has an interest in supporting Spanish attempts to redirect European interest southward once again, both over economic and security matters.[25]

The Northern European Response

The two northern European states that have an influence on European policy toward the south Mediterranean region, because of their role in funding the Euro-Mediterranean Partnership Initiative, are Britain and Germany. Their interests in the western Mediterranean beyond this policy arena traditionally have been marginal to their interests elsewhere in the European periphery. Germany has always placed the East as a high priority, and Britain has been far more involved in the eastern Mediterranean. This is not to suggest, however, that they have had no interests in the Maghreb. Germany has long had a special relationship with Tunisia, largely because of German firms that outsourced there during the 1960s. Britain has been concerned about the strategic significance of Gibraltar, particularly after Spain closed its borders with the colony in the 1960s and Morocco provided essential labor and food and water supplies instead.

Britain, however, has also been forced to widen its western Mediterranean horizons since the 1980s because of its increasingly tense relationship with Libya. Formal diplomatic relations were broken in 1984, and Britain joined the United States in 1992 in condemning Libya for its alleged involvement in the destruction of an airliner over the Scottish town of Lockerbie in December 1988. Britain has, since then, refused to allow Libya to be brought into the Barcelona process and has made it clear that this will not be acceptable until the Lockerbie issue is cleared up, despite pressure from south Mediterranean states and from some of its partners within the European Union. Britain has also been at the forefront of demands to trim back the MEDA funding program (as has Germany) and has argued that more efforts must be made to stimulate private foreign investment into the region. It has also begun to develop specific links with Morocco, both because of the political reforms taking place there and because of the privatization program now being undertaken by the Moroccan government, in which British advisers have played an important role.

Germany has expressed reservations about the Barcelona process similar to Britain's, and initially it was Germany that was most reluctant to go ahead with it, largely because Germany would be expected to provide 30 percent of the MEDA funding program. There are also serious domestic reservations about a significant involvement in the Mediterranean because of regional instability and domestic prejudices against the Islamic world.[26] Yet in the final analysis, Germany, like Britain, recognizes that south Mediterranean security and development are essential if the threat of migration is to be reduced and that this will depend on a successful outcome to the Euro-Mediterranean Partnership Initiative.

The Outlook

It is clear that the European Union agenda over the Maghreb is driven essentially by Spain and France, with Germany and Britain maintaining ultimate control. It is for this reason that the economic aspect that characterizes all European common policy formulation is so strong. It reflects, too, the predominantly defensive nature of European policy toward the region, with its emphasis on exclusion and the role of the market in fostering economic development. One consequence of this attitude is that the policy itself may well fail in the terms it has set itself. Indeed, this will certainly be the case if Europe cannot persuade south Mediterranean states to form their own integrated economic groupings by 2015, when the current agreements come to an end.

It may turn out, however, that other aspects of the Barcelona process will have greater significance in the long run, whatever the economic prospects may be. As suggested above, the very nature of the economic transformation being imposed on the states of the Maghreb may threaten established power relations there by breaking up the traditional patronage-clientage patterns that dominate both the economy and government. This, of course, depends on the degree to which governments are prepared to embrace such change, but the pressure will be there, nonetheless. It will be intensified by internal and external pressure for political change—partly because of the nature of the agreements themselves, but much more significantly because of changes in cultural and information links between Europe and the Maghreb. Indeed, it is extremely difficult to quantify the role that these might play in the future, whatever indigenous political developments in the region might be.

Indeed, the uncertainties implicit in the overall Barcelona process are far greater than in its economic dimension alone. One of the main reasons for this is that, despite its defensive nature, the process will force Europe and the Maghreb to engage in an increasingly shared policy process. Of course, this is of far greater importance for the Maghreb than it is for Europe. Nonetheless, there is a profound irony in the fact that it has been the European Union, with its nonexistent common foreign and security policy, which has imposed on European states the necessity of formulating national policies to the south Mediterranean region. It is a further irony that these policies now coincide to such an extent that they give meaning to the otherwise empty rhetoric that defines the third pillar of Maastricht. It remains to be seen, however, whether or not this is a pointer toward a common European future and what its real implications for the Maghreb might be.

Notes

This chapter is a revised and extended version of an article originally published in *Cambridge Review of International Affairs* 10, no. 2 (winter–spring 1997).

1. A good analysis of the problems of migration from North Africa into Europe is provided by Collinson, *Shore to Shore.*

2. Lorca, "The EU and the Mediterranean."

3. Spencer, "Reconceptualizing or Re-Orientating Europe's Mediterranean Security Focus?"

4. *Eurofor* and *Euromarfor* are land-based and maritime forces drawn from France, Spain, Italy, and Portugal that are designed for collective Mediterranean security issues and for humanitarian purposes. They came into formal operation—to intense southern Mediterranean suspicion and hostility—in late 1996. This experience parallels that of NATO, which is also developing its own southern Mediterranean dialogue, against a background of suspicion and disbelief among southern Mediterranean nonmember states. These states have little confidence in hints of a southern "partnership-for-peace" initiative from what they consider to be a fundamentally European instrument of collective security, which, almost by definition, eventually will be directed against them. Many persons in the southern Mediterranean still recall former NATO secretary-general Willy Claes's assertion that political Islam would eventually turn out to be as great a threat as communism once was.

5. Spencer, "Reconceptualizing or Re-Orientating Europe's Mediterranean Security Focus?"

6. Camier, *Les pays du Grand Maghreb et la Communauté Européenne.* The willingness to do this was enshrined in the Treaty of Rome, signed in 1957, in which the new European entity agreed to sign economic agreements with countries in the franc zone, "dans le souci de maintenir et d'intensifier les courants traditionnels d'échanges et de contribuer au développement économique de ces pays" (12).

7. An excellent account of the history of the relationship is provided in Marks, "High Hopes and Low Motives," 1–24.

8. Collinson, *Shore to Shore,* appendix for numbers (although these almost certainly significantly underestimate the true figures).

9. In reality, North Africans make up roughly 2.6 million of Europe's estimated

10 million foreign emigrant workers. Indicative figures are given in Oualalou, *Après Barcelone . . . le Maghreb est nécessaire,* 174.

10. Tunisia, Algeria, and Morocco are conventionally considered to be the Maghreb states, although they have been joined by Libya and Mauritania in the Maghreb Arab Union (UMA).

11. Joffé, "Algeria in the New World Order," 49. "Valhyd" stands for "Valorisation des hydrocarbures."

12. European Commission, *SEC* (89), 1958.

13. European Commission, *Strengthening the Mediterranean Policy of the European Union.*

14. Mauritania, Morocco, Algeria, Tunisia, Egypt, Jordan, Israel, Lebanon, Syria, Turkey, and Malta. Libya was excluded because of its continuing dispute with Britain, France, and the United States over airborne terrorism and the UN sanctions against it.

15. *Maghreb Quarterly Report* 19 (June–October 1995): 42.

16. Joffé, "Integration or Peripheral Dependence," 181.

17. Joffé, "Algeria in the New World Order," 49.

18. Ruf, "The Flight of Rent," 11.

19. British Petroleum, *BP Statistical Review of World Energy 1996,* 18–28.

20. Gillespie, "Spain and the Mediterranean," 193–211.

21. Eberhardt Rhein, former head of DG-1 in the European Commission, quoted in *El Pais,* international. ed., November 27, 1995.

22. Howorth, "France and the Mediterranean in 1995," 157–75.

23. Joffé, "Jacques Chirac and France's Middle East Policy," 23–37.

24. Lesser, "Southern Europe and the Maghreb," 231–42.

25. Faria, "The Mediterranean: A New Priority in Portuguese Foreign Policy," 212–30.

26. Jünemann, "The Mediterranean Policy of the Federal Republic of Germany."

Bibliography

Books

Addi, Lahouari. *L'Algérie et la démocratie: Pouvoir et crise du politique dans l'Algérie contemporaine* (Algeria and democracy: Power and political crisis in contemporary Algeria). Paris: La Découverte, 1995.

Aguirre, José Ramón Diego. *Historia del Sahara Espanõl—La Verdad de una Traición* (History of Western Sahara: The truth about a treason). Madrid: Kaydedas Ediciones, 1988.

Ait-Embarek, Moussa. *L'Algérie en murmure: Un cahier sur la torture* (Algeria in whispers: A notebook on torture). Geneva: Hoggar, 1996.

Aktouf, Omar. *Algérie: Entre l'exil et la curée.* Paris: Editions L'Harmattan, 1989.

Amin, Samir, ed. *Le Maghreb: Enlisement ou nouveau départ?* (The Maghreb: Sinking or a new departure?). Paris: L'Harmattan, Forum du Tiers Monde, 1996.

Amnesty International. *Algeria: Deteriorating Human Rights under the State of Emergency.* London: Amnesty International, 1993.

———. *Amnesty International Report.* London: Amnesty International, 1993.

———. *Amnesty International Report.* London: Amnesty International, 1996.

———. *Libya: Amnesty's Prisoner Concern in the Light of Recent Legal Reforms.* London: Amnesty International, 1991.

———. *Libya: Further Information on Political Detention.* London: Amnesty International, 1991.

———. *Morocco: Breaking the Wall of Silence. The "Disappeared" in Morocco.* London: Amnesty International, 1993.

———. *Morocco: Human Rights Violations in* Garde à Vue *Detention.* London: Amnesty International, 1990.

———. *Tunisia: Women Victims of Harassment, Torture and Imprisonment.* London: Amnesty International, 1993.

Amsden, Alice H. *Asia's Next Giant.* New York: Oxford, 1989.

Anderson, Lisa. *The State and Social Transformation in Tunisia and Libya, 1830–1980.* Princeton, N.J.: Princeton University Press, 1986.

Arkoun, Mohammed. *L'Islam, morale et politique.* Paris: UNESCO/Desclée de Brouwer, 1986.

———. *Ouvertures sur l'Islam.* 2nd ed. Paris: J. Grancher, 1992.

Attali, Jacques. *Verbatim—Chronique des années 1981–1986.* Paris: Fayard, 1993.

Badie, Bertrand. *L'état importé. Essai sur l'occidentalisation de l'ordre politique.* Paris: Fayard, 1992.

Badie, Bertrand, Christian Coulon, Bernard Cubertafond, et al. *Contestations en pays islamiques* (Opposition in Islamic countries). Paris: CHEAM, 1984.

Balta, Paul. *Le Grand Maghreb—Des indépendances à l'an 2000.* Paris: La Découverte, 1990.

Béji, Hélé. *Le désenchantement national: Essai sur la décolonisation* (National disenchantment: Essay on decolonization). Paris: Maspero, 1982.

———. *L'imposture culturelle* (The cultural imposture). Paris: Editions Stock, 1997.

Benani, Boubker Jala. *L'islamisme et les droits de l'homme* (Islamism and the rights of man). Lausanne, Switzerland: Aire, 1984.

Ben Jelloun, Tahar. *Harrouda.* Paris: Denoël, 1973.

———. *L'homme rompu* (Worn-out man). Paris: Editions du Seuil, 1994.

Bennabi, Malek. *La démocratie en Islam* (Democracy in Islam). Algiers: Mosquée Beni Messous, n.d.

Bennoune, Mahfoud. *The Making of Contemporary Algeria, 1830–1987: Colonial Upheavals and Post-Independence Development.* Cambridge: Cambridge University Press, 1988.

Bennoune, Mahfoud, and Ali El-Kenz. *Le hasard et l'histoire—Entretiens avec Belaïd Abdessalem* (Fate and history: Interviews with Belaïd Abdessalem). Vol. 2. Algiers: ENAG, 1990.

Bensidoun, Isabelle, and Agnes Chevallier. *Europe-Méditerranée: Le pari de l'ouverture* (Europe-Mediterranean: The challenge of opening). Paris: Editions Economica, 1996.

Berque, Jacques. *Le Maghreb entre deux guerres* (The Maghreb between two wars). Paris, 1962.

Berramdane, Abdelkhaleq. *Le Sahara Occidental—Enjeu maghrébin* (Western Sahara: a Mahgreb stake). Paris: Karthala, 1992.

Binder, Leonard. *Crises and Sequences in Political Development.* Princeton, N.J.: Princeton University Press, 1971.

Boudjedra, Rachid. *FIS de la haine* (FIS of hatred). Paris: Denoël, 1992; Paris: Folio, 1994.

———. *La répudiation.* Paris: Denoël, 1969.

———. *Lettres algériennes.* Paris: Grasset, 1995.

———. *L'insolation.* Paris: Denoël, 1972.

Boukhoubza, M'hammed. *Octobre 88—Evolution ou rupture?* Algiers: Editions Bouchène, 1991.

Brahimi, Brahim. *Le pouvoir, la presse et les intellectuels en Algérie.* Paris: L'Harmattan, 1989.

British Petroleum. *BP Statistical Review of World Energy 1996.* London: BP, 1996.

Brown, L. Carl. *The Tunisia of Ahmad Bey, 1837–1855.* Princeton, N.J.: Princeton University Press, 1974.

Brynen, Rex, Bahgat Korany, and Paul Noble. *Political Liberalization and Democratization in the Arab World. Vol.1. Theoretical Perspectives.* Boulder, Colo.: L. Rienner, 1995.

Buci-Glucksmann, Christine. *Gramsci and the State.* Translated by David Fernbach. London: Lawrence and Wishart, 1980.

Burgat, François. *L'Islamisme en face* (Islamism on the other side). Paris: La Découverte, 1995.

———. *The Islamic Movement in North Africa.* Translated by W. Dowell. Austin: Center for Middle Eastern Studies, University of Texas, 1993.

Camau, Michel. *La notion de démocratie dans la pensée des dirigeants maghrébins* (Maghrebi rulers' conception of democracy). Paris: CNRS, 1971.

Camier, A. *Les pays du Grand Maghreb et la Communauté Européenne.* Brussels: Commission of the European Communities, DE 68, 1991.

Carlier, Omar. *Entre nation et jihad. Histoire sociale des radicalismes Algériens* (Between nation and jihad: Social history of Algerian radicalism). Paris: Presses de Sciences Po, 1995.

Chalabi, El-Hadi. *L'Algérie, l'état et le droit* (Algeria: The state and the law). Paris: Arcantère Edition, 1989.

Charef, Abed. *Algérie-Le Grand dérapage* (Algeria: The big skid). Paris: Editions de l'Aube, 1994.

———. *Octobre '88—Un chahut de gamins?* (October '88—screaming kids?). 2nd ed. Algiers: Editions Laphonic, 1990.

Charte Nationale, 1976. Algiers: FLN Editions, 1977.

Collinson, Sarah. *Shore to Shore: The Politics of Migration in Euro-Maghreb Relations.* London: Royal Institute of International Affairs, 1996.

Comité National Contre la Torture. *Cahier noir d'Octobre* (October notebook). Algiers: 1989.

Confluences Méditerranée. *Le Maghreb face à la mondilisation* (The Maghreb facing globalization). No. 21 (spring 1997). Paris: L'Harmattan.

Country Commercial Guides. *Morocco: Trade and Project Financing.* National Trade Data Bank. STAT-USA. Document I.D. 1263.

Dean, David D. *The Air Force Role in Low-intensity Conflict.* Maxwell Air Force Base, Ala.: Air University Press, 1986.

Deeb, Mary-Jane. *Libya's Foreign Policy in North Africa.* Boulder, Colo.: Westview Press, 1991.

de Froberville, Martine. *Sahara Occidental: La confiance perdue* (Western Sahara: lost trust). Paris: L'Harmattan, 1996.

Delmasure, Dominique. *L'économie tunisienne: De l'état-providence à l'ambition libérale* (Tunisian economy: From welfare state to liberal ambition). Paris: Centre d'Etudes Prospectives et d'Informations Internationales (CEPII), 1990.

de Villers, Gauthier. *L'état démiurge—Le cas algérien* (Demiurgic state: The Algerian case). Paris: L'Harmattan, 1987.

Dwyer, Kevin. *Arab Voices—The Human Rights Debate in the Middle East.* Berkeley: University of California Press, 1991.

Economist Intelligence Unit. *Libya: Country Profile 1992–1993*. London: EIU, 1992.

El-Fathally, Omar I., and Monte Palmer. *Political Development and Social Change in Libya*. Lexington, Mass.: Lexington Books, 1980.

El-Kenz, Ali. *Algerian Reflections on Arab Crises*. Translated by R. W. Stookey. Austin: Center for Middle Eastern Studies, University of Texas, 1991. Simultaneously published as *Au fil de la crise—5 études sur l'Algérie et le monde arabe*. 2nd ed. Algiers: ENAL, 1991.

———, ed. *L'Algérie et la modernité*. Dakar, Senegal: CODESRIA, 1989.

———, ed. *The Challenge of Modernity*. London: CODESRIA Book Series, 1991.

Entelis, John. *Comparative Politics of North Africa: Algeria, Morocco and Tunisia*. Syracuse: Syracuse University Press, 1980.

Etienne, Bruno. *L'Islamisme radical* (Radical Islamism). Paris: Hachette, 1987.

European Commission. *Strengthening the Mediterranean Policy of the European Union. Establishing a Euro-Mediterranean Partnership*. Brussels: Com(94) 427, October 19, 1994.

Eveleth, Stimson G., et al. *The Private Sector Strategy for USAID/Tunisia*. Bureau for Private Enterprise, USAID. Project number 940–2028.03, 1988.

Farès, Zahir. *Algérie—Le bonheur et son contraire* (Algeria: Happiness and its opposite). Paris: L'Harmattan, 1996.

Freedom House. *Freedom in the World 1991–92*. New York: Freedom House, 1992.

Fuller, Graham E. *Algeria—The Next Fundamentalist State?* Santa Monica, Calif.: RAND, Arroyo Center, 1996.

Garon, Lise. *L'obsession unitaire et la nation trompée—La fin de l'Algérie socialiste* (Totalitarian obsession and the deceived nation: The end of socialist Algeria). Sainte-Foy, Quebec: Les Presses de l'Université Laval, 1993.

Gerschenkron, Alexander. *Economic Backwardness in Historical Perspective*. Cambridge, Mass.: Harvard University Press, 1962.

Ghalioun, Burhan. *Le malaise arabe—Etat contre nation* (Arab quandary—State against nation). Algiers: ENAG, 1991.

Gorbachev, Mikhail. *Perestroika: New Thinking for Our Country and the World*. London: Collins, 1987.

Goumeziane, Smaïl. *Le mal algérien—Economie politique d'une transition inachevée, 1962–1994* (The Algerian affliction—Political economy of an unfinished transition). Paris: Fayard, 1994.

Gramsci, Antonio. *Selections from the Prison Notebooks*. Edited and translated by Quintin Hoare and Geoffrey Nowell Smith. New York: International Publishers, 1971.

Grandguillaume, Gilbert. *Arabisation et politique linguistique au Maghreb*. Paris: Maisonneuve et Larose, 1983.

Greffou, Malika Boudalia. *L'école algérienne de Ibn Badis à Pavlov*. Algiers: Editions Laphomic, 1989.

Grimaud, Nicole. *La politique extérieure de l'Algérie*. Paris: Karthala, 1984.

———. *La Tunisie à la recherche de sa sécurité*. Paris: Presses Universitaires de France, 1995.

Guerrid, J. *L'Algérie: L'une et l'autre société* (Algeria: The one and the other society). Oran, Algeria: Editions CRASC, 1995.

Haggard, Stephan. *Pathways to the Periphery*. Ithaca, N.Y.: Cornell University Press, 1990.

Haggard, Stephan, and Robert R. Kaufman, eds. *The Politics of Economic Adjustment*. Princeton, N.J.: Princeton University Press, 1992.

Haggard, Stephan, and Steven B. Webb, eds. *Voting for Reform*. New York: Oxford University Press, 1994.

Hall, John A., ed. *Civil Society—Theory, History, Comparison*. Cambridge: Polity Press, 1995.

Halliday, Fred. *Islam and the Myth of Confrontation: Religion and Politics in the Middle East*. London and New York: I. B. Taurus, 1996.

———. *Rethinking International Relations*. Basingstoke: Macmillan, 1994.

Harbeson, John W., Donald Rothchild, and Naomi Chazan, eds. *Civil Society and the State in Africa*. Boulder, Colo.: L. Rienner, 1994.

Harbi, Mohammed. *L'Algérie et son destin—Croyants et citoyens* (Algeria and its destiny—Believers and citizens). Paris: Arcantère Editions, 1993.

Harik, Ilya, and Denis J. Sullivan, eds. *Privatization and Liberalization in the Middle East*. Bloomington: Indiana University Press, 1992.

Hegel, G. W. F. *The Phenomenology of Mind*. Translated by J. P. Bailie. New York: Macmillan, 1949.

Henni, Ahmed. *Le Cheikh et le patron* (The sheikh and the executive officer). Alger: OPU, 1993.

Henry, Clement M. *The Mediterranean Debt Crescent*. Gainesville: University Press of Florida, 1996.

Hidouci, Ghazi. *Algérie, la libération inachevée* (Algeria, the unfinished liberation). Paris: La Découverte, 1995.

Hirschman, Albert O. *The Strategy of Economic Development*. New Haven, Conn.: Yale University Press, 1958.

Hodges, Tony. *Western Sahara: The Roots of a Desert War*. Westport, Conn.: Lawrence Hill, 1983.

Huitième plan en bref. Tunis: Ministère du Plan et du Développement Régional, 1993.

Human Rights Watch World Report, 1993. New York: Human Rights Watch, 1992.

Huntington, Samuel. *Political Order in Changing Societies*. New Haven: Yale University Press, 1968.

Ignasse, Gérard, and Emmanuel Wallon, eds. *Demain l'Algérie* (Tomorrow Algeria). Paris: Syros, 1995.

IMF Staff. *Tunisia: Recent Economic Developments*. Country Report No. 96/27. Washington, D.C.: International Monetary Fund, April 1996.

International Market Insight. *Economic Trends: Morocco*. National Trade Data Bank. STAT-USA. March 12, 1997. Document I.D. 1784.

Jowitt, Ken. *New World Disorder: The Leninist Extinction.* Los Angeles: University of California Press, 1992.

Kaye, Jacqueline, and Abdelhamid Zoubir. *The Ambiguous Compromise: Language, Literature, and National Identity in Algeria and Morocco.* London: Routledge, 1990.

Keane, John, ed. *Civil Society and the State: New European Perspectives.* London: Verso, 1988.

Khader, Bishara. *Le Grand Maghreb et l' Europe: Enjeux et perspectives* (The greater Mahgreb: Stakes and perspectives). Paris, France, and Ottignies, Belgium: Editions Publisud and Editions Quorum, 1992.

Al-Khalil, Samir. *The Republic of Fear.* New York: Pantheon, 1990.

Khatibi, Abdelkébir. *Penser le Maghreb* (Thinking the Maghreb). Rabat: Société Marocaine des Editeurs Réunis, 1993.

Khelladi, Aïssa. *Les islamistes algériens face au pouvoir.* Algiers: Editions Alfa, 1992.

Killick, Tony. *A Reaction Too Far.* Boulder, Colo.: Westview Press, 1989.

Kramer, Martin, ed. *The Islamism Debate.* Tel Aviv: Dayan Center Papers, Moshe Dayan Center for Middle Eastern and African Studies, Tel Aviv University, 1997.

Labat, Séverine. *Les islamistes algériens—Entre les urnes et les maquis* (Algerian Islamists: Between ballots and bullets). Paris: Seuil, 1995.

Labdaoui, Abdellah. *Les nouveaux intellectuels arabes* (The new Arab intellectuals). Paris: L'Harmattan, 1993.

Laroui, Abdallah. *Idéologie arabe contemporaine* (Contemporary Arab ideology). Paris, 1967.

Layachi, Azzedine. *State, Society and Democracy in Morocco.* Washington, D.C.: CCAS, Georgetown University, 1998.

Lerner, Daniel. *The Passing of Traditional Societies.* New York: Free Press, 1958.

Leveau, Rémy, ed. *L'Algérie dans la guerre* (Algeria at war). Paris: Editions Complexe, 1995.

———. *Le fellah marocain défenseur du trône* (The Moroccan peasant defender of the throne). Paris: FNSP, 1975.

———. *Le sabre et le turban—L'avenir du Maghreb* (The sabre and the turban—The future of the Maghreb). Paris: Editions François Bourin, 1993.

Louraoui, Lafifa, and Karima Hammoud. *Industry Sector Analysis, Morocco: Franchising.* National Trade Data Bank. STAT-USA. August 1, 1996. Document I.D. 5730.

Malek, Rédha. *Tradition et révolution. Le véritable enjeu* (Tradition and revolution. The true stake). Algiers: Editions Bouchène, 1991.

Malloy, James M., ed. *Authoritarianism and Corporatism in Latin America.* Pittsburgh, Pa.: University of Pittsburgh Press, 1977.

Manceron, Gilles, ed. *Algérie: Comprendre la crise* (Algeria: Understanding the crisis). Paris: Interventions, Editions Complexe, 1996.

Mayer, Ann. *Islam and Human Rights.* London: Westview, 1991.

Medhar, Slimane. *Tradition contre development.* Algiers: ENAP Editions, 1992.

Memmi, Albert. *The Colonizer and the Colonized.* Translated by H. Greenfield. New York: Orion Press, 1965.

Micaud, Charles A., with Leon Carl Brown and Henry Clement Moore. *Tunisia: The Politics of Modernization.* New York: Praeger, 1964.

Mimouni, Rachid. *De la barbarie en général et de l'intégrisme en particulier* (On barbarity in general and fundamentalism in particular). Paris: Le Pré aux Clercs, 1992.

———. *La malédiction* (The curse). Paris: Editions Stock, 1993.

Moore, Clement Henry. *Politics in North Africa.* Boston: Little, Brown, 1970.

———. *Tunisia since Independence.* Berkeley: University of California Press, 1965.

Nelson, Joan M., ed. *Economic Crisis and Policy Choice.* Princeton, N.J.: Princeton University Press, 1990.

Nsouli, Saleh M., et al. *The Path to Convertibility and Growth: The Tunisian Experience.* Washington, D.C.: International Monetary Fund, 1993.

O'Donnell, Guillermo, and Philippe Schmitter. *Transitions from Authoritarian Rule—Tentative Conclusions about Uncertain Democracies.* Baltimore: Johns Hopkins University Press, 1986.

Oualalou, F. *Après Barcelone . . . le Maghreb est nécessaire* (After Barcelona: Maghrebi construction is essential). Paris: L'Harmattan, 1996.

Parker, Richard B. *North Africa: Regional Tensions and Strategic Concerns.* New York: Praeger, 1987.

Perrault, Gilles. *Notre ami le roi* (Our friend the king). Paris: Gallimard, 1990.

Petroleum Finance Company. *Country Report: Libya Critical Period Ahead.* Washington, D.C.: PFC, 1995.

Pierre, Andrew J., and William B. Quandt. *The Algerian Crisis: Policy Options for the West.* Washington, D.C.: Carnegie Endowment for International Peace, 1996.

Reporters sans Frontières. *Le drame algérien* (The Algerian tragedy). Paris: Editions La Découverte, 1994.

Rouadjia, Ahmed. *Les frères et la mosquée* (The brothers and the mosque). Paris: Karthala, 1990.

Ruedy, John, ed. *Islamism and Secularism in North Africa.* New York: St. Martin's Press, 1994.

———. *Modern Algeria. The Origins and Development of a Nation.* Bloomington: Indiana University Press, 1992.

Saghir, Jamal. *Privatization in Tunisia.* CFS Discussion Paper Series. Washington, D.C.: World Bank, 1993.

Salamé, Ghassan, ed. *Démocraties sans démocrates—Politiques d'ouverture dans le monde arabe et islamique* (Democracies without democrats: Policies of opening in the Arab and Islamic world). Paris: Fayard, 1994.

Sanson, Henri. *Laïcité islamique en Algérie* (Islamic secularism in Algeria). Paris: CNRS, 1983.

Stepan, Alfred. *The State and Society.* Princeton, N.J.: Princeton University Press, 1978.

Strange, Susan. *The Retreat of the State—The Diffusion of Power in the World Economy.* Cambridge: Cambridge Studies in International Relations, Cambridge University Press, 1996.

Tibi, Bassam. *Islam and the Cultural Accommodation of Social Change.* Boulder, Colo.: Westview Press, 1991.

Toumi, Mohsen. *La Tunisie de Bourguiba à Ben Ali.* Paris: Presses Universitaires de France, 1989.

United Nations Development Program. *Human Development Report 1997.* New York: Oxford University Press, 1997.

U.S. Department of Energy, Energy Information Administration. *Algeria: Country Analysis Brief.* National Trade Data Bank. STAT-USA. July 25, 1995. I.D. Number: EN CABS ALGERIA.

U.S. Department of State. *Background Notes: Morocco.* National Trade Data Bank. STAT-USA. August 22, 1995. I.D. Number: ST BNOTES MOROCCO.

———. *Economic Policy and Trade Practices: Morocco.* National Trade Data Bank. STAT-USA. April 20, 1995. I.D. Number: ST ECOPOL MOROCCO.

———. *Economic Policy and Trade Practices: Tunisia.* National Trade Data Bank. STAT-USA. April 20, 1995. I.D. Number: ST ECOPOL TUNISIA.

U.S. International Trade Administration. *Algeria: Domestic Economy.* National Trade Data Bank. STAT-USA. August 23, 1995. I.D. Number: IT CCG ALGERIAA02.

———. *Algeria: Economic Trends and Outlook.* National Trade Data Bank. STAT-USA. August 23, 1995. I.D. Number: IT CCG ALGERIA02.

———. *Morocco: Economic Trends and Outlook.* National Trade Data Bank. STAT-USA. August 23, 1995. I.D. Number IT CCG MOROCC002.

———. *Morocco: Executive Summary.* National Trade Data Bank. STAT-USA. August 23, 1995. Document I.D. IT CCG MOROCC001.

———. *Morocco: Investment Climate.* National Trade Data Bank. STAT-USA. August 23, 1995. Document I.D. IT CCG MOROCC007.

———. *Tunisia: Domestic Economy.* National Trade Data Bank. STAT-USA. August 23, 1995. I.D. Number: IT CCG TUNISIAA02.

———. *Tunisia: Economic Trends and Outlook.* National Trade Data Bank. STAT-USA. August 23, 1995. I.D. Number IT CCG TUNISIA02.

———. *Tunisia: Investment Climate.* National Trade Data Bank. STAT-USA. August 23, 1995. I.D. Number: IT CCG TUNISIA07.

U.S. Senate, Committee on Foreign Relations. *The Western Sahara: The Referendum Process in Danger.* Washington, D.C.: Government Printing Office, 1992.

Vandewalle, Dirk, ed. *North Africa: Development and Reform in a Changing Global Economy.* New York: St. Martin's, 1996.

———, ed. *Qadaffi's Libya 1969–1994.* New York: St. Martin's Press, 1995.

Wade, Robert. *Governing the Market.* Princeton, N.J.: Princeton University Press, 1990.

Waltz, Susan. *Human Rights and Reform. Changing the Face of North African Politics.* Berkeley: University of California Press, 1995.

Waterbury, John. *The Commander of the Faithful.* New York: Columbia University Press, 1970.

Waterbury, John, and Alan Richards. *A Political Economy of the Middle East.* 2nd ed. Boulder, Colo.: Westview Press, 1996.

Weaver, Ole, Barry Buzan, Morten Kelstrup, and Pierre Lemaître, eds. *Identity, Migration and the New Security Agenda in Europe.* Copenhagen and London: Center for Peace and Conflict Research, and Pinter Publishers, 1993.

World Bank. *Claiming the Future: Choosing Prosperity in the Middle East and North Africa.* Washington, D.C.: World Bank, 1995.

———. *Republic of Tunisia. Towards the 21st Century. Country Economic Memorandum.* Report No. 14375-TUN. Washington, D.C.: The World Bank.

———. *World Debt Tables, 1994–95.* 2 vols. Washington, D.C.: World Bank.

———. *World Development Report 1995.* New York: Oxford University Press, 1995.

———. *World Development Report 1997.* New York: Oxford University Press, 1997.

Yacoubian, Mona. *Algeria's Struggle for Democracy.* New York: Council on Foreign Relations, Studies Department Occasional Paper. Series No. 3, 1997.

Zartman, I. William, ed. *The Political Economy of Tunisia.* New York: Praeger, 1991.

———. *Ripe for Resolution: Conflict and Intervention in Africa.* New York and Oxford: Oxford University Press, 1985.

———, ed. *Tunisia: The Political Economy of Reform.* Boulder, Colo.: Lynne Rienner, 1991.

Zartman, I. William, and W. Mark Habeeb, eds. *Polity and Society in Contemporary North Africa.* Boulder, Colo.: Westview Press, 1993.

Zoubir, Yahia H., and Daniel Volman, eds. *International Dimensions of the Western Sahara Conflict.* Westport, Conn.: Praeger, 1993.

Articles

Abzahad, M. "Activité et chômage des jeunes citadins au Maroc: Diagnostic" (Activities and unemployment among urban youth in Morocco). In *Démographie: Problèmes de la jeunesse et de l'enfance maghrébines* (Demography: problems of Maghrebi children and youth). Algiers: ONS, 1994, 486–510.

Addi, Lahouari. "Les intellectuels qu'on assassine" (Those intellectuals who are assassinated). *Esprit* (January 1995): 130–37.

Ahmad, Mumtaz, and I. William Zartman. "Political Islam: Can It Become a Loyal Opposition?" *Middle East Policy* 5, no. 1 (January 1997): 68–84.

Alexander, Christopher. "State, Labor, and the New Global Economy in Tunisia." In *North Africa: Development and Reform in a Changing Global Economy,* edited by Dirk Vandewalle. New York: St. Martin's Press, 1996.

Al-Ghannouchi, Rachid. "Towards Inclusive Strategies for Human Rights Enforcement in the Arab World—A Response." *Encounters* 2, no. 2 (1996):190–94.

Anderson, Lisa. "The Traditions of Imperialism: The Colonial Antecedents of the Authoritarian Welfare State in the Arab World." Paper presented at the annual meeting of the American Political Science Association. New York, 1995.

Arkoun, Mohammed. "Islam, Europe, Occident." In *The Mediterranean Revisited,* edited by Tuomo Melasuo. Tampere, Finland: Tampere Peace Research Institute. Research Report no. 57, 1994.

Babadji, Ramdane. "Le phénomène associatif en Algérie: Genèse et perspectives" (The advent of associations in Algeria: Genesis and perspectives). *Annuaire de l'Afrique du Nord 1989.* Vol. 28. Paris: CNRS, 1991.

"Banking in Emerging Markets Survey." *The Economist* (April 12–18, 1997).

Barrouhi, Abdelaziz. "Tunisia Makes First Share Offering to Foreigners." *ClariNet e.News.* Group: Clari.World.Africa. February 22, 1996. Item 21989.

———. "Tunisia's Central Bank Calls for Higher Growth." *ClariNet e.News.* Group: Clari.World.Africa.Northwestern. February 3, 1996. Item 576.

Béji, Hélé. "Hélé Béji par elle-même" (Hélé Béji by herself). *Cahier d'études maghrébines.* I. "Dossier Assia Djebar" (May 1990): 31–36.

———. "La langue est ma maison" (Language is my home). *La quinzaine littéraire* (March 16–31, 1985).

Bekri, Tahar. "On French-Language Tunisian Literature." Translated by Richard E. Morris. *Research in African Literatures* 23, no. 2 (summer 1992): 177–82.

Bellin, Eva. "Civil Society: Effective Tool of Analysis for Middle East Politics?" *PS* 27, no. 3 (September 1994): 509–10.

———. "Tunisian Industrialists and the State." In *Tunisia: The Political Economy of Reform,* edited by I. William Zartman. Boulder, Colo.: L. Rienner, 1991.

Benachenou, A. "Inflation et chômage en Algérie" (Inflation and unemployment in Algeria). In *Maghreb-Machrek* (Paris) 139 (January–March 1993): 29–41.

Ben Jelloun, Tahar. "Le français tel qu'on le rêve" (French as we dream of it). *Le Nouvel Observateur* 1220 (March 25–31, 1988): 60–61.

Benmouhoub, Louisa. "Une interview de Tahar Djaout à la revue *Tin Hinan.*" Report in *Algérie Littérature/Action* 1 (May 1996): 205–12.

Bennani, M. Ch. "Les représentations du monde des jeunes marocains" (The Moroccan youth's images of the world). Ph.D. dissertation. Institut d'Etudes Politiques. Paris, 1993.

Benrabah, Mohammed. "La langue perdue" (The lost language). *Esprit* (January 1995): 35–47.

Berman, Sheri. "Civil Society and the Collapse of the Weimar Republic." *World Politics* 49, no. 3 (April 1997): 401–29.

Bill, James A. "The Study of Middle East Politics, 1946–1996: A Stocktaking." *Middle East Journal* 50, no. 4 (Autumn 1996): 501–12.

Bobbio, Noberto. "Gramsci and the Conception of Civil Society." In *Gramsci and Marxist Theory,* edited by Chantal Mouffe. London and New York: Routledge and Kegan Paul, 1979.

Diamond, Larry. "Toward Democratic Consolidation." *Journal of Democracy* 5, no. 3 (July 1994).

Djerejian, Edward. "The U.S. and the Middle East in a Changing World." *Dispatch* 3, no. 3 (1992).

Donnelly, Jack. "Cultural Relativism and Human Rights." *Human Rights Quarterly* 6, no. 6 (1984): 400–419.

Dourian, Kate. "Banker Says North African Markets Stir but Need Reform." *ClariNet eNews*. Group: Clari.World.Africa.Northwestern. March 19, 1996. Item 691.

———. "Moroccan Banks Gear Up for Competition." *ClariNet eNews*. Group: Clari.World.Africa.Northwestern. February 8, 1996. Item 352.

Dryden, Douglas Kring. "The Western Sahara: Can the UN Turn Failure into Success?" Remarks at the Defense Forum Foundation Lunch on the Occasion of the Visit of Mohammed Abdelaziz of the Saharan Republic to Capitol Hill. Washington, D.C., March 14, 1997.

Durch, William J. "Building on Sand: UN Peacekeeping in the Western Sahara." *International Security* 17, no. 4 (spring 1993): 151–71.

Eckstein, Harry. "Case Study and Theory in Political Science." In *Handbook of Political Science. Vol. 7. Strategies of Inquiry,* edited by Fred I. Greenstein and Nelson W. Polsby. Reading, Mass.: Addison-Wesley, 1975.

El-Alaoui, Hicham Ben Abdellah. "La monarchie marocaine tentée par la réforme" (The Moroccan monarchy tempted by reform). *Le Monde Diplomatique* (September 1996).

El-Benna, Abdelkader. "Les partis politiques au Maroc" (The political parties of Morocco). In *La société civile au Maroc,* edited by Noureddine El-Aoufi. Rabat, Morocco: SMER, 1992.

El-Din Hassan, Bahey. "Towards Inclusive Strategies for Human Rights Enforcement in the Arab World" *Encounters* 2, no. 2 (1996): 171–89.

"État, ville et mouvements sociaux au Maghreb et au Moyen Orient" (State, city, and social movements in the Maghreb and in the Middle East). *Maghreb-Machrek* 115 (1987): 53–69.

Evans, Peter. "The State as Problem and Solution: Predation, Embedded Autonomy, and Structural Change." In *The Politics of Economic Adjustment,* edited by Stephan Haggard and Robert E. Kaufman. Princeton, N.J.: Princeton University Press, 1992.

Faria, Fernanda. "The Mediterranean: A New Priority in Portuguese Foreign Policy." *Mediterranean Politics* 1, no. 2 (Autumn 1996): 212–30.

Farsoun, Smith K., and Christina Zacharia. "Class, Economic Change and Political Liberalization in the Arab World." In *Political Liberalization and Democratization in the Arab World: Theoretical Perspectives,* edited by Rex Brynen, Bahgat Korany, and Paul Noble. Boulder, Colo.: Lynne Rienner, 1995.

"Foreign Investment in Morocco Triples in 1997." *ClariNet eNews*. Group: Clari.World.Africa. December 26, 1997. Item 964.

"France Presses Algeria on Reforms After Massacres." *ClariNet e.News.* Group: Clari.World.Africa.Northwestern. January 5, 1998. Item 1097.

Friedman, Thomas L. "Oops! Wrong War." *New York Times,* April 7, 1997.

Gafaïti, Hafid. "Rachid Boudjedra: The Bard of Modernity." Translated by Patricia Geesey. *Research in African Literatures* 23, no. 2 (summer 1992): 89–102.

———. "Rachid Mimouni entre la critique algérienne et la critique française." *Itinéraires et contacts de cultures* 14, "Poétiques croisées du Maghreb" (1991): 26–34.

Geddes, Barbara. "The Effect of Political Institutions on the Feasibility of Structural Adjustment." Paper prepared for the World Bank Project on the Political Economy of Structural Adjustment in New Democracies, 1991.

Geertz, Clifford. "Comment." *Daedalus,* Plenary Session (winter 1989): 238–39.

Gereffi, Gary. "Big Business and the State." In *Manufacturing Miracles,* edited by Gary Gereffi and Donald L. Wyman. Princeton, N.J.: Princeton University Press, 1990.

———. "Paths of Industrialization: An Overview." In *Manufacturing Miracles,* edited by Gary Gereffi and Donald L. Wyman. Princeton, NJ: Princeton University Press, 1990.

Gharssali, N. "Les jeunes de 15 à 29 ans en Tunisie" (The youth between 15 and 29 in Tunisia). In *Démographie: Problèmes de la jeunesse et de l'enfance maghrébines.* Alger: ONS, 1994, 389–401.

Gillespie, R. "Spain and the Mediterranean: Southern Sensitivity, European Aspirations." *Mediterranean Politics* 1, no. 2 (Autumn 1996): 193–211.

Goldberg, Ellis. "Smashing Idols and the State: The Protestant Ethic and Egyptian Sunni Radicalism." *Comparative Studies in Society and History* 33 (1991): 3–35.

Grandguillaume, Gilbert. "Arabisation et démagogie en Algérie." *Le Monde Diplomatique* 515 (February 1997): 3.

Gress, David R. "The Subtext of Huntington's 'Clash'." (Review Essays) *Orbis* (spring 1997): 285–99.

Grimaud, Nicole. "Algeria and Socialist France." *Middle East Journal* 40, no. 2 (spring 1986).

———. "La diplomatie sous Chadli ou la politique du possible" (Diplomacy under Chadli; policy of the achievable). *Annuaire de l'Afrique du Nord 1991.* Paris: CNRS, 1994, 401–35.

Grissa, Abdessatar. "The Tunisian State Enterprises and Privatization Policy." In *Tunisia: The Political Economy of Reform,* edited by I. William Zartman. Boulder, Colo.: L. Rienner, 1991.

Harik, Ilya. "Privatization and Development in Tunisia." In *Privatization and Liberalization in the Middle East,* edited by Ilya Harik and Denis J. Sullivan. Bloomington: Indiana University Press, 1992.

Hermassi, Elbaki. "The Islamicist Movement and November 7." In *The Political Economy of Tunisia,* edited by I. William Zartman. New York: Praeger, 1991.

———. "The Rise and Fall of the Islamist Movement in Tunisia." In *The Islamist Dilemma*, edited by Laura Guazzone. London: Ithaca, 1995, 105–28.

———. "La société tunisienne au miroir Islamiste" (Tunisian society in the Islamist mirror). *Maghreb-Machrek* 103 (1984): 39–56.

Hermassi, Elbaki, and Dirk Vandewalle. "The Second Stage of State Building." In *Polity and Society in Contemporary North Africa*, edited by I. William Zartman and W. Mark Habeeb. Boulder, Colo.: Westview Press, 1993.

Hodges, Tony, and James Ball. "Is There Oil in the Western Sahara?" *African Business*, no. 48 (August 1982): 14.

"Hommage á Tahar Djaout." *Cahiers du CISIA* (Comité International de Soutien aux Intellectuels Algériens) 1 (September 1993).

Howorth, J. "France and the Mediterranean in 1995: From Tactical Ambiguity to Inchoate Strategy?" *Mediterranean Politics* 1, no. 2 (Autumn 1996): 157–75.

Huntington, Samuel P. "Social and Institutional Dynamics of One-Party Systems." In *Authoritarian Politics in Modern Society*, edited by Samuel P Huntington and Clement H. Moore. New York: Basic Books, 1970.

Ibrahimi, Hamed. "Les libertés envolées de la Tunisie" (Gone liberties in Tunisia). *Le Monde Diplomatique*. URL: (http://www.monde-diplomatique.fr/md/1997/02/IBRAHIMI/ 7752.html), 1997.

———. "Une presse asphyxiée, des journalistes harcelés" (Asphyxiated press, harassed journalists). *Le Monde Diplomatique*. URL: (http://www.monde-diplomatique.fr/ md/1997/02/IBRAHIMI/7753.html), 1997.

International Monetary Fund. "Tunisia's Four-Year-Old Reform Plan Produces Remarkable Turnaround." *IMF Survey* (June 18, 1990): 178–81.

Joffé, George. "Algeria in the New World Order." *Journal of Algerian Studies* 1 (1996).

———. "Facing New Sanctions." *Middle East International* (August 28, 1993).

———. "Integration or Peripheral Dependence: The Dilemma Facing the South Mediterranean States." In *Co-operation and Security in the Mediterranean: Prospects after Barcelona*, edited by A. Bin. Malta: University of Malta, 1996.

———. "Islamic Opposition in Libya." *Third World Quarterly* 10, no. 2 (1988).

———. "Jacques Chirac and France's Middle East Policy." *Jime Review* 29 (summer 1995): 23–37.

———. "Qadhafi Ups the Ante." *Middle East International*, October 8, 1993.

Jünemann, A. "The Mediterranean Policy of the Federal Republic of Germany." *L'Europe et la Méditerranée: L'après-Barcelone*. Geneva: Institut Européen de l'Université de Genève, 1996.

Khan, Amin. "Algerian Intellectuals: Between Identity and Modernity." In *Algeria: The Challenge of Modernity*, edited by Ali El-Kenz. London: CODESRIA Book Series, 1991, 281–306.

Klare, Michael. "Itching for a Fight: Washington Prepares for War against the 'Rogues'." *The Progressive*, September 1996.

Korn, David A. "The Middle East: Islam vs. the Established Order." *Freedom Review* 24, no. 1 (January/February 1993).

Krueger, Anne O. "The Political Economy of the Rent-Seeking Society." *American Economic Review* 64 (1974): 291–303.

Lacoste, Yves. "Les causes spécifiques du drame algérien" (Specific causes of the Algerian tragedy). *Herodote* 77 (April–June 1995): 3–27.

Lake, Anthony. "Confronting Backlash States." *Foreign Affairs* 73, no. 2 (March–April 1994).

Lamchichi, Abderrahim. "Les incertitudes politiques et sociales: L'islamisme s'enracine au Maroc" (Political and social uncertainties: Islamism takes roots in Morocco). *Le Monde Diplomatique,* May 1996.

Laurent, Michel, and Guilain Denoeux. "Campagne d'assainissement au Maroc" (Cleaning campaign in Morocco). *Maghreb-Machrek* 154 (October–December 1996): 125–35.

Lavenue, Jean-Jacques. "Le FIS et la constitution algérienne." *Praxis juridique et religion* 10, no. 2 (1993): 127–43.

"Le chômage, données statistiques" (Unemployment: statistical data). *Statistiques officiels 1995.* Algiers: Office National des Statistiques, 1995.

Leander, Anna. "Bertrand Badie: Cultural Diversity Changing International Relations?" In *The Future of International Relations,* edited by Iver B. Neumann and Ole Wæver. London and New York: Routledge, The New International Relations Series, 1997.

Leca, Jean. "État et société en Algérie" (State and society in Algeria). In *Le Maghreb—Les années de transition,* edited by Bassma Kodmani-Darwish. Paris: IFRI/MASSON, 1990.

Lesser, Ian O. "Southern Europe and the Maghreb: US Interests and Policy Perspectives." *Mediterranean Politics* 1, no. 2 (Autumn 1996): 231–42.

Limam, Ziyad. "Focus: Interview with Ben Ali." *Jeune Afrique* 1752 (August 4–10, 1994): 4–5.

"Loi no. 89–11 du 5 Juillet 1989 relative aux associations à caractère politique," (Law no. 89–11 of July 5, 1989, relative to political associations). *Journal officiel de la république algérienne* (July 5, 1989): 604–7.

"Looking to Join the Caravan." *The Economist* (June 7–13, 1997): 75.

Lorca, A. V. "The EU and the Mediterranean: Is an 'Us' and 'Them' Situation Inevitable?" *The International Spectator* 31, no. 3 (July–September 1996).

Lustick, Ian. "Hegemony and the Riddle of Nationalism: The Dialectics of Political Identity in the Middle East." Working Paper No. 001. Philadelphia: University of Pennsylvania, Christopher Browne Center for International Politics, 1997.

Magnuson, Douglas K. "Islamic Reform in Contemporary Tunisia: Unity and Diversity." In *The Political Economy of Tunisia,* edited by I. William Zartman. New York: Praeger, 1991.

Mahjoub, Azzam. "État, secteur public et privatisation en Tunisie" (State, public sector, and privatization in Tunisia). *Annuaire de l'Afrique du Nord.* Paris: Editions du CNRS, 1987, 299–315.

Mahroug, Moncef. "A quand la relance?" *Jeune Afrique* 1887 (March 5–11, 1997).
———. "Par-delá l'UMA." *Jeune Afrique* 1878 (January 1–7, 1997).
Marks, Jon. "High Hopes and Low Motives: The New Euro-Mediterranean Partnership Initiative." *Mediterranean Politics* 1, no. 1 (1997).
———. "Special Report: Tunisia." *Middle East Economic Digest* (MEED) (November 17, 1995): 12–15.
Mediene, Benamar. "Une société en mal d'expression" (A society in need of expression). In *Demain l'Algérie,* edited by Gérard Ignasse and Emmanuel Wallon. Paris: Syros, 1995, 105–20.
"Minister Says Non-economic Factors behind Free-fall of Rupiah." *ClariNet e.News.* Group: Clari.World.Africa.Northwestern. December 19,1997. Item 3164.
Moore, Clement H. "Tunisia: The Prospects for Institutionalization." In *Authoritarian Politics in Modern Society,* edited by Samuel P. Huntington and Clement H. Moore. New York: Basic Books, 1970.
"More Resources Given to Defence." *Jane's Defence Weekly.* July 1, 1995, 14.
"Morocco's Economy Seen at Zero Growth in 1997." *Jordan Times* (June 21, 1997).
Mortimer, Robert. "The Greater Maghreb and the Western Sahara." In *International Dimensions of the Western Sahara Conflict,* edited by Yahia H. Zoubir and Daniel Volman. Westport, Conn.: Praeger, 1993.
———. "Islamists, Soldiers, and Democrats: The Second Algerian War." *Middle East Journal* 5, no. 1 (winter 1996): 18–39.
———. "Maghreb Matters." *Foreign Policy* (fall 1989): 160–75.
———. "Regionalism and Geopolitics in the Maghreb." *Middle East Report* 184 (September–October 1993): 16–19.
Naylor, Phillip C. "Spain, France, and the Western Sahara: A Historical Narrative and Study of National Transformation." In *International Dimensions,* edited by Yahia H. Zoubir and Daniel Volman. Westport, Conn.: Praeger, 1993.
Nelson, Joan M. "Introduction: The Politics of Economic Adjustment in Developing Nations." In *Economic Crisis and Policy Choice,* edited by Joan M. Nelson. Princeton, N.J.: Princeton University Press, 1990.
Nsouli, Saleh M., et al. "The European Union's New Mediterranean Strategy." *Finance and Development* (September 1996): 14–17.
O'Donnell, Guillermo A. "Tensions in the Bureaucratic-Authoritarian State and the Question of Democracy." In *The New Authoritarianism in Latin America,* edited by David Collier. Princeton, N.J.: Princeton University Press, 1979.
O'Sullivan, Edmund. "Grappling with the Legacy of the Past." *MEED* (January 10, 1992): 4–5.
Ouazani, Cherif. "UMA: 3 + 2." *Jeune Afrique* 1832 (February 14–20, 1996): 25–27.
Pelletreau, Robert. "U.S. Policy toward North Africa." *Department of State Dispatch* 5, no. 40 (October 3, 1994).
Pfeifer, Karen. "Between Rocks and Hard Choices: International Finance and Eco-

nomic Adjustment in North Africa." In *North Africa: Development and Reform in a Changing Global Economy,* edited by Dirk Vandewalle. New York: St. Martin's Press, 1996, 25–63.

Pons, Olivier. "L'Islam politique: Mouvement unitaire ou multiforme?" (Political Islam: Unitary or multifaceted movement?). *Défense nationale* (July 1997): 125–37.

"The Race for Competitiveness and High Growth." *Newsletter of the Economic Research Forum for the Arab Countries, Iran & Turkey* 3, no. 2 (June 1996).

Ramonet, Ignacio. "Main de fer en Tunisie" (Iron fist in Tunisia). *Le Monde Diplomatique* (July 1996).

Roberts, Hugh (interview with). "Under Western Eyes: Violence and the Struggle for Political Accountability in Algeria," *Middle East Report* 206 (spring 1998): 39–42.

Rodrik, Dani. "Credibility of Trade Reform: A Policy Maker's Guide." *The World Economy* 12 (March 1989): 1–17.

Rossevsky-Wickham, Carrie. "Beyond Democratization: Political Change in the Arab World." *PS* 27, no. 3 (September 1994): 507–9.

Rothkopf, David. "In Praise of Cultural Imperialism?" *Foreign Policy* 107 (summer 1997): 38–53.

Rouadjia, Ahmed. "L'UMA mise à mal." *Annuaire de l'Afrique du Nord, 1994.* Paris: CNRS, 1996, 849–55.

Rueschemeyer, Dietrich, and Peter B. Evans. "The State and Economic Transformation: Toward an Analysis of the Conditions Underlying Effective Intervention." In *Bringing the State Back In,* edited by Peter Evans, Dietrich Rueschemeyer, and Theda Skocpol. Cambridge, Mass.: Harvard University Press, 1985, 44–77.

Ruf, Werner. "The Flight of Rent: The Rise and Fall of a National Economy." *Journal of North African Studies* 2, no. 1 (spring 1997).

Saadi, Djamila. "Le linguicide algérien." *Algérie Littérature/Action* 5 (November 1996): 98–100.

Sabagh, George. "The Challenge of Population Growth in Morocco." *MERIP* 23, no. 2 (March–April 1993): 181.

Santucci, Jean-Claude. "État et société au Maroc: Enjeux et perspectives de changement" (State and society: Stakes and perpectives of change). In *Le Maroc actuel: Une modernisation au miroir de la tradition?* (Morocco today: Modernization in the mirror of tradition?) edited by Jean-Claude Santucci. Paris: CNRS, 1992.

Satloff, Robert. "Islamism Seen from Washington." In *The Islamism Debate,* edited by Martin Kramer. Tel Aviv: Dayan Center Papers. No. 120. Tel Aviv: Tel Aviv University, Moshe Dayan Center for Middle Eastern and African Studies, 1997, 101–14.

Sayad, Abdelmalek. "Intellectuels à titre posthume" (Intellectuals posthumously). *Liber: Revue européenne des livres.* Supplement 101–2 (March 1994): 5.

Schemeil, Yves. "Préface: Passeurs entre deux rives: Les énonciateurs de la culture politique arabe" (Ferrymen between two shores: Communicators of Arab political culture). In *Les nouveaux intellectuels arabes*, edited by Abdellah Labdaoui. Paris: L'Harmattan, 1993, 7–15.

Schmitter, Philippe C. "Still the Century of Corporatism?" In *The New Corporatism*, edited by Frederick B. Pike and Thomas Stritch. Notre Dame, Ind.: University of Notre Dame Press, 1974.

Scholte, Jan Aart. "Global Capitalism and the State." *International Affairs* 73, no. 3 (July 1997).

Seddon, David. "Morocco at War." In *War and Refugees—The Western Sahara Conflict*, edited by Richard Lawless and Laila Monahan. London and New York: Pinter, 1987.

———. "Riot and Rebellion in North Africa: Political Responses to Economic Crisis in Tunisia, Morocco and Sudan." In *Power and Stability in the Middle East*, edited by Berch Berberoglu. London: Zed Books, 1989.

Shahin, Emad Eldin. "Secularism and Nationalism: The Political Discourse of Abd al-Salam Yassin." In *Islamism and Secularism in North Africa*, edited by John Ruedy. New York: St. Martin's Press, 1996.

Shils, Edward. "The Virtue of Civil Society." *Government and Opposition* 26, no. 1 (winter 1991).

Shirley, Edward. "Is Iran's Present Algeria's Future?" *Foreign Affairs* 74, no. 3 (May/June 1993).

Soudan, François. "Algérie-Maroc: Faut-il craindre le pire?" (Algeria-Morocco: Should we fear the worst?) *Jeune Afrique* 1673 (January 28–February 3, 1993): 6–9.

———. "Quand le Maghreb retrouve ses Juifs . . . La loi du retour?" (When the Maghreb rediscovers its Jews: The law of return?). *Jeune Afrique* 1692 (June 10–16, 1993): 14.

Spear, Thomas. "Politics and Literature: An Interview with Tahar Ben Jelloun." *Yale French Studies.* "Post/Colonial Conditions," edited by Françoise Lionnet and Ronnie Scharfman. 83 (1993): 30–43.

Spencer, Claire. "Reconceptualizing or Re-Orientating Europe's Mediterranean Security Focus?" In *Reconceptualizing European Security*, edited by W. Park and W. Rees. London: Longmans, 1997.

Stenberg, Leif. "The Revealed Word and the Struggle for Authority: Interpretation and Use of Islamic Terminology among Algerian Islamists." In *Questioning the Secular State—The Worldwide Resurgence of Religion in Politics*, edited by David Westerlund. London: Hurst & Company, 1996.

Suleiman, Michael W. "Attitudes, Values and Political Process in Morocco." In *The Political Economy of Morocco*, edited by I. William Zartman. New York: Praeger,1987.

Taylor, Michael. "Fringe Benefits." *Far Eastern Economic Review* (June 28, 1990).

Tengour, Habib. "Le fourvoiement des elites" (The going astray of elites). *Intersignes* 10 "Penser l'Algérie" (spring 1995): 67–77.

Tessler, Mark A. "The Origins of Popular Support for Islamist Movements: A Political Economy Analysis." Milwaukee: University of Wisconsin, Center for International Studies, 1993.

———. "Regime Orientation and Participant Citizenship in Developing Countries: Hypothesis and a Test with Longitudinal Data from Tunisia." *Western Political Quarterly* 34 (December 1981): 479–98.

———. "Youth in the Maghrib: Social Mobilization, Unrealized Expectations and Political Alienation." In *Polity and Society in Contemporary North Africa*, edited by I. William Zartman and W. Mark Habeeb. Boulder, Colo.: Westview Press, 1993.

Tessler, Mark A., John P. Entelis, and Gregory W. White. "Kingdom of Morocco." In *The Government and Politics of the Middle East and North Africa*, edited by David E. Long and Bernard Reich. Boulder, Colo.: Westview Press, 1995.

Tozy, Mohammed. "Champ et contre-champ religieux au Maroc" (Religious field and counter-field in Morocco). Ph.D. dissertation. University of Paris, 1984.

"Tunisie: Le trop bon elève." (Tunisia: The too-good student) *Le Monde* (May 11, 1993): 11.

Vandewalle, Dirk. "Autopsy of a Revolt: The October Riots in Algeria." Hanover, N.H.: Institute of Current World Affairs, 1988.

———. "Ben Ali's New Era: Pluralism and Economic Privatization in Tunisia." In *The Politics of Economic Reform in the Middle East*, edited by Henri J. Barkey. New York: St. Martin's Press, 1992.

———. "Breaking with Socialism: Economic Liberalization and Privatization in Algeria." In *Privatization and Liberalization in the Middle East*, edited by Iliya Harik and Denis J. Sullivan. Bloomington: Indiana University Press, 1992.

———. "From the New State to the New Era: Toward a Second Republic in Tunisia." *Middle East Journal* 42 (Autumn 1988).

———. "Uneasy and Unequal Partners: A European Perspective on Change and Development in North Africa," in *North Africa: Development and Reform in a Global Society*, edited by Dirk Vandewalle. New York: St. Martin's Press, 1996.

Verges, Meriem. "La Casbah d'Alger: Chronique de survie dans un quartier en sursis" (The Casbah of Algiers: Chronicle of survival in a sentenced quarter). *NAQD* (Algiers) 6 (March 1994): 37–43.

Volman, Daniel. "The Role of Military Assistance in the Western Sahara War." In *International Dimensions of the Western Sahara Conflict*, edited by Yahia H. Zoubir and Daniel Volman. Westport, Conn.: Praeger, 1993.

Waller, Robert. "Qadhafi Ahead on Points." *Middle East International* (June 23, 1995).

Walzer, Michael. "The Civil Society Argument." In *Dimensions of Radical Democratic Pluralism, Citizenship, Community*, edited by Chantal Mouffe. London: Verso, 1992.

———. "The Idea of Civil Society." *Dissent* (spring 1991).

Waterbury, John. "Une démocratie sans démocrates? Le potentiel de libéralisation politique au Moyen-Orient" (Democracies without democrats? The potential for political liberalization in the Middle East). In *Démocraties sans démocrates—Politiques d'ouverture dans le monde Arabe et Islamique*, edited by Ghassan Salamé. Paris: Fayard, 1994.

White, Gregory W. "The Mexico of Europe? Morocco's Partnership with the European Union." In *North Africa: Development and Reform in a Changing Global Society*, edited by Dirk Vandewalle. New York: St. Martin's Press, 1996.

"World Bank Chief Ends Algeria Visit on High Note." *ClariNet e.News*. Group: Clari.World.Africa.Northwestern. March 22, 1996. Item 724.

"World Population Data Sheet." Washington, D.C.: Population Reference Bureau, 1994.

"The World's Emerging Markets All at Sea." *The Economist*. January 28, 1995.

Yared, Marc. "Kaddafi–Israel: Qui a piégé qui?" (Qadaffi–Israel: Who tricked whom?) *Jeune Afrique* 1692 (June 10–16, 1993).

Zartman, I. William. "King Hassan's New Morocco." In *The Political Economy of Morocco*, edited by I. William Zartman. New York: Praeger, 1987.

Zghal, Abdelkader. "Le concept de société civile et la transition vers le multipartisme" (The concept of civil society and the transition to multiparyism). *Annuaire de l'Afrique du nord 1989* (Paris: C.N.R.S) 28 (1991): 225–26.

———. "The New Strategy of the Movement of the Islamic Way: Manipulation or Expression of Political Culture." In *Tunisia: The Political Economy of Reform*, edited by I. William Zartman. Boulder, Colo.: Lynne Rienner, 1991.

Zoubir, Yahia H. "Algeria: Ballots Not Bullets." *Jane's Defence Weekly* (February 7, 1996).

———. "Algerian Islamists' Conception of Democracy." *Arab Studies Quarterly* 18, no. 3 (summer 1996): 65–85.

———. "Political Economy of the Western Sahara Conflict." In *Economic Crisis and Political Change in North Africa*, edited by Azzedine Layachi. Westport, Conn.: Greenwood Press, 1998.

———. "Stalled Democratization of an Authoritarian Regime: The Case of Algeria." *Democratization* 2, no. 2 (summer 1995): 109–39.

———. "The U.S., the Algerian Crisis, and the Question of Radical Islamism." Paper presented at the 38th International Studies Association Annual Convention. Toronto, Canada, March 18–22, 1997.

———. "The Western Sahara Conflict: Regional and International Dimensions." *Journal of Modern African Studies* 28, no. 2 (1990): 225–43.

Zoubir, Yahia H., and Anthony G. Pazzanita. "The United Nations' Failure in Resolving the Western Sahara Conflict." *Middle East Journal* 49, no. 4 (fall 1995): 614–28.

Zoubir, Yahia H., and Daniel Volman. "The New World Order and the Case of the Western Sahara: US Foreign Policy in Transition." *Mediterranean Quarterly* 4, no. 2 (spring 1993): 108–20.

———. "The United States and Conflict in the Maghreb." *Journal of North African Studies,* 2, no. 3 (winter 1997–98): 10–24.

Zunes, Stephen. "Arab Nationalism and the Persian Gulf Conflict." *Peace Review* 3, no. 2 (spring 1991).

———. "Rogue States in U.S. Middle East Policy." *Middle East Policy* 5, no. 2 (May 1997): 150–67.

———. "The United States in the Saharan War: A Case of Low-Intensity Intervention." In *International Dimensions of the Western Sahara Conflict,* edited by Yahia H. Zoubir and Daniel Volman. Westport, Conn.: Praeger, 1993, 53–92.

———. "The United States and the Western Sahara Peace Process." *Middle East Policy* 5, no. 4 (January 1998): 131–46.

Contributors

Mohamed Farid Azzi is an associate professor of sociology at the University of Oran, Algeria. He received a degree in sociology from the Université d'Oran in 1977, an M.A. in sociology from the University of Wales in 1982, and finished his Ph.D. studies in political science at the Institut d'Etudes Politiques in Paris. He has published various articles on young people in the Maghreb.

Youcef Bouandel is a lecturer in politics at the School of Policy Studies, University of Lincolnshire and Humberside (Hull), England. He is a graduate of the University of Algiers (Institut des Sciences Politiques et des Relations Internationales), 1986. He received his M.A. in 1988 and his Ph.D. in 1993 from the University of Glasgow, Scotland, and has published the book *Human Rights and Comparative Politics*.

Nora Ann Colton is an assistant professor of international economics at Drew University, Madison, New Jersey. She earned her Ph.D. from St. Anthony's College, Oxford. Dr. Colton's publications include "The New Middle East: Open for Business," "The North African Miracle: Privatization and Liberalization in the Maghreb," and "Coping with Supply Shocks: The Case of Jordan." She is completing a book on Yemen, entitled *Invisible Markets: The Informal Sector and Migration in Yemen*.

Mary-Jane Deeb, a professor of international relations at the American University in Washington, D.C., received her Ph.D. in international relations from the School of Advanced International Studies of Johns Hopkins University. She is the editor of *The Middle East Journal*, author of *Libya's Foreign Policy in North Africa*, and co-author of *Libya Since the Revolution*. Dr. Deeb has written more than fifty articles, book chapters, and book reviews for academic publications and is currently co-editing a manuscript entitled *Gender and Politics in the Middle East.*

Patricia Geesey received her Ph.D. in French from Ohio State University in 1991 and is an associate professor of French at the University of North Florida. Her articles on North African French-language literature and Algerian women immigrants in France have appeared in *The French Review, SubStance, Dalhousie French Studies*, and *Research in African Literatures.* She is currently working on a manuscript about Algerian women writers.

Clement Moore Henry, who received his Ph.D. in political science from Harvard University, is a professor at the University of Texas at Austin. Dr. Henry specializes in the Middle East and North Africa, where he has conducted research on political parties, the engineering profession, and financial institutions. He has written four books (some under the name of Clement Henry Moore), including *The Mediterranean Debt Crescent: Money and Power in Algeria, Egypt, Morocco, Tunisia, and Turkey,* and has co-authored or co-edited five other books as well as having contributed more than three dozen articles to other books and journals.

E. G. H. Joffé is deputy director of the Royal Institute of International Affairs and teaches at the School of Oriental and African Studies at London University. He is the author of more than eighty articles published in academic journals and books, and has been co-editor of six studies on the Middle East and North Africa. Professor Joffé is editor of the *Journal of North African Studies* and co-editor of *Mediterranean Politics.*

Robert King, who earned his M.A. in linguistics from the University of Florida, is currently completing his Ph.D. at Emory University. Most recently he taught international relations and Middle East politics at Oglethorpe University. His research presentations have included "The State, the Private Sector, and State-Led Reform in North Africa" and "Tunisia's Political Persistence in a Rapidly Changing Environment."

Azzedine Layachi is an assistant professor at St. John's University in New York. He holds a Ph.D. and M.A. in politics from New York University and a B.A. from the Institut d'Etudes Politiques, University of Algiers, Algeria. He is the author of *Civil Society and Democratization in Morocco* (1996). His articles on North Africa have been published in *Middle East Quarterly* and *Arab Studies Quarterly*, among other journals.

Robert A. Mortimer, professor of political science at Haverford College in Pennsylvania, received both his M.A. and Ph.D. from Columbia University. He has written several books and dozens of chapters in books, book reviews, and articles that have appeared in publications such as *Middle East Insight, Foreign Policy*, and the *Middle East Journal*.

Claire Spencer is deputy director of the Center for Defense Studies at King's College, University of London, specializing in Mediterranean and North African affairs. She has held appointments in various foundations and has published a number of articles, including "The Maghreb in the 1990s" in IISS Adelphi Paper 247 and "The Roots of Maghrebi Unity and Disunity" in *Morocco*.

Daniel Volman received his Ph.D. in African history from the University of California, Los Angeles, in 1991 and is director of the Africa Research Project in Washington, D.C. He is the author of numerous articles on African security issues and is co-editor of *International Dimensions of the Western Sahara Conflict* (1993).

Yahia H. Zoubir is an associate professor of international studies at Thunderbird, the American Graduate School of International Management, Glendale, Arizona, and is the director of the European program of the Thunderbird French Geneva Center in France. He holds a bachelor's degree from the Institut d'Etudes Politiques, University of Algiers, and an M.A. and Ph.D. from the American University, Washington, D.C. He is editor in chief of the *Thunderbird International Business Review* (formerly *The International Executive*) and co-editor of and main contributor to *International Dimensions of the Western Sahara Conflict*. Dr. Zoubir has written dozens of articles that have appeared in publications such as the *Canadian Journal of History, The Middle East Journal, Democratization*, and *Arab Studies Quarterly* and has been a contributing author of many book chapters. He is currently writing a book on the Algerian crisis.

Stephen Zunes, who received his Ph.D. from Cornell University, is an assistant professor of politics at the University of San Francisco. He has written about North Africa for scholarly journals such as *Middle East Policy, Arab Studies Quarterly*, and *Peace Review*. He is completing a book on Western Sahara.

Index